Ideology in the Language of Judges

OXFORD STUDIES IN ANTHROPOLOGICAL LINGUISTICS
William Bright, General Editor

Editorial Board

Wallace Chafe, University of California, Santa Barbara
Regna Darnell, University of Western Ontario
Paul Friedrich, University of Chicago
Dell Hymes, University of Virginia
Jane Hill, University of Arizona
Stephen C. Levinson, Max Planck Institute, The Netherlands
Joel Sherzer, University of Texas, Austin
David J. Parkin, University of London
Andrew Pawley, Australian National University
Jef Verschueren, University of Antwerp

Volumes Published in the Series

Ideology
in the Language
of Judges

•——•

How Judges Practice Law, Politics,
and Courtroom Control

SUSAN U. PHILIPS

New York • Oxford

Oxford University Press

1998

Oxford University Press

Oxford   New York

Athens   Auckland   Bangkok   Bogota   Bombay   Buenos Aires
Calcutta   Cape Town   Dar es Salaam   Delhi   Florence   Hong Kong
Istanbul   Karachi   Kuala Lumpur   Madras   Madrid   Melbourne
Mexico City   Nairobi   Paris   Singapore   Taipei   Tokyo   Toronto   Warsaw

and associated companies in
Berlin   Ibadan

Copyright © 1998 by Susan U. Philips

Published by Oxford University Press, Inc.
198 Madison Avenue, New York, New York 10016

Library of Congress Cataloging-in-Publication Data
Philips, Susan Urmston.
Ideology in the language of judges : how judges practice law,
politics, and courtroom control / Susan U. Philips.
p.   cm. — (Oxford studies in anthropological linguistics ; 17)
Includes bibliographical references and index.
ISBN 0-19-511340-3; ISBN 0-19-511341-1 (pbk.)
1. Judges—United States.   2. Judicial process—United States.
3. Law and politics.   4. Law—Language.   I. Title.   II. Series.
KF8775.P49   1998
347.73'14—dc21   97-48671

1 3 5 7 9 8 6 4 2

Printed in the United States of America
on acid-free paper

To my mother,
Mary Jane Urmston

• —————— •

Acknowledgments

I would like first to acknowledge Robert Edgerton's influence on my thinking about American culture, which came through my working with him and Craig McAndrew as an undergraduate research assistant when they were studying the culture of patients at a southern California hospital for the mentally retarded. Through participation in their ethnographic research, I came to be able to think about my own culture anthropologically.

The research itself was supported by two postdoctoral fellowships—a Russell Sage Residency in Law and Social Sciences and a National Science Foundation National Needs Postdoctoral Fellowship. During the year I took courses at the University of Arizona College of Law, I learned a great deal from my professors Joel Finer, David Wexler, Charles Ares, and Dan Dobbs. Charles Ares guided some of my initial inquiries into the judiciary and introduced me to the Honorable William Druke, who at that time was associate presiding judge of the Pima County Superior Court. Judge Druke, in turn, agreed to supervise my research in that court. He arranged meetings for me with prospective subjects for my study. Judge Druke also obtained an oral ruling from the Honorable Stanley Feldman, chief justice of the Arizona Supreme Court, that my tape recording in court, not allowed by outsiders at that time, could be carried out as an exception for educational purposes. My greatest debt is to the nine judges who participated in this study. They gave generously and thoughtfully of their time and ideas, each offering distinctive perspectives. Their staff members reflected the high morale surrounding all of these judges in their kindness and hospitality on the many occasions when I visited judges' chambers.

I am also grateful to graduate students at the University of Arizona for research assistance of various kinds. Jean Florman did most of the transcription of recordings of court proceedings from a summer of initial pilot work. Terry Reichardt Betancourt did the bulk of transcription of the guilty pleas and interviews with judges that form the heart of the data analyzed here. Anne Reynolds coded and counted patterns in questions and answers in the guilty pleas. Claudia Bartz did some preliminary analysis of similarities and differences in career history interviews with judges. Helen Robbins helped with the references.

I was supported in the write-up of this material by a sabbatical, a Socio-Behavioral Research Institute Research Professorship, and a Udall Center for Policy Studies Fellowship, all through the University of Arizona. Doris Sample typed and retyped a good deal of material for me during the early stages of writing the manuscript.

A number of people read and/or discussed all or parts of this manuscript with me. William O'Barr, Jane Hill, Sheila Slaughter, Deborah Tannen, Greg Matoesian, and the Honorable Margaret Houghton read the entire work. I am particularly grateful to Deborah for her careful reading and fine editing of the manuscript. Dave Wexler, Charles Ares, and Patricia MacCorquodale commented on various sections of the text. I benefited from discussions with Sally Merry, Sue Hirsch, and Niko Besnier about issues in the book. And I have also been helped by the comments from Bill Bright, editor of the series in which this book appears, and the anonymous readers to whom he sent the book for review. I very much appreciate the efforts of all these people.

Finally I thank my husband, Wes Addison, and our son, Charlie Addison, for being supportive of this work, and I also thank Charlie for his help with the final preparation of the book manuscript.

Contents

Introduction xi

1 Ideology in Discourse 3
2 The Myth of the Trial Court Judge as Nonideological 14
3 Intertextual Relations between Written and Spoken Genres of Law 27
4 Two Ideological Stances in Taking Guilty Pleas 48
5 Judges' Ideologies of Courtroom Control 87
6 Ideological Diversity in Legal Discourses 116

Appendixes
    Appendix A: Social Background Questionnaire 127
    Appendix B: Career History Interview 133
    Appendix C: Rule 17, *Arizona Rules of Criminal Procedure*:
                   Pleas of Guilty and No Contest 135
    Appendix D: Plea Agreement 137
    Appendix E: Transcription Notations 141
    Appendix F: Four Changes of Plea / Guilty Plea Transcripts 147
    Appendix G: Refusal of Plea Agreement in Aborted Sentencing Transcript 187

Notes 193
References 197
Index 203

Introduction

This book began as an anthropological study of judicial behavior in an American trial court. It became more than that. It became an analysis of the way ideological diversity is organized in legal discourses, both spoken and written. Throughout, my approach is to look at how meaning is constituted through the organization of discourse structure. I describe here each of these aspects of the study as an introduction to this book.

In the 1960s and 1970s, studies of the judicial behavior of trial court judges focused on recorded outcomes of legal procedures, specifically on sentencing behavior. Social scientists were interested in how much judges varied in their sentencing practices and in factors that might explain the variation, particularly the possible factor of bias against ethnic minorities. This work was motivated by public policy debates over how much leeway judges should be allowed in sentencing criminal defendants, a debate that led to laws creating greater constraints on judges' sentencing practices around the country. As public policy has gone this route, the interest in judges' behavior has waned. This book aims to revive the interest in judicial behavior but with a very different concept of "behavior." I found the earlier concept of behavior odd, for it usually referred to written residues of actual behavior—to records of what judges had done in court. Sentencing, for example, could be examined without ever setting foot in a trial court or encountering a trial court judge face to face. As a linguistic anthropologist interested in how speakers create realities through language use, to me behavior means people actually talking to one another, not the residue of their actions on paper. And this study as a whole argues for the idea that when we examine judges' courtroom behavior, we see judges constituting richly complex legal and nonlegal realities.

As I see it, then, speech by judges in the courtroom *is* judicial behavior. Stimulated in part by students of judicial behavior, but also by sociolinguistic studies of language variation, when I began this study I wanted to understand how judges varied in their courtroom language use and what that variation meant, particularly to the judges themselves. To pursue this goal, I focused on the guilty plea as a distinct procedure and bounded discourse unit. In the guilty plea, judges hear criminal defendants plead guilty to crimes. I tape-recorded multiple instances of such hearings done by a group of judges with whom I worked closely. One important role of the judge in this procedure is to make sure the criminal defendant's due process constitutional rights to a fair trial are being knowingly and voluntarily waived. When, in interviews, I asked the judges why they did the procedure the way they did, they consistently focused on this due process issue: they saw themselves as making sure the defendant's plea of guilty was knowing and voluntary; they saw themselves as individually implementing the written law that interpreted the constitutional right to due process. Their concern with due process led me to include the written law that "governed" the spoken law in my study. The chapters that follow, then, deal with several different kinds of discourse and the relations among them: spoken guilty pleas, interviews with judges, and several kinds of written law.

I found diversity in the way the judges interacted with defendants that was related to their interpretations of the written law. This diversity was organized and socially systemic, rather than individual, in that small groups of judges did the procedure in similar ways and gave similar reasons for why they did the procedure as they did. Yet the groups differed in both their behavior and their reasoning. The judges used two clearly different interactional strategies in taking guilty pleas. One group elaborated the procedure and involved the defendant more. The judges in this group interpreted the written law as requiring of them that they individually establish *during the procedure* that the defendant was knowingly and voluntarily waiving the right to trial, and they did this by involving the defendant more. The second group abbreviated the procedure and involved the defendant very little; this group interpreted the written law as requiring that they determine that there was evidence *in the written record* of the case as a whole that the plea met due process law. Thus, this group did not feel the perceived burden to engage the defendant that the first group felt. I characterize the two as "procedure-oriented" and "recorded-oriented" strategies for meeting due process requirements.

I found a diversity within the written law that was parallel to this diversity in the spoken law. This parallel meant that judges with different approaches could all find a basis for their positions when they looked to the written law for guidance. At the same time, many of the reasons they gave for doing what they did could not be found in the written law. Thus it became evident that the spoken law really has an interpretive life and a culture of its own and is not just a reflection of the written law.

It should already be apparent that this project became not only a study of judicial behavior but also a study of the way ideological diversity is organized in legal discourses. But there is more to this ideological diversity than what I have suggested so far.

Clearly the judges saw what they did as enacting law and as thinking within legal interpretive frameworks. This view is consistent with one permeating the legal profession that what they are doing is law and nothing but law, and particularly not politics. The trial court judges with whom I worked acknowledged that they had become judges through a process influenced by party politics and political ideologies, and they acknowledged having political ideologies themselves. But they did not feel their political ideologies should influence what they did in the courtroom, and they could not see that their political ideologies affected how they took guilty pleas. Their position was consistent with the idea promulgated by the organized bar (i.e., by federal and state-based professional organizations of practicing lawyers) that trial court judges do not make law. Rather, they implement the law that is made by state legislatures and appellate courts.

Paralleling this distinction is the idea that although it is reasonable to expect appellate court judges to be "ideological" in the political sense of conservative versus liberal, and to expect this to influence the law they make, it is not appropriate for trial court judges to be so because their function or role is different. This distinction has been important in the organized bar's success in convincing state legislatures that trial court judges should be appointed, not elected by voters on the basis of political party affiliations or their associated political ideologies.

I argue to the contrary that the judges can be seen as enacting political ideological stances, whether consciously or not. Procedure-oriented judges take a more liberal stance: as representatives of the state, they are willing to assume the role of protector of the individual, who is seen as needing the help of the state to obtain due process. Record-oriented judges take a more conservative stance: they eschew this role of protector and do not see it as called for. The more elaborate procedures of the liberal judges do expand the moments of state involvement, whereas, by comparison, the more abbreviated procedures contract those same moments of state involvement. Political ideology may be erased by rhetoric about the nature of the trial court judge's role, then, but it is nevertheless present, and we see that these efforts of the organized bar to carefully construct boundaries and barriers between the trial court and the appellate court and between the political and the legal are vulnerable to challenge.

Moreover, in addition to the polysemy or the multiple meanings of the judges' courtroom discourse as both legal and political, there is a third interpretive framing of the judges' guilty pleas that became apparent in interviews with them, and this is the ideology of courtroom control. Record-oriented judges see involving the defendant verbally in the guilty plea as increasing the likelihood that the judge will lose control of the procedure and risk spoiling it. Procedure-oriented judges realize there is such a risk of spoiling the procedure if the defendant says the wrong thing, but they expressly deny being concerned about losing control of the courtroom. Defendants do try to contribute information during the procedure that the judges do not want them to, and the judges discourage such contributions in one way or another. According to the procedure-oriented judges, a friendly egalitarian chatty judge is seen by some as inviting rebellion and disorder from defendants and by others as making people feel comfortable and free to talk in a courtroom that they should see as theirs.

Judges conceptualize these differences in views on courtroom control as having to do with personal judicial style, not the law and not political ideology. I argue that these control ideologies are related to everyday ideologies of control that permeate American life and the way Americans think about hierarchical relations—relations that range from the parent–child relation through school classrooms through the bureaucratic hierarchies within which the life of work takes place. Once again, the boundaries drawn by the legal profession between law and not law seem permeable, if not illusory.

Three different ideological frameworks, then, inform the judicial behavior of the judges and can be seen as enacted by the way judges take guilty pleas. *Legal ideology* clearly predominates. *Political ideology* is denied. And *everyday ideologies of control* are quite explicit but viewed by the judges as of marginal relevance to the legal task at hand. Here I argue that all are relevant, all are present, and really, to understand the nature of the legal system, we cannot accept the legal profession's characterizations of what lawyers are doing as only law. Law is richly and pluralistically ideological.

The final dimension to this study, which I mentioned at the beginning of this preface, is its exploration of the role of language and discourse structure, particularly as these are understood in linguistic anthropology, in constituting this multiplicity of ideologies. I show how different genres of discourse—written law, spoken law, and interviews—constitute ideology differently. Speech genre boundaries are also interpretive boundaries, so to some extent different genres of discourse can be associated with different interpretive frames. At the same time, the spoken and written genres of law index one another and create intertextual relations among genres. Using the speech genre of the guilty plea, I show how distinct topics form sequentially ordered discourse units. It is through judges' manipulation of those topical discourse units that they constitute their procedure- and record-oriented strategies for taking pleas and enact different ideological stances.

I take linguistic anthropologists to task for their failure to give serious attention to how interpretive diversity in discourse is socially organized, particularly into power relations of domination and subordination. I turn theoretically to Marxist conceptualizations of ideology as involving contestation and struggle to help me think about the influence of power relations on the organization of the ideological diversity I document.

There are several levels of struggle and opposition that emerge as relevant for understanding the organization of ideological diversity in the legal discourses considered here. First, there is the struggle of the judge to maintain control over his courtroom, and more specifically over the defendant. Second, there is the struggle among the judges for ideological dominance in interpreting the due process law—who is right, the procedure-oriented judges or the record-oriented judges, the less controlling judges or the more controlling judges, the liberal judges or the conservative judges? Third, there is a historical struggle between political parties and the organized bar, not only for control over the ideological definition of the trial court judge's role but also for actual control over the process that determines who will become a judge. What is most striking about these struggles is that they are largely hidden, denied, unrecognized, and unacknowledged. Only the disagreement among judges over courtroom control is overt and recognized, and this disagreement is defined as of little legal consequence. Through discussion of the relevance of ideological struggle for our understanding of discourse structure, I show how power relations shape the organization of discourse.

The book consists of six chapters, followed by appendices, including transcripts of four pleas that illustrate the distinction between record- and procedure-oriented strategies for meeting due process requirements.

Chapter 1, "Ideology in Discourse," introduces the theory and method of the study. I discuss the two theoretical traditions drawn upon in this work, linguistic anthropological approaches to culture in discourse and Marxist approaches to ideological diversity, and I show how they are relevant to the way data for the project were collected and analyzed. From linguistic anthropology I take the idea that different forms of discourse constitute different cultural realities. From Marxist treatments of ideological diversity I take the idea that ideological diversity is socially organized, specifically into dialectical relations of opposition, contestation, and domination and subordination.

Chapter 2, "The Myth of the Trial Court Judge as Nonideological," focuses on the position taken by judges in this study that they should be nonideological in their work, particularly in the courtroom. I argue that this position suggests the success of the organized bar in defining what judges do as law, not as politics. The judges I worked with clarified their nonideological role by contrasting the trial court judge's role with that of the appellate judge, saying that whereas appellate court judges make law, they, as trial court judges, merely implement the law. In various social scientific and organized bar-supported literatures, this distinction between appellate and trial court judges is used to justify different criteria for selecting judges at the different levels. At the appellate level, candidates' political ideologies are considered relevant to the job. At the trial court level, political ideologies should not matter because trial court judges are not making law. In these same literatures, trial court judges are argued to have only been negatively affected by the influence of party politics on their judicial behavior and only positively affected by adherence to legal professional standards. These views have been the basis for a historic shift since World War II in methods for selecting trial court judges in state courts across the country—from election to appointment of judges. I interpret this shift as a gaining of power by the organized bar and a waning of power by political parties.

About half the judges in this study were elected and half were appointed. I show how the impact of this shift in selection process can be seen in their accounts of the ways they came to be judges, in their characterizations of their own political ideologies, and in the nature of their denials of the influence of political ideologies on their work. The ultimate impact, I argue, is the denial of political ideology coupled with the actual continuing relevance of political ideology for the way they behave in the courtroom.

Having established that the clearest ideological stance the judges take is that they are not ideological, I proceed to argue in the remaining chapters of the book that their speech is, to the contrary, very ideologically laden, and pluralistically so. Each of the four remaining chapters deals with ideological diversity in a different way.

Chapter 3, "Intertextual Relations between Written and Spoken Genres of Law," examines the diversity in interpretations of due process in the written law governing guilty pleas and in the spoken guilty plea. I show how the judges organize the plea into a sequence of topics, each of which indexes elements of a state procedural rule that spells out how due process rights are to be secured in the guilty plea. Then I discuss how the genre of case law interpreting that rule differs from the genre of the rule itself. The rule requires the judge to determine that the defendant is knowingly and voluntarily waiving his due process rights to a trial in the procedure, but case law allows for the judge to merely find evidence in the record of the case as a whole that these rights have been knowingly and voluntarily waived. The judges draw on both the procedural rule and case law in their spoken pleas.

Chapter 4, "Two Ideological Stances in Taking Guilty Pleas," shows how the range of due process strategies allowed by case law is represented in spoken pleas. Even though the judges have common elements in the way they do guilty pleas, as I discuss in chapter 3, they also differ systematically in the ways they manage the topics that constitute sequentially ordered discourse units within the plea. One group of judges believes the plea should be done more in the way the written procedural rule requires that it be done—that is, in the procedure itself—so, as stated, I call this group *procedure oriented*. These judges elaborate certain topics by giving the defendant more information and by eliciting from the defendant more information through questioning. The other group of judges believes this elaboration is unnecessary, and, consistent with case law produced by appellate judges, believes it is sufficient that there be evidence in the written record of the case as a whole that the defendant's due process rights have been secured. I call this group *record oriented*. These judges abbreviate the same topics that are elaborated by the first group, giving less information to the defendants and eliciting less information from the defendants through questioning.

And although, as I have noted, the judges do not see a political ideological dimension to the due process interpretations they enact, I argue that their strategies do enact liberal and conservative concepts of the state. Procedure-oriented judges enact a liberal view of the state: as representatives of the state, they assume personal responsibility for protecting the rights of individuals. Record-oriented judges enact a more conservative view of the state: as representatives of the state, they do not assume such personal responsibility for protecting individuals but, rather, see this responsibility as shared with lawyers and the individual defendants who appear before them. They also show much less interest in what is at issue here than do the procedure-oriented judges, so their position is less elaborated in interviews, as well as in the courtroom. I ask whether it is reasonable to see these two positions as in opposition—struggle or conflict—and conclude that although it is, such conflict is not overtly recognized or at least not acknowledged as such by the judges themselves.

Chapter 4 is in many ways the pivotal chapter of the book. The earlier chapters lead up to this one, and the later chapters lead away from it. Furthermore, it is in this chapter that the way ideological stances can be enacted through discourse practice in the courtroom is thoroughly developed.

Chapter 5, "Judges' Ideologies of Courtroom Control," describes judges' ideologies of courtroom control as a third way of making sense of how they do their guilty pleas. All the judges in this study agreed that the more the defendant is involved in the guilty plea, particularly in the factual basis where there must be evidence that a crime was committed, the greater the risk that the procedure will be spoiled by the defendant saying something inconsistent with what the law requires for the procedure to be legally binding. I show how the various ways that the defendants resist confessing to crimes in the factual basis threaten the legal validity of the guilty plea and how judges respond to such threats.

I argue that the judges respond to this threat to legal validity differently through their use of record-oriented versus procedure-oriented strategies in protecting due process rights. The record-oriented judges minimize the threat by minimizing defendant involvement in the plea. The procedure-oriented judges feel they must involve the defendant and so they do. But unlike the record-oriented judges, this group developed and articulated ideologies of courtroom control that to me seem designed to counter criticisms that they and/or others like them do not maintain control over the courtroom. I show how the procedure-oriented judges deny that they lose control of the courtroom in interviews (although I never suggested they did), question whether judges seen as in control are good judges, and characterize themselves as more informal in the courtroom than controlling judges and as endeavoring to make the average citizen more comfortable and willing to talk in their courtrooms. And I suggest that the oppositionally organized ideologies of courtroom control, both voiced solely by the procedure-oriented judges, draw on ways of thinking and talking about control and formality that are widespread in American culture.

Again, as in chapter 4, we find that the procedure-oriented judges have much more ideologically elaborated positions on why they do things as they do than the record-oriented judges, so that the positions of the two groups are not really parallel. But whereas opposition and conflict between the two groups of judges are not directly acknowledged for legal or political ideologies, they are very overt when ideologies of courtroom control are being discussed.

Chapter 6, "Ideological Diversity in Legal Discourses," pulls together the arguments from the previous chapters in an overview of the way ideological diversity is organized in the legal discourses considered throughout the book.

Does it matter that judges are one way rather than another when they are on the bench in the courtroom? I think it does. This book encourages us to think about what kinds of judges we want in our courtrooms in a different way than the organized bar does. Do we want liberal judges who are friendly and believe the courtroom is for all of us, yet expand the role of the state in their friendliness and spend more of our taxpayers' money? Do we want conservative judges who are distant and may be intimidating, but respect our privacy and try to limit the role of the state and the expenditure of state funds? This book invites consideration of these questions.

Tucson, Arizona   S.U.P.
January 1997

Ideology in the Language of Judges

1

.———.

Ideology in
Discourse

A Narrative of Problem and Method

During the time I spent studying judges' use of language in the Pima County Superior Court, in Tucson, Arizona, judges and lawyers occasionally expressed surprise that an anthropologist was doing research in their courts. Some of them may have been surprised because they associate anthropology with archaeology, which is a highly visible area of endeavor in Arizona, and other kinds of anthropologists usually do ethnographic studies of communities in small-scale non-Western societies. So what was I doing in court? My own single major study up to that time had been an ethnographic study of language use on a small Indian reservation in Oregon (Philips [1983] 1993). In that study I combined the classic ethnographic method of participant observation in a community with what has come to be called *microethnography*, which is the study of culture and social structure in face-to-face interaction (Philips 1993). Usually, microethnographic work involves tape recording or videotaping an activity in a bounded setting. In my case the settings were classrooms where I tape-recorded as well as observed.

Sometime in the mid-to-late 1970s I decided to change my areal and substantive foci of research. I was really more interested in law than in education. And I found that people on Indian reservations generally did not care to be "studied." But when I began observing in the courts in downtown Tucson, much of what went on was unintelligible to me.[1] I couldn't tell how much of this unintelligibility was due to my lack of background in law and how much it was due to shared knowledge about specific cases that courtroom personnel were privy to but I was not. I decided to go to law school for a year to find out how much the legal interpretive perspective was contributing to sense making in the courtroom and to better understand the interpretive perspective of the members of the culture I wanted to study.

3

Well before I spent a year as a regular student at the University of Arizona College of Law (Philips 1982), I envisioned my future research as focusing on the language use of judges. The group category "judges," or "the Pima County Superior Court Bench," was in my mind my "community" rather than, say, Tucson, or the Pima County Superior Court in its entirety, or the legal community of Tucson. In actuality, however, the Pima County Superior Court building became my ethnographic setting and the broader context in which I functioned self-consciously as a participant observer. During the times I and many others were waiting for legal procedures to begin, or on breaks in the middle of court proceedings, I sat in courtrooms and in the halls outside courtrooms where the public waits—sometimes watching and listening, and sometimes talking to those close to me. I rode up and down the elevator to the coffee shop in the basement, where I often lingered. I hung out in the judges' outer chambers and chatted with their secretaries, clerks, and bailiffs while waiting to talk with the judges in their inner chambers. I talked to court administrators in their offices about the vagaries of court calendars. I thought about the judges as an interpretive community, regularly engaged in interaction with one another and influenced by one another's ways of thinking about how to conduct themselves as judges. As time passed, I realized it would have been good had I been able to observe the judges in the full range of activities that constituted their jobs, but I had a definite time frame within which to carry out the study and I had already committed myself to a particular set of information-gathering strategies that were primarily microethnographic in nature.

At the time this research was being developed, several major studies that I knew about had already been done on language use in courts (Danet et al. 1976; O'Barr 1982; Atkinson & Drew 1979). All this work focused on language use in trials, and more particularly on the interaction between lawyers and witnesses. I thought it would be useful to look at other courtroom activities and to focus on other courtroom-defined speaking roles to see whether and how dimensions of language use other than those addressed in earlier work would become salient. I chose to focus on judges as a way of "studying up" (Nader 1972), looking at the most powerful person in the courtroom rather than the least powerful, as anthropologists had been criticized for doing. I wanted to look at many instances of the same procedure to understand the nature of variation in judicial behavior, which I felt had not been done and could not as easily be done with trial data. To more readily obtain information on multiple instances of a legal activity, I wanted to look at short procedures in which judges played an active role.

The project was originally formulated as a study of the relations among judges' judicial behavior, social background, and political ideologies, under the influence of the judicial behavior literature available at the time, but only on one level. On another level I saw the project as a study of the way in which variation in language use constitutes variation in culture and social structure. The three-way connections between judicial behavior on the one hand and social background and political ideologies of judges on the other had been developed primarily in studies of appellate judges. Written decisions by such judges were treated as or equated with "judicial behavior." In the research that had been done on trial court judges, the only "behavior" that had been examined was sentencing, and sentencing was looked at primarily in relation to "attitudes" (e.g., Hogarth 1971).[2] I had a different concept of behavior, namely behavior as actual face-to-face interaction rather than as traces of human activity on paper. I wanted to look at courtroom activity as judicial behavior. I also felt judges' "attitudes" were not richly represented in the trial court literature because they were usually captured as answers to questions formulated by researchers on written questionnaires. I thought that more face-to-face, open-ended interviewing strategies with judges would yield something more and other than political ideology as revealed by attitudes toward, say, capital punishment. I also expected that a more exploratory approach to judges' social backgrounds than that taken in the literature on appellate judges would yield richer and more diverse evidence of the influence of their social backgrounds on their judicial behavior. From the beginning I thought in terms of both culture and ideology rather than attitudes, and to me these terms represented a more careful, coherent, and in-depth approach to the point of view of the judges than the concept of attitudes suggests, in keeping with the ethnographic research goal of representing the experience of the people with whom one works. I also expected that judges' courtroom behavior would be ideological and would reveal and enact meaning. This expectation came from my training in linguistic anthropological approaches to meaning, which involved the idea that cultural realities are constituted through language use in communication in face-to-face interaction. Central to that tradition is the idea that speakers use language in different ways in different contexts to constitute different social realities.

My original plan was to tape different procedures multiple times and to tape the same judges doing them. I also wanted to compare the judges' socially occurring speech in the courtroom with their speech in interviews. The most systematic examination of "contextual variation" in language use at that time had been done with interviews, focusing on phonological variables using the sentence as the linguistic unit and the speaker as the social unit (e.g., Labov 1964). Speakers' class and gender identities had been shown to covary with phonological variation, so that part of the "meaning" of pronunciation *was* class and gender. But this approach was not rich regarding the cultural meaning of the speaking activity examined, and it was not clear how variation captured in interviews would be manifested in routine socially occurring speech. I wanted to see how the role of language (in the constitution of social realities) differed in interviews and socially occurring speech, and I expected to give a great deal of attention to the sequential structure of discourse and to the role of the discourse context in the cultural construction of meaning.

One of my law professors who was from Tucson approached the Pima County Superior Court judges on my behalf. I met with the associate presiding judge of the court, who agreed to supervise my project, recruit judges for it, and get permission from the chief justice of the Supreme Court of Arizona for the project to be carried out.[3] With this supervising judge's assistance, I then began my research, carried out from 1978 to 1980, with a summerlong pilot project. In this pilot project I observed and tape-recorded four superior court judges hearing guilty pleas and two county commissioners handling initial appearances in criminal cases. I met with the judges after each observation or taping and discussed with them why they had handled the cases as they did. I felt I would have more comparability in the criminal cases and a better chance of understanding the law that governed them than in the civil cases. I envisioned myself capturing the criminal process at two stages—the first stage (initial appearance) and the stage that substituted for the trial (the change of plea or guilty plea). I wanted to see whether the organization of interaction and meaning differed at the different stages. I also obtained social background data from the case files on each of the defendants to see how the nature of the criminal change and the social identity of the defendant might be affecting the nature of the activity I recorded. During the several months following this data collection, my research assistant and I transcribed the guilty pleas and two of the initial appearance proceedings and I analyzed them in a preliminary way.

Although this material was useful for some comparative purposes (see Philips 1984a, 1984b, 1987a), the initial appearance data was problematic for me in several respects. There were so many participants in these proceedings that it was difficult to be sure who was speaking, despite my best efforts to code this information during the procedures, and much of the speech was hard to hear on the tape, even though my microphones and I were situated right next to the judge, as in my other taping activities. This comparative taping also did not allow me to see the same judges doing different procedures because temporarily appointed county commissioners rather than regular supreme court judges did the initial appearances.

The following plan for the rest of the project emerged during this pilot effort: I would tape a larger number of the regular judges doing two procedures, the guilty plea and the voir dire, when prospective jurors are questioned and actual jurors are selected. I would interview the judges after each of two periods of observation and each subsequent taping. I aimed to get more than one instance of each procedure from each judge. I also planned to tape-record social background interviews and career history interviews with each judge. Both of my interview schedules were reviewed by the associate presiding judge and by each judge in the study before I went forward with the interviews. I ended up working with nine judges, who made up slightly more than half of the total number on the bench at the time.

During the period in which I then endeavored to do all of what I had mapped out, I still had to make further changes in my plans. The courtroom taping took more time than I expected because of constant scheduling changes in the courtroom procedures, and some judges were doing the procedures I was interested in much more often than were others. Although I taped a total of five voir dires and one complete trial, I had to let go of my plans to tape more instances of the voir dires because getting them was taking too much time. I also found that my taping of interviews was taking too long. I was afraid that if I burdened the tightly scheduled judges with too much interviewing, I would lose my access to them. So I made the social background interview into a Social Background Questionnaire (appendix A, Social Background Questionnaire), which the judges filled out, and continued to tape the career history interviews (appendix B, Career History Interview). I also ended up taping short procedures that occurred at the same time as the guilty pleas, such as motions and sentencings, because this made it easier to capture the beginnings and endings of the guilty pleas and was less disruptive than constantly turning the recorder off and on.

I ended up with a total of 25 to 30 hours of tapings, which included 44 guilty pleas (about 7 hours of taping) and 9 career history interviews (about 12 hours of taping). I also had notes from numerous post-taping interviews with the judges, eight Social Background Questionnaires, and copies of various forms of written law associated with the guilty plea. These "texts" form the basis for comparative and intertextual analysis in this book.

Over the period during which this database was examined again and again and the book was written, my analytical focus changed. I went through a shift in theoretical orientation from thinking of judicial behavior and ideology as connected to thinking predominantly in terms of ideology being enacted through and in the language use that constituted both the courtroom behavior and the interviews. I came to see the different forms of discourse that constituted my database as differing in the way legal and nonlegal ideologies were made manifest in them. I ended up giving less analytical attention to the information about social background that I had obtained from the judges than I had originally intended because there were too few judges to generalize about them with great confidence and the data did not seem very rich, although the career history information emerged as more fruitful. I had been skeptical about the importance of the liberal–conservative distinction used to characterize appellate court judges' political ideologies when I began the study and expected to see other cultural distinctions emerge in judges' language use that would have ideological dimensions to them. Other cultural distinctions with ideological dimensions did emerge in their speech, but the liberal–conservative distinction turned out to be more alive in judges' discourse practices than I had imagined and also emerged as deeply connected to other ways of thinking and talking about judicial behavior.

This book, then, came to be about how judges in the Pima County Superior Court in Tucson, Arizona, produce and organize ideology and ideological diversity in legal discourses that center around criminal defendants' due process rights in the guilty plea. In this study I find ideology and ordered ideological diversity in a range of forms of talk and in multiple instances of the same form of talk. The courtroom guilty pleas are themselves intertextually related to other legal discourses and to my interviews with the judges about why they do guilty pleas as they do. Here ideology is conceptualized as located in and across a range of discourses rather than located in an ungrounded way in society as a whole or in a single text.[4]

The trial court judges in this study take the position that, although they see themselves as subscribing to particular political ideologies, such ideologies should not influence the way they handle guilty pleas. Their position is consistent with the legal view of the role of trial court judges compared to the role of appellate judges in the American legal system, as I learned it in law school and as it is expressed in the literature on judicial behavior. Appellate judges are seen as deciders of law. They are understood to be influenced in deciding what the law is by their political philosophies, and selection of appellate judges attends to that aspect of their background. Trial court judges, on the other hand, are seen as deciders of fact, and as (mere) implementers of the law decided on by the appellate courts. In the selection of trial court judges, their political views and their party affiliations are backgrounded. This inconsistency between levels of courts reflects the influence of both the political party system and professional bar associations on the judicial selection process and to some extent reveals an ideological struggle between these two types of organizations for control of the legal process.

But I argue here that, regardless of whether judges recognize they are enacting political philosophies in the way they do guilty pleas, they *are* enacting such political philosophies. Although legal interpretive perspectives or ideologies are dominant in the way judges think about what they are doing, judges are enacting nonlegal ideologies in the guilty plea as well. Political and everyday ideas about state and individual exercise of power are realized through judges' enactments of different interpretations of defendants' due process rights, so that courtroom discourse is ideologically polysemic. However, political and everyday ideologies are suppressed and peripheralized in a variety of ways that sustain the interpretive salience and domination of legal ideology in the legal discourses about the guilty plea.

Language and Ideology

To conceptualize ideology in discourse in this book, I have drawn primarily on and tried to integrate two rather disparate theoretical traditions—that of anthropological approaches to language as encoding culture and that of Marxist approaches to ideology.[5] Within each of these traditions the idea has emerged that ideologies are constituted and enacted in social practices rather than being the nonmaterial mental phenomena that can be correlated with behavioral practices. This fundamental source of common orientation provides the basis for the integration of these two traditions. Each tradition has both strengths and weaknesses, and I try here to compensate for the weaknesses I see in each tradition by drawing upon the strengths of the other tradition. In brief, the strength of anthropology is that it offers a theory and method for understanding the role of language in the constitution of social realities at the level of actual human social interaction. But this tradition has only recently begun to come to grips with intrasocietal interpretive diversity and with the way in which power relations shape the nature of interpretive practices. The Marxist tradition offers a theory of how ideological diversity is socially ordered in terms of relations of domination and subordination involving struggles for ideological control. These struggles shape the nature of ideology and its diverse manifestations and help explain how ideologies change over time. But, although many Marxists today are generally sympathetic to the idea that symbolic practices, including language, carry ideology, they have not developed a theory of how ideology is constituted through language in actual discourse practices. Marxist thought about ideology has been little influenced by actual close examination of the life of ideology in social practices. My goal, then, is to conceptualize ideology and ideological diversity as grounded in actual discourse practices that are socially ordered by various kinds of power struggles between dominant and subordinate social forces and ideologies.

Marxists on Ideology

In general, Marxist theory of ideology today envisions ideology as shaped by dominant and subordinate sectional interests engaged in a power struggle. The model is basically dualistic; however, although Marx-influenced scholars used to locate this struggle in class relations, it is now looked for in a variety of kinds of relationships. In the Marxist tradition, dominant ideologies are developed and promulgated by groups in power. Such ideologies justify the present political order and the place of subordinated interests within it. A dominant ideology also hides or conceals the vested interest of the dominant group, and if the subordinated group is to perceive its true interest, the dominant ideology must be critiqued and its vested interests revealed as a necessary step in the resistance of the subordinated group against its own oppression. Thus, although the subordinate group may subscribe to the dominant ideology, ideological critique will lead to the emergence of an oppositional ideology, which will play a role in the resistance of the subordinated against the dominant. Anthropologists have recently shown a keen interest in documenting this process of resistance and are debating what counts as resistance (e.g., Comaroff 1985; Abu-Lughod 1985; Martin 1987; Kennedy & Davis 1993).

In the last two decades, Marx-influenced scholars have paid increasing attention to the role of ideology in the political domination of nation states over their citizens, under the influence of the work of Antonio Gramsci (1971). Gramsci is known for his critique of Marx's failure to acknowledge the role of the state in shaping the nature of relations of domination and subordination. He argued that in advancing a revolutionary cause, it is not enough for a revolutionary party to be able to take over nation state structures by force to achieve its goals. State control depends not only on coercion but also on the hegemony, or ideological domination, that creates and maintains the consent of the governed. Hegemony, a kind of ideological consensus, was envisioned by Gramsci as achieved by creating coalitions among classes who were both inside the state and outside it, particularly in civil structures strongly connected to the state, including political parties, the church, and labor unions. In Gramsci's view, both legal and educational structures were seen as organs of the state with important hegemonic functions. Althusser (1971) used the term "ideological state apparatuses" to refer to organizational structures with important hegemonizing roles, and he argued that these must be connected to and deeply penetrate family life to be effective forces of state hegemony.

Gramsci emphasized that hegemony was never total and required constant effort to maintain, notably through the co-optation of resistance from various competing interests. He saw struggle in relatively nondualistic terms, portraying a range of organizational structures involved in an ideological struggle for control of the state, and he represented the boundary between state and civil organizations and activities as amorphous and blurred. Some scholars, however, have reproduced the dualism in Marx's own work in their interpretation of Gramsci by representing the state as in an oppositional relationship with nonstate social entities.

Some interpreters of Gramsci, notably Raymond Williams (1977), have also attributed to his concept of hegemony a kind of "naturalized" unconscious and pervasive quality. Such a concept of hegemony is evident in the work of several influential French social theorists who hold that the most powerful interpretive perspectives are those with a taken-for-granted quality constituting a lived reality (Barthes 1972; Bourdieu 1977; Foucault 1972, 1980). But Gramsci's own writing is not clear on this point, and a concept of hegemonic ideology more consistent with his vision of multiple struggles for ideological control of the state is one of varying degrees of implicitness and explicitness in the ideologies being fought over.

The specific although unelaborated place for law as an ideological state apparatus in Gramsci's work has contributed to the emergence of a vision of law as a form of ideology among students of law influenced by Marxist thought (Tigar & Levy 1977;

Hay 1975; Sumner 1979). The critical legal studies movement has also developed a vision of law as ideology (e.g., Kairys 1982; Jeorges & Trubek 1989; Fineman 1988), although not all of this work is overtly Gramscian. In both Marxist and non-Marxist developments of a view of law as ideology there has been attention to the pluralism of legal ideologies, to struggle and conflict among legal ideologies, and to change over time in dominant legal interpretive perspectives emerging from that struggle, so that the law of a given time and place can be seen as historically contingent and culturally local (Starr & Collier 1989; Amherst Seminar 1988; Just 1992; Sarat & Kearns 1991; Lazarus-Black & Hirsch 1994).

Legal scholarship that focuses on the language of law emphasizes the constitutive role of language and recognizes that specific interpretive frames are invoked in legal uses of language. Law itself is treated as a specific interpretive framework (O'Barr 1982; Conley & O'Barr 1990) and legal cases are conceptualized as involving conflicting views of reality constituted by prosecution and defense (Bennett & Feldman 1981; Maynard 1984). There is also increasing conceptualization of interpretive perspective as ideology, connecting power relations and conflict to multiple legal interpretive perspectives (Philips 1994). Those who focus on the constitutive role of language in the production of ideologies have been particularly interested in what happens when the ideologies of members of the legal profession about law come into contact with citizens' ideas about justice as they seek help from the legal system (Merry 1990; Conley & O'Barr 1990; Mertz 1992; Hirsch 1994). This study shares their concern with the constitutive role of language in the production of ideology and ideological diversity, but it is focused primarily on legal ideological diversity *within* the state (Carnoy 1984) and only secondarily on the way in which state and civil society mutually influence one another in the courtroom.

To summarize, then, Marxist and Gramscian traditions offer a way of grounding ideological diversity in a social order conceived in terms of relations of domination and subordination. Many legal scholars now think of law as ideology and as ideologically plural, and they recognize the role of language in the constitution of legal ideologies. Some scholars recognize the hegemonizing role of law as a vehicle of the state in Gramscian terms. As yet, however, discussions of the ways in which language use constitutes legal ideologies have not foregrounded relations of domination and subordination. And these discussions have not been grounded in a coherent approach to actual discourse practices, with the notable exception of Matoesian (1993).

Linguistic Anthropologists on Culture in Discourse

Anthropological theories of culture as practice offer promise for such grounding of the social construction of legal ideologies in actual discourse practices. In recent decades both cultural and linguistic anthropologists have moved in the direction of seeing culture as located in social practices (Sherzer 1987; Urban 1991) rather than as knowledge located in the minds of individuals, although how they characterize practice varies. Many cultural anthropologists have been influenced by Bourdieu's (1977) concept of practice and Foucault's (1972) concept of discourse in envisioning culture in practice. For Bourdieu, individuals' involvement in social experiences constantly transforms their mental (culturally structured) worlds. For Foucault the individual exists experientially in actual discourses that form a broad societal discourse, which is thought of as reality and as truth but is actually historically contingent and constantly undergoing transformation. Both these scholars offer a vision of a cultural whole that is constantly shifting processually and changing through discourse practices.

Linguistic anthropologists and some cultural anthropologists equate practice with actual spoken discourse or language use. In this view, speakers and hearers engaged in face-to-face interaction jointly produce meaning. Thus, to understand how meaning is produced, it is necessary to examine actual discourse, in the form of transcripts of tape recordings of socially occurring speech.

In work that examines socially occurring discourse, the concepts of genre and text have emerged as particularly useful for showing how shifts in speakers' interpretive perspectives are organized. The term *speech genre* refers to forms of talk that are recognized as discrete or distinct by members of a culture.[6] The fact that genres are often named and referred to by speakers is taken as evidence that there is in some sense conscious awareness that talk comes in different forms. Commonly cited examples of speech genres include stories, poems, speeches, and lectures.[7] Discourse realizations of genres are seen by language users and analysts alike as sequences of contiguous utterances which are usually although not always separable from or marked off from surrounding discourse by clear beginnings and endings. Many genres are also identifiable in discourse through their internal coherence, which is achieved in part through an internal sequential structure that constrains relations between language form and content.

The internal sequential structuring of speech genres in actual discourse has both global and local dimensions (Matoesian 1993). *Global structure* refers to the idea that a genre of discourse involves an abstract schema or script entailing a predictable sequence of topics or smaller units of discourse that, when adhered to, allow for recognition of speech as constituting a particular form of talk. *Local structure* refers to the idea that all talk, whether realizing such a global schema or not, is locally managed on a turn-by-turn basis, so that what a speaker says is heard as related to what the preceding speaker has said.

There are several ways in which the structuring of speech genres plays a role in constituting multiple points of view or interpretive diversity in discourse practices. First, genres themselves are recognized to entail different interpretive framings of social reality. Thus, a story is a different way of framing reality than a lecture or a court trial, even when the events being represented are the same events. Genre-specific linguistic and discourse conventions cue listeners as to the kinds of interpretive conventions they need to be using to make sense of what they are hearing. The idea that individual genres entail genre-specific framings of reality tends to be taken for granted rather than problematized in most work on speech genres. Of greater theoretical interest to linguistic anthropologists has been the idea that *within* a given speech genre, particular linguistic forms and discourse conventions provide contextualization cues (Gumperz 1982) or frames (Goffman 1974) for shifts in interpretive perspective or point of view in the sequential structure of discourse.[8]

Linguistic anthropologists also recognize that the process through which speaker and listeners connect what is said to their knowledge of immediate and past contexts raises the possibility of both systematic variation and great individual open-endedness in interpretive practices.[9]

Recently anthropologists have begun to write about the way in which speech is connected to other speech as a relation among genres, using the term *intertextuality* to refer to such connections (Briggs & Bauman 1992). Speakers and hearers make both regular and systematic, as well as new, connections between genres to produce or make sense of a given text, thus generating new interpretations of past textual productions. To understand how speakers and hearers relate genres in producing meaningful talk and in making sense out of talk, anthropologists have developed methods of comparative analysis of texts that in themselves create new forms of intertextuality or new relations among texts and genres. Thus, intertextuality can refer both to a process of meaning making in which we all engage and to a method of analysis used by anthropologists to better understand that process. Such analysis can focus on relations among multiple instances of the same genre of speech, relations among different genres of speech, and relations between different genre-ed renderings of the "same" events or content.

Some linguistic anthropologists, particularly those trained in the ethnography of communication (Gumperz & Hymes 1964) demonstrate a strongly developed awareness that speech genres are socially ordered in their intertextual relations into domains and institutions of language use.[10] In their productive and interpretive practices, speakers and hearers draw on their awareness of such relations. Scholars in this tradition show the greatest methodological commitment to the analysis of multiple genres from within a single community that locates those genres within the larger sociocultural organization of the community. Representing genres in relation to one another and placing them in a broader sociocultural context involves a thick, rich intertextual analysis representing a level of social ordering of interpretive diversity intermediate between a single text and "the discourse" of an entire society. It is with this tradition that the present work is aligned.

Characterizations of such social ordering of discourse practices have only recently become concerned with issues salient in Marxist traditions, however—that is, with a social ordering seen as involving relations of domination and subordination shaped by political economic processes that include a residential community's articulation with the world outside it.[11] Without these Marxist concerns, anthropologists are addressing the constitution of culture, rather than of ideology.

Conclusion

The integration of Marxist and anthropological approaches to meaning in discourse in this work entails viewing judges as representatives of the state who promulgate a legal ideology that is hegemonic in the sense that it is imposed by them on those they engage in courtroom discourse to achieve a single salient sociolegal reality. But these same judges also constitute ideological diversity through the range of ways that the structuring of speech genres have been shown by anthropologists to contribute to multiple interpretive perspectives in language use: Different legal interpretations of due process rights are evident in the spoken and written legal genres devoted to the guilty plea. Different judges enact different legal ideological stances in the way they hear guilty pleas by making different intertextual connections between the written genres of law and their own spoken pleas. They do this by including or omitting and expanding or abbreviating certain topics in the guilty plea. Moreover, intertextual connections between the pleas and my interviews with the judges about their work show that they are enacting not only due process legal ideologies but also political ideologies concerning the role of the state in relation to the individual and more society-wide commonsense ideologies about social control.

As I display how this ideological diversity is ordered in the forms of talk analyzed, I attend specifically to the utility of Marxist conceptualizations of the ordering of ideological diversity, asking: In what ways and to what extent is the ideological diversity I document dualistically organized, and to what extent is there evidence of opposition and conflict among the ideologies and their promulgators? In what ways do relations of domination and subordination shape the nature of the ideological diversity I find? What does it mean to talk about ideological stances as being constituted relatively explicitly as opposed to implicitly? In general, I find that when ideological diversity can be seen as oppositionally organized in relations of domination and subordination, such conflict and struggle are largely concealed or hidden from view in a variety of ways that contribute to a sometimes misleading projection of law as ideologically monolithic.

Next I take up the idea raised earlier that political ideology has no place in the work of trial court judges, who do not make law but rather implement law that is made by others. I argue that this way of viewing trial court judges is in itself ideological and reflects the present-day success of professional organizations of trial court lawyers in defining the job of judge in professional terms rather than in the political terms of political parties.

2

The Myth of the
Trial Court Judge
as Nonideological

Well at the trial level, while we are vested with some measure of discretion, we don't have as much discretion as most lay people would suppose we do. We are governed by statutes which are the creatures of the legislature. We are governed by appellate court decisions, state appellate court decisions, the United States Supreme Court decisions. What I am trying to say is that in most cases, what our own philosophical bent is, or what our particular background may lead us to by way of feelings about a particular matter, don't mean a great deal. Because as I say, at the trial level we are simply trying to apply the law as it's presented to us.

(Judge 6, Career History Interview, p. 32)[1]

In this chapter I show how the Tucson judges with whom I worked operate in a political climate in which they present themselves, as in the previous quote, as mere implementers of law, uninfluenced by their own political and social backgrounds. Yet what they must do to become judges, their routes to the trial court bench, requires a significant involvement in local political processes that makes it highly unlikely they are not so influenced.

Historically, in the United States, there has always been a tension in the selection of trial court judges—between wanting judges who are responsive to local community values and political ideologies and wanting judges who are impartial and somewhat removed from such influences. In recent decades, the political tide has moved, and is still moving, toward emphasizing impartiality over local community responsiveness. I suggest this is largely due to the growth in influence of professional organizations of lawyers, such as the State Bar of Arizona, and the lessening (though by no means the disappearance) of the influence of state and county political party organizations over these same processes. This emphasis has intensified the judges' need to appear uninfluenced by anything other than the law itself.

In the discussion to follow I show how organized state bars in general and the State Bar of Arizona in particular succeeded in changing the selection of judges from an elective to an appointive system heavily influenced by the bar and talk about the ideological debates that have influenced this shift. I interlace this discussion with the views and experiences of the nine judges with whom I worked. I compare and contrast those who came onto the bench under the elective system (Judges 1 through 5) with those who came onto the bench under the current appointive system (Judges 6 through 9) to show how they reflect the change.[2]

I conclude, as have others, that the process of becoming a judge is no less political than it was before, but the politics is now more the politics and ideology of the organized bar and less the politics and ideology of Republican and Democratic political party organizations. Judges' denial of ideological influence on their judicial behavior itself reflects the current ideological influence of the lawyers of the organized bar.

The purpose of this discussion is to help explain why judges interpret their own judicial behavior in legal terms yet are still influenced by other kinds of ideologies, including political ideologies.

The Shift from Elected to Appointed Judges

During the 19th century, the majority of states elected judges. The turn of the century saw calls for reform in judicial selection because of the way it was controlled by political party machines in some parts of the country, notably New York. Judges were rewarded for political party service, which critics of judicial selection processes saw as hindering their impartiality and contributing to their corruption (Schmidhauser 1979; Roll 1990).

With the growing sense of professional identity among lawyers and the increasing strength of the national American Bar Association and organized state bars during this century came their additional critique of elective systems as failing to select professionally well-qualified judges. This failure led to the organized lobbying of legislatures and the public by organized bars for changes from elective to appointive selection of judges that was clearly present by the 1940s but peaked in the 1960s and 1970s.

Basically, there are three modes of selection of state trial court judges in this country: partisan election, nonpartisan election, and appointment. In both partisan and nonpartisan election systems, candidates run against each other and are elected by registered voters in their jurisdictions. In the 1940s, Missouri introduced a new appointive system that was supported by the organized bar because of the way it incorporated attention to the professional qualifications or merit of lawyers considered for appointment. Missouri's plan, which came to be called *merit selection*, in contrast to elective systems involved appointment by an elected official, usually the governor of the state for state courts of general jurisdiction. It typically is distinguished by three characteristics: (1) candidates are nominated by a commission of lay and lawyer members; (2) selection is by appointment; (3) tenure is by vote of the electorate, which periodically votes to retain or not retain each judge (Winters 1973).

The clearest and most influential argument of organized bars as they campaigned for merit selection to be instituted in other states besides Missouri was that under older earlier systems of judicial selection, local political party organizations selected and supported candidates on the basis of their past contributions to those parties and not on their personal and legal professional qualifications, so that the candidates were not the best candidates from a legal point of view. Note that in taking this position, those campaigning for merit selection were able to sidestep the issue of corruption (i.e., they did not have to claim the judges selected by local party organizations were corrupt, only that they were incompetent).

In addition, it was common practice nationally for sitting judges to time their retirements so that the person temporarily appointed to fill their positions until an election would be of the same party (Dolbeare 1967). This person, as the incumbent, would then have an advantage over his opponent of the opposing party when election time came. Three of the five Tucson judges in my study who came onto the bench under the elective system were first appointed by the governor of Arizona in this way.

In the excerpt that follows, Judge 2 reveals the careful calculations of party-loyal judges leaving the bench, who wanted to make sure someone of the same party would be appointed to the positions they were leaving. He[3] is talking about how he as a Democrat came to be appointed by the governor of Arizona at a time when a Republican governor was about to go out of office and a Democratic governor was about to come in.

(1) Harrison [a Republican], at the same time, ran for the Appeals Court and was elected and everybody knew that he was going to resign to allow the outgoing Republican governor replace him with a Republican. Johnson, being a Democrat, everybody knew he was going to stay and let the new governor do it. So, both on the Republican side and the Democratic side, this jousting was going on all fall. But neither one of them had a formal process at that time. . . . Now how it came about with me, ever since everybody knew that those two positions were going to be open, and on the Democratic side, some people came along, like Davidoff called me and a couple of other lawyers called me and said, "Would you be interested in being considered if this informal search committee that the governor has announced wanted to consider your name?" And I said "Yes, I would like to be considered." And the reason they asked me, I think, they knew I had run for office for one of these two years before and so they were familiar with it. (Judge 2, Career History Interview, pp. 34–35)

While this particular judge, then, was rather passive in the immediate context of his appointment, Judge 3 was more active:

(2) I had some inside information that there was going to be a vacancy probably, because Mathews was going to retire from the Court of Appeals and come back into the law firm that I was in. And I knew that was coming up and I suspected that when it did that one of the judges here would be appointed to take his place. So I got to the governor, Jolly, early, wrote him myself and told him that I would be interested in the appointment if it came up, and I contacted three people that I knew were close to him, that I knew, that I asked to contact him on my behalf and they all did. (Judge 3, Career History Interview, pp. 49–50)

Social scientific research supports the organized bar's claims that party organizations dominated judicial selection. During the most intense period of organized bar campaigning for merit selection across the country, the 1960s and 1970s, a flurry of studies described the significant extent to which local party organizations controlled the selection of judges for trial courts of general jurisdiction, although those studies also made it clear that this influence varied considerably from city to city (Dolbeare 1967; Levin 1977; Eisenstein & Jacob 1977).

The Arizona Experience with Merit Selection

Arizona voters approved a change from an elective to an appointive system in 1974. The emergence of the Arizona merit selection system and the features particular to it have been well documented (Dunn 1967; Cameron 1976; Lee 1973; Slavin 1976; Roll 1990). Until 1975, Arizona judges were nominated in party primaries, then ran in the general election without party designation. Technically, then, Arizona could be said to have had a nonpartisan election system of judicial selection, but the modes of appointment of the judges with whom I worked show how partisan it actually was. In 1976, the Arizona Constitution was revised to provide for a merit selection system (Ariz Rev. Stat. §§ 36–38) with the following features: nomination commissions, with a separate commission for each county with a population of more than 150,000 (which meant only the counties that include Phoenix and Tucson actually appoint judges) were to consist of nine persons. Three attorneys were to be nominated by the State Bar of Arizona Board of Governors and appointed by the governor of Arizona, with advice and consent of the Senate. Five laypeople (nonattorneys) were to be appointed by the governor with advice and consent of the Senate.[4] Both commissions were to be chaired by the chief justice of the Arizona State Supreme Court, who was to vote only on tie votes. I was told that the greater number of lay relative to lawyer members of the commission reflected the historically populist background in Arizona State politics. For each available position, the commission was to submit to the governor at least three nominations, and then the governor was to choose one person from among those nominated.

Party politics were constrained by the changes in the state constitution rather than eliminated in Arizona's system, both in the composition of the commissions and in the list of nominees submitted. The changes specified that not more than two of the three attorneys and not more than three of the five lay members can be members of the same party. This allowed for the party of the appointing state governor to dominate the commission but prevented the total exclusion of other political parties. Similarly, the nominating commission's three nominations must consist of no more than two-thirds members of the same political party. Typically, two of the nominees come from the governor's party, while the third comes from the party out of power, and the governor selects one of the two from his own party, unless there are overriding considerations such as the need to respond to pressures for ethnic minority representation on the bench or the exceptionally impressive reputation of a particular candidate.

In Arizona, judges are brought to the electorate for approval of continued tenure or disapproval and removal from office every 3 years. As in other states, the State Bar of Arizona developed a judicial evaluation process conceived as a companion to the merit selection system in which lawyers are polled by the bar regarding their views on the judges up for reelection (Slavin 1976). The results of that poll are publicized before the election with the intent that the opinions of those considered by the organized bar to be most knowledgeable (i.e., themselves) about judges' performance on the bench will influence the electorate. Evaluation criteria, which convey a good deal about lawyers' ideas of merit, include punctuality, attentiveness in court, promptness of rulings, fairness, courteousness, courtroom discipline, knowledge and application of the law, consideration of briefs and authorities, and judicial temperament and demeanor (*Arizona Daily Star* 1978).

Soon after the introduction of the merit selection system, Cameron (1976) noted that although the approval rates of voters generally followed the same pattern as those of the bar polls—those the bar polls condemned were given lower ratings than those the bar polls approved of—none of the judges that the bar poll recommended removing from office were in fact removed by the voters. This pattern continues to the present and has been noted in other states with merit selection systems (Jacob 1978). In other words, never does a majority of the electorate disapprove of judges whom the lawyers evaluate as doing a poor job. The organized bar, which is so committed to this approach to judicial selection and retention, considers this voting pattern to be a problem because so far there is no evidence that the merit selection system can get rid of judges who are deemed lacking in merit. Recently, the Chief Justice of the Arizona Supreme Court appointed a commission to look into alternative ways in which to evaluate judges and disseminate the results of those evaluations to the public, and their efforts are being observed with interest by proponents of merit selection in other parts of the country (Commission on Judicial Performance Review 1994).

The merit selection system has not been without its critics, and there have been intermittent political efforts in Arizona to alter or get rid of it since its inception (Roll 1990).

Appointed Judges versus Elected Judges

Are the judges who are now appointed under the merit selection system in Tucson different from the judges who came onto the bench under an elective system? Of course, the issue for the organized bar should be whether the judges are better, more meritorious, more punctual, impartial, more knowledgeable of the law, and so on. Interestingly enough, to my knowledge the bar polls have not addressed this issue. There are no comparisons of those who have been selected under the different systems in these terms, nor does the social scientific literature on judicial behavior address this issue. Among the judges with whom I worked on the Pima County Superior Court Bench, those selected under different systems are not evaluated as better or worse in the bar polls I have seen. In other words, judges who came in under the merit selection system do not as a group get higher evaluations than the other judges.

However, some other kinds of differences exist within the small group with which I worked—in the way they talk about how they came to be judges and how they conceptualize their roles as judges—that suggest some impact from a change in selection processes. First, the judges who were appointed indicate more distance from party politicians in the way they were selected. As earlier quotes suggest, at least some of the judges who came in under the elective system (but were in fact appointed by the governor) were close friends with party activists who aided their selection. The judges who were appointed under the merit selection system do not suggest such intimacy, although the contrast is not absolute:

(3) At the point that there were vacancies, the commissions had been empaneled and I simply sent in an application together with a resume and they screened the application. If they thought you were an interesting candidate, they'd invite you for an interview. (Judge 6, Career History Interview, p. 28)

(4) I'm sure [the governor] didn't even know what a Judge 8 was or is, and I had only contributed like seventy-five dollars to his campaign. But I had the support of a broad base
of good lawyers down here in town, several of whom had (   ) good connections with
him. And they recommended, after my name got on the list, that he take a good look at
me. I'm sure that helped. (Judge 8, Career History Interview, pp. 33–34)

(5) Once the three names came out I didn't ask one person to lobby for me with the
governor or anything. (Judge 7, Career History Interview, p. 20)

Second, the four judges who were selected under the "new" system also discussed
planning their careers so that they would look to the commission like the kind of lawyer who should become a judge, an idea not discussed by Judges 1 through 5. This
planning meant getting a broad rather than narrow base of legal experience, plenty of
trial practice, and, if possible, lower-level judicial experience.

(6) I told him ["him" refers to the Superior Court judge who appointed Court Commissioners, who are part of the same court system but more restricted jurisdictionally in
legal matters they can handle] that I was practicing by myself and he said, "Gee sure
love to have you over here as a Court Commissioner", and I said, "Well the problem is
I don't know that I could live on what you're paying." . . . I did some fast calculating
and said, "Well, gee, this might be a start of where I've always wanted to be anyway
and I'll give it a whirl. The family won't suffer too much, at least for awhile until the
funds ran out." (Judge 6, Career History Interview, p. 17)

(7) I was just trying to become as good a lawyer as I could become and give myself as much
and as diverse an experience as I could, because I had decided, oh, five years anyway,
before I became a judge that that's what I really wanted to do. And by going with the
Franken firm, which is the one that I was with last, they had a different kind of practice
than, say Mahoney [the firm he had been with] had. Mahoney [lawyers] are known
generally in the community as a plaintiff's law firm, whereas Franken is generally known
as a defense firm. And so I had experience on both sides of the fence. It was good for
me and, you know, allowed me to check some of my own thoughts about myself in terms
of my attitude and aptitude, as well as get some good experience. I think it helped me,
at my age, seem credible to the selection committee. . . . Not being a politician I had to
do that. (Judge 8, Career History Interview, pp. 20–21)

(8) The experience I had as a special commissioner and the years on the bench pro tem,
you know, made me better qualified than a lot of guys. Look, I'd wanted to be a judge
for a long time. You know, I decided to do the things that would help me get the job.
. . . Probably six, seven years ago. I decided this is what I wanted to do. . . . Anything
that I did prior to six, seven years ago was just because I wanted to do it. But the last
five or six years a lot of it has been geared towards what my ultimate goal was. And that
was to be a judge. It took lots of patience if nothing else. (Judge 9, Career History Interview, pp. 25–27)

Third, a difference between the two groups of judges which reflects a greater distance from party politics under the new selection system lies in the way they characterized their political ideological orientations. The older judges who came in under
the elective system were comfortable associating themselves with political labels, with
representing themselves as politically coherent, and a few were even comfortable with

acknowledging that their politics had some influence on their judicial behavior, although usually only vaguely and as a matter of style rather than substance.

(9) I certainly am a partisan Democrat. . . . I see humanity and human things of more importance than property. . . . In studying about the Supreme Court it sort of horrifies me how the whole history of it has been guided by property interests rather than human interests and that bothers me. . . . As a trial judge I don't follow that. (Judge 1, Career History Interview, pp. 61–62)

(10) I've been a member of the Democratic Party. I resent very much being referred to as a liberal, because I'm not sure what a liberal or a conservative really is except I've watched other people who claim they are and both of them are, in my opinion, ridiculous. I consider myself a Populist. I'm interested in people. . . . And whether you want to call that a political [orientation] or not, I'm not interested in politics per se in my professional job. I'm interested in seeing it from that standpoint. (Judge 2, Career History Interview, pp. 59–62)

One of these five judges who came in under the elective system talked about the difficulties he experienced when he was expected to sentence people for crimes in a way that went against his political orientation.

(11) I did at one time anyway, have real philosophical problems or dilemmas with prosecuting, or sentencing or dealing with cases involving quote-unquote victimless crimes. Prostitution, pornography, all of that kind of stuff. . . . I know that I cannot in good conscience put somebody in jail or prison for a marijuana offense. I just can't do that and the prosecution knows that and so does the defense and so they don't bring cases to me or let cases come to me where they want somebody to go to prison for such an offense. . . .

Because philosophically I can conceptualize what it is to lose your freedom and think that that's probably the most important thing that we have, I had reservations about putting people in jail, unless I thought it was a serious transgression. . . . You have to have some adjustment period to that so that you feel, hopefully you never feel comfortable about it because taking somebody's liberty is a pretty traumatic thing. But you do. You have to. You can't ignore the responsibility that you have that some people just have to be locked up, some require extensive punishment or whatever. . . . I'm sure that my track record would reflect it to some extent, that I had high propensity or incidence of probation disposition at the early part of my Superior Court time. (Judge 5, Career History Interview, pp. 46–50)

But, whereas the judges who came in under elective systems were more likely to be holistic in their representations of their political ideological stances, the four judges who were appointed under merit selection presented themselves as more fragmented or less coherent in their political ideologies.

(12) You know you can be liberal on one thing and conservative on another. . . . Right now it depends on the issue that's being presented as to, you know, what my position would be. . . . If you ask me, am I for an amendment to the Constitution requiring a balanced budget, I'm against that. If you ask me, am I for cutting down the bureaucracy, I'll say "Yeah, I am for that". So you know, you can sort of divide the issues as you go along. So I reject this simple terminology of, you know, liberal or conservative. Probably [I'm]

somewhere in the middle and reacting to the issue as it arises. (Judge 7, Career History Interview, pp. 33–34)

(13) You know, of course, judges are people. We have our own, I'm entitled to my own opinions and thoughts on issues and subjects, whether they relate to the law or some other subject. And I suppose generally I consider myself to be liberal, although I'm not all that label conscious. Kind of depends on the given issue. I sometimes think more in terms of the singer rather than the song, for instance, when I'm voting. (Judge 8, Career History Interview, pp. 49–50)

These judges, unlike those who came in under an elective system, also cited and elaborated on the importance of impartiality in their role and the constraint of law on them when asked about their political ideologies and the impact of those ideologies on their judicial behavior. They were less willing than the group that came in under the elective system to acknowledge such an impact, and when they did acknowledge the possibility, they were clear that it was wrong. They supported the legal constraint imposed on them and gave it as a reason why their political ideologies should not affect their judicial behavior. Here is what another merit-selected judge had to say on this issue:

(14) But as far as I'm concerned the number one criterion for doing my job right is impartiality, and I should not let my own given thoughts or leanings on a particular issue influence how I decide that. That has nothing to do with what the facts in the case are essentially. The facts are established at this level. And once those are established, then I'll apply the law as I see that it is, even if I don't happen to agree with it or wish that it were some other way. I think that's important. So I like to think that my own orientation politically or philosophically or whatever you want to say doesn't affect my behavior in the courtroom. However, I don't doubt that sometimes it's apparent. (Judge 8, Career History Interview, pp. 50–51)

One judge who came in under the elective system also articulated such a view. Ironically, this is the same judge who talked about his initial reluctance to provide harsh sentences for some kinds of crimes. But that was earlier in his career, and what follows conveys his basic commitment to follow the law rather than his own ideological inclinations.

(15) When I get into that position I try to follow the law. I don't think it's for me to legislate. It's for me to decide what the law has concluded in that regard, what the Supreme Court is saying, even though I may philosophically disagree with 'em. I mean I'm a Justice Black, Hugo Black, kind of person when it comes to pornography. The Constitution says you can't have any law abridging freedom of speech. Not withstanding that, the majority of the court has said otherwise: pornography can be prosecuted or controlled and so forth. So I follow that and try to arrive at a decision in the case that's consistent with what I think the case is like. So I try to get my personal philosophy out of it. And I don't think that that's the way for me to change it, to be a judicial activist, so to speak, and say, "Not withstanding what everybody along the line has said, I think to the contrary." (Judge 5, Career History Interview, p. 44)

In sum, the four appointed judges were more distant from party politics in the selection process, planned their careers so they would look good professionally to judicial selection commissions, were more ideologically fragmented than elected judges, and were more explicit about their impartiality and the constraints on them from written law than the elected judges.

But Selection of Judges Is Still "Political"

In spite of the greater distance from the political process in the experience of the judges appointed under merit selection, the process is still very political, even in the narrow sense of party politics. As the selection of judges is presently institutionalized, the party affiliations of lay members appointed to nominating commissions by the governor are controlled in a way that allows the governor's party to dominate numerically. And clearly the governors of Arizona still regularly appoint far more members of their own party than of the opposing party.

The judges with whom I worked were in general agreement that the process is still very political in this narrower sense, regardless of the system under which they had been selected. Here again, quotes reveal the judges' views.

(16) And there's no question about my political activity had a lot to do with my appoint-ment by the governor. (Judge 9, Career History Interview, p. 23)

(17) You know, when you see a judgeship developing in the next six months and the [po-litical party] county chairman calls you and asks you to do something, you do it. . . . But you know, every judge who has been appointed to the Superior Court certainly, even under the Merit Selection system, he has to have the political contact that finally brings the appointment down and without that contact he's not gonna get the appoint-ment. . . . When Bennett goes to the federal court, when Jarrold retires or resigns . . . three names, at a minimum, are gonna come out of the nominating commission, and if people were betting on it, if you try to figure out . . . does Jones or Smith have the better chance? Who's paid their political dues? . . . So he can contact someone assum-ing he is at someone's favor, say Randall, for example, who's probably the most powerful Democratic person in Pima County, to call the governor and say, "Hey, Gov, you got three names up there, I think Donatello is entitled to it this time." . . . That's the way mine finally came down. . . . This is my pure speculation on the backroom politics. . . . You know obviously there are many other considerations and there's the equal oppor-tunity aspect of it. That certainly is a very heavy consideration. (Judge 4, Career His-tory Interview, pp. 28–32)

(18) I think it [the political process] comes into play at the governor's level. I don't think it comes into play at all at the level of the commission. . . . Anyhow I don't see anything wrong with that necessarily as long as the committee which is bi-partisan and objec-tive says there are three people qualified for a job, I don't see anything wrong with the governor then saying, "Well, I'm going to lean towards someone in my own party or someone I know, because at least he's been certified as being qualified." (Judge 6, Career History Interview, pp. 28–29)

The continued involvement of party politics in the process of selection of judges, yet now more covert and without democratic electoral involvement, is one of the major complaints about merit selection in Arizona that has motivated political campaigns in favor of returning to an electoral process (Roll 1990).

My own view, however, one shared by some other students of judicial behavior (e.g., Schmidhauser 1979; Levin 1977), is that we must broaden the concept of the "political" to include bar politics. In the literature produced on merit selection, which appears to be dominated by bar activists, there is no acknowledgement that their success in instituting merit selection is a political success, nor is there acknowledgement that their political influence over judicial selection and retention has grown relative to that of party organizations. Nor did the judges with whom I worked ever suggest that bar activity be considered political. Rather, such activity was kept analytically separate in my discussions with judges about their career histories, both by them and by me, a separation I did not question at the time.

But as my earlier account of the formal structure for merit selection suggests, the organized bar has succeeded in institutionalizing its involvement in the selection process through its representation on every commission that submits judicial nominees to the governor of the state. And although those representatives may be outnumbered by lay members of the commission, no other kind of organized group in the state has such regular and collective representation—not the real estate developers, not the police, not welfare workers, and so on. Nor do lay members have the professional authority that the representatives of the bar have on these commissions.

The Arizona State Bar's control over the process of evaluating sitting judges is another important way in which lawyers institutionalized their control over the selection and retention of judges. Of greatest relevance to this study's focus on ideology in the court is the organized bar's success in having its concepts of what makes a good judge, as manifest in the bar poll criteria for merit, dominate public and not-so-public discourses in the judicial selection and retention processes.

Moreover, in addition to the institutionalization of greater organized bar control of merit selection and retention, evidence from my interviews suggests that work for the organized bar is replacing work for political parties as an important prerequisite for nomination for judgeships.

In general, the first five judges, who came onto the bench under the electoral system, show much higher levels of political party activity than the last four judges, who came onto the bench under the appointive system. In the first group, three held party offices, including elective offices (precinct committeeman; county party vice chairman; county party chairman; county committee chairman; county central committee member) and the other two were active in political party campaigning before coming onto the bench. In the second, merit-selected group of judges, only one had held a party office, and two reported not being active at all.

Conversely, overall the first group of judges shows much less prior involvement in local and state bar organizations than the second group. In the first group of five judges, who came to the bench under an electoral system, only one was active in bar affairs, whereas three reported no bar activity at all other than participation in state bar seminars and attendance at state bar conventions. In the second group of four judges, who came in under the appointive system, two were very active (Pima County Bar Association President; Pima County Bar Association Secretary–Treasurer; Arizona Bar Association Board of Governors, which appoints the lawyer members of the commissions that nominate judgeship candidates to the governor. In fact, both these judges were on the Arizona State Bar Association Board of Governors at the time they were appointed. Only one judge in this group reported not being active in bar affairs prior to becoming a judge, and this one, an ethnic minority candidate, said, "I think most of the other [nominees] were very active in either bar politics or democratic political situations" (Judge x, Career History Interview, pp. 19–20).

In general, then, we see a lessening of political party involvement and an increase in bar association activity with the shift in Arizona from an *electoral* to an *appointive* judicial selection process, parallelling the decrease in the role of party politics and the increase in bar involvement in the selection of judges in Arizona. This shift suggests that the nature of judges' "political background" is changing.

Bear in mind that by participating in different kinds of activities, lawyers may also become different kinds of people. Schmidhauser (1979), in an analysis of what kind of men [*sic*] get to be Supreme Court Justices, argues that men who are active in party politics and held political office before becoming justices are historically strongly represented on the Supreme Court because such activity turns them into clear and consistent party ideologues. Ideological clarity and consistency are qualities we look for in our highest appellate court because we understand these justices to make, not just implement, law, and we want our law to be informed by political philosophical positions. Moreover, there is considerable evidence that appellate court justices' party affiliations are manifest in their decisions (Nagel 1961; Ulmer 1962).

I suggest, by analogy, that the more coherent political ideological identities of the judges who came in under the elective system and the more fragmented ideological identities of the merit-selected judges were shaped by their greater and lesser involvement in political party activity. However, students of judicial behavior have never argued that trial court judges, like Supreme Court justices, manifest political party ideology in their judicial behavior. Rather, they actively deny (e.g., Levin 1977; Dolbeare 1967) or simply do not address this argument (Eisenstein & Jacob 1977), a point to which I return shortly.

Of those students of judicial behavior who take a broader view of the political than just party politics, Schmidhauser (1979) is among the few who express any degree of concern over the broadened influence of the organized bar in judicial selection, and his analytical focus was the Supreme Court. As at the state level, the American Bar Association has, since the 1940s, increased its influence over the selection of Supreme Court nominees (see also Grossman 1965). Schmidhauser (1979) said:

> Although politics in judicial selection are condemned as evil, what the Bar groups essentially suggest is a substitution of the partisan ideological influences dominant in the affairs of the organized Bar associations for the partisan ideological influences which prevail in political parties at the state or national level. . . . Modern professional associations have acquired many of the attributes of governments. . . .
>
> The status of the major public professions in modern America considerably enhances the ability of leaders of their major associations to influence public policy making. (p. 29)[5]

That lawyers *have* group-specific political ideologies is little documented, but in one rare empirical study of lawyers' political attitudes, the authors argue that they do:

Attorneys want certain kinds of judges on the bench who will interpret rules in a particular way because such matters affect their individual law practices. . . . In judicial selection, as in the handling of legal affairs generally, attorneys act as spokesmen of the social and economic interests they represent. (Watson & Downing 1969: 43, *quoted in* Schmidhauser 1979: 33)

Just as there is little concern with or evidence of political party ideology influence on trial court judicial behavior in literatures on judicial behavior, so too there is little concern with organized bar political ideological influence on judicial behavior. The reasons this is so are clearly related to pervasive, deeply rooted views on the differences between the roles of appellate and trial court judges that the Tucson judges articulate so clearly. Appellate justices, with broader powers, can implement political ideologies, whereas trial court judges, with narrower powers, are not expected to be able to implement their political ideologies. Dolbeare's views on this issue seem typical:

We have found the criteria for selection of judges here to be service to the party rather than policy preference or program orientation of any kind. *We have found no reason to consider this lack of policy concern to be unique to partisan election courts,* and we have seen that participants in local politics generally are unlikely to seek to influence selection of judges on a policy basis. This is only consistent with most assumptions about local politics, which are to the effect that the motivations of activists are more likely to be extractive (jobs, contracts, power, patronage, etc.) than programmatic (ideological, policy preferences, comprehensive programs, etc.). The political activist whose motivation stems from ideological or program goals is more likely to focus on state or national levels of government, suggesting in effect a continuum of relatively greater proportions of policy orientation among activists from the local through the state to federal levels. Some participants at the local level are active there because of ideological or program goals, of course, but the proportion of persons taking part for purely economic self-interest or other extractive purposes seems highest at the local level. (1967: 124 (emphasis added))

In other words, in Dolbeare's view, whether judges are appointed as a reward for labor for the political party or as a reward for organized bar labor, the motives of the rewarders and the rewarded are "extractive," not ideological, at local political levels. However, as is typical in non-Marxist treatments of political ideology, Dolbeare equates the ideological with explicit intentionally motivated policy orientations that can be associated with recognized institutionalized organizational structures. He does not allow, as Marxists do, that much of what is "ideological" does not have these qualities but is rather hidden, covert, unconscious and unrecognized, and effective by virtue of such qualities. I find it stunning that the same processes acknowledged to be ideologically laden at the appellate court level are widely asserted to be free of ideology at the trial court level. If trial court judges are so lacking in agency, why have them at all? If judgeships are merely extractive spoils, just another set of jobs to go after, why not go after spoils that are easier to get?

Conclusion

The main ideological stance of the Tucson judges with whom I worked is that their work, their legal action on the bench, is nonideological. They take this position because of the political climate in which they function as judges. This climate is one in which there is a tension between the need for trial court judges to be responsive to local community values and political processes and their need to be impartial in the resolution of conflicts. But in recent decades, the political campaigning of the organized bar has created pressure on judges to stress their impartiality and to downplay their political nature and succeeded in obscuring the political nature of judicial appointments. Thus, lawyers who must be political animals to become judges deny the political nature of their actions on the bench. In chapter 4, however, I show how even in the guilty plea, a procedure highly constrained by the many forms of written law that supposedly render trial court judges agentless, systematic differences among the judges in the way they hear pleas can be interpreted as enactments of conservative and liberal political philosophies. We turn first though to the written law that constrains the judges and its impact on their spoken law in the guilty plea in the next chapter.

3

·———·

Intertextual Relations between
Written and Spoken
Genres of Law

In chapter 2, I described how the legal profession, particularly legislatures and appellate courts and including the judges in this study, sees trial court judges as implementers of written law made by others. In this chapter and the next, I discuss how the judges in this study implement the written law in the spoken guilty plea. Both of these chapters then focus on the way legal ideologies, rather than political and everyday ideologies, dominate the practical consciousness of these judges. From the judges' point of view, the key issue in the guilty plea is to make sure defendants are waiving their constitutionally guaranteed due process rights to a trial knowingly and voluntarily as they plead guilty to a crime.

The salient kind of law the judges must follow, and which they see the procedure as "governed" by, is procedural law—law that tells them what they must do in the procedure to make sure the defendant's constitutional rights are protected. The key piece of state legislation that tells them what they must do is Rule 17, *Arizona Rules of Criminal Procedure:* Pleas of Guilty and No Contest (Arizona Revised Statutes). In this chapter I show how the judges organize the spoken guilty plea into a sequence of topics, each of which indexes and meets a different part of Rule 17. But I argue that although on the face of it their courtroom work is a straightforward implementation of Rule 17, these judges are still engaged in interpreting the law. They must be responsive not only to Rule 17 but also to state appellate case law that interprets Rule 17. Their spoken procedures in turn show the influence of both the *procedural rule* and *case law*, as well as elaborations and abbreviations of specific topics in the procedure that are not dictated by either form of law.

Thus, there is ideological diversity across the written and spoken forms of law that address the same due process issues. And the spoken form, the guilty plea itself, indicates that the judges' interpretive practices do not depend entirely on the written law; thus, to some extent the spoken law has a life of its own.

The legal interpretive activity in which these judges engage is part of a much broader interpretive tradition in Western European history, rooted in the Judaic and Christian traditions of Talmudic and Biblical interpretation. Just as individual judges see themselves as interpreting the written law in the way they handle legal procedures, so too preachers offer individual interpretations of the Bible in their sermons. But whereas ministers and members of congregations recognize that there is also a denominational and even a congregational dimension to the individual preacher's interpretation of the Bible, there is little acknowledgement by lawyers or those who study them of the *collective* and local (but not universal) nature of interpretations of the written law that we see in my legal data.

In exploring the connections between written and spoken law, I view the spoken procedure as a speech genre and the two kinds of written law as written genres of law and the relations among them as intertextual relations between different genres of language use. In their discussion of intertextual relations between genres of language use, Briggs and Bauman (1992) introduce the concept of "intertextual gap." They talk about how closely genres dealing with the same information are related to one another, a concept useful for discussing the relations among the genres considered here. If the gap between genres is small, they suggest, then there is a sense of oneness between them, the sense that one genre is being reproduced in another. For example, if I read a quote from the Bible, there is only a small gap between the written and spoken renditions, although my broader framing of the quote could create a gap. And as they point out, when there is such unity, one genre can draw on the authority of another. When the gap is larger, there is more of a sense that something different is happening, and here one genre can be seen as transforming another and as involving innovation and creativity.

As I discussed in Chapter 2, trial court judges represent their implementation of the law as involving little or no gap among written forms of law and between written law and spoken law, which gives their words authority. But, as should be evident from this idea of degree of gap, I argue here that there are significant gaps between the genres of law I examine. And drawing on Marxist ideas about the hiddenness of ideology, I conclude this chapter by suggesting that this diversity is obscured and hidden from members of the lay public because they see only the spoken law and do not have access to the interpretive practices of the judges as they index the written law in their spoken procedures. In this way the impression that the law is monolithic and singular is sustained.

In the sections to follow I first show how parts of Rule 17 are indexed in the string of topics that constitutes the internal sequential structure of the spoken guilty plea. Then I explain how this procedural rule and the case law differ in their interpretations of how due process requirements must be met in the spoken procedure, as well as how the spoken procedure draws on both genres of written law and is independent of them. Finally, I conclude by discussing the intertextual gaps between these forms of due process law and the ways these gaps are hidden from the view of the lay public.

Indexing Rule 17 in the Spoken Guilty Plea

As already noted, the internal sequential structure of the spoken guilty plea is organized as a string of topics, each of which addresses a different part of the procedural rule governing the guilty plea, Rule 17. Rule 17 is reproduced in whole at the end of the book in appendix C (Rule 17, *Arizona Rules of Criminal Procedure:* Pleas of Guilty and No Contest). Here I present those parts of the rule that focus on what must be done by judges when defendants appear before them to plead guilty, highlighting in italics those parts that are specifically relevant to the topical organization of the spoken plea, which I then discuss.

Rule 17.2   Duty of court to advise defendant of his rights and of the consequences of pleading guilty or no contest.

Before accepting a plea of guilty or no contest, the court shall address the defendant personally in open court, informing him of and determining that he understands the following:

    a. The *nature of the charge* to which the plea is offered.
    b. The *nature and range of possible sentence* for the offense to which the plea is offered, including any special *conditions* regarding sentence, parole, or commutation imposed by statute.
    c. The *constitutional rights* which he forgoes by pleading guilty or no context, including his right to counsel if he is not represented by counsel.
    d. His right to plead not guilty.

Rule 17.3   Duty of court to determine voluntariness and intelligence of the plea.

Before accepting a plea of guilty or no contest, the court shall address the defendant personally in open court and determine that he wishes to forego the constitutional rights of which he has been advised, that his plea is voluntary and *not the result of force, threats or promises* (other than a plea agreement) and that there is a *factual basis* for the plea.

Rule 17.4   Plea negotiations and agreements. . . .

    c. Determining the Accuracy of the Agreement and the Voluntariness and Intelligence of the Plea. The parties shall file the *agreement* with the court, which shall address the defendant personally and determine that he *understands* and agrees to its *terms,* that the written document contains all the terms of the agreement, and that the plea is entered in conformance with Rules 17.2 and 17.3. . . . (Ariz. Rev. Stat. Rule 17)

The topics that comprise the procedure and the aspects of Rule 17 that these topics index now follow, listed here in their most commonly occurring sequential order. The topics in brackets are those that do not always occur.

  I. Opening
      Call of the Case
      Self-Identification by Lawyers
      [repair slot]

II. Substance of Procedure
    [Social Background Questions]

Nature of Charge	Rule 17.2a
Plea Agreement Comprehension Questions	Rule 17.4c
Conditions of Plea Agreement	Rule 17.2b
Sentencing Possibilities	Rule 17.2b
Constitutional Rights	Rule 17.2c
	17.3
Coercion Questions	Rule 17.3
Factual Basis	Rule 17.3

    [repair slot]
    Findings

III. Closing
    Sentencing Arrangements
    Probation Investigation Arrangements

This listing of topics can be used in several key ways to point out how the guilty plea has genre-like properties. The substance of the procedure is framed by genre boundary-creating activities that mark both the beginning and the end of the procedure. Thus, the guilty plea procedure always begins with an opening and ends with a closing. While the internal sequential structure of the substance of the procedure is quite variable, the larger sequential structure of the procedure as a whole is fixed in that one always gets first the opening, then the substance, then the closing.

These three parts of the procedure also differ in their structuring of participation of the judge, the two lawyers, and the defendant. The opening and the closing that bracket the procedure regularly and predictably involve interaction between the judge and the two lawyers, whereas the substance of the procedure is conceptualized as, and the judges' procedure formats are primarily designed as, two-party interactions between the judge and the defendant. The judges' formats are designed to be co-interactant-proof: they are structured so that no matter what the defendant says in response to the judge, it is still appropriate for the judge to move to the same next utterance of his own.

As noted, the substance of the procedure consists of a string of topics, each of which meets some element of the due process requirements that Rule 17 lays out for procedurally acceptable pleas. By "topic" I refer to a series of contiguous or adjacent utterances which can be understood to be and are thought of by judges as related to one another and as being topically about the same thing. Groups of contiguous utterances have topical coherency by virtue of the fact that they are made sense of by the speaker and hearer understanding them to be mutually interdependent. In other words, the intelligibility of any given utterance within a topic depends on having heard other utterances within the same topic to a greater extent than on having heard utterances across topical coherencies. That concepts of topics are *shared* among the judges is apparent: although they differ in their preferred sequential orderings of topics, they all use the same specific topics made up of similar contiguous utterances.

Both judges and lawyers display their perception that such groups of utterances belong together by making efforts to preserve their contiguity or their adjacency. Thus, judges who vary the order of the topics in their pleas from instance to instance of the plea, and the majority do this, keep the utterances within a topic together—that is, the utterances that comprise a topical coherency "move" together. This kind of variability is discussed further in the next chapter.

Both judges and lawyers also try to repair a topic either within that topic or between topics. Repairs of the substance of the procedure, initiated by both the judge and the lawyers, complicate the internal sequential structure of guilty pleas. The occurrence of such repairs is not predictable in some respects, although their local management as side sequences does involve their being contingently related to what precedes and follows them. Sometimes any sense of topical coherency and of a sequential structure of topics gets lost in the repair process as one experiences the procedure, rendering it temporarily incomprehensible to the listener, although it may be possible to see structure in a transcript examined under non-real-time conditions.

Even though repairs of the procedure are not entirely predictable, it is possible to talk about a preference structure to these repairs. Both lawyers and judges prefer to repair the procedure just before moving into the substance of the procedure and just at the end of the substance of the procedure before the judge makes the finding that the plea has been knowing and voluntary, which is the performative part of the procedure (i.e., what makes it legally binding). For this reason I have identified "repair slots" at these sequential junctures. These slots are at topic boundaries as well as being close to the boundaries of openings and closings. Topics are also repaired within the topic. Finally, repair occurs at topic boundaries within the substance of the procedure. What does not occur is the repair of one topic within another topic, strong evidence of the efforts of judges and lawyers to maintain topic coherency. All three kinds of repairs that do occur appear in the example of the spoken plea, to which I now turn, to illustrate the sequential structure of the plea.[1]

The Spoken Guilty Plea in Practice

Appendix F (Four Changes of Plea/Guilty Pleas) contains four complete changes of plea, so that readers can assess the nature of routinization and variability in this discourse form. Two of the pleas are from Judge 8 and two are from Judge 4. For each judge I have included a plea of guilty to the charge of robbery and a plea of guilty to the charge of prescription falsification to make them more comparable. Following is a detailed analysis of Judge 8's robbery plea, to illustrate the properties of the spoken plea that I have been describing. (See also appendix E for transcription notations.) In this case a young woman acted as the driver of the getaway car for a "friend" who did the actual robbery.

Opening   (*lines 1–13 of Judge 8 Robbery in Appendix F*)

Judge:	Fine. [2 secs] A-00000, State versus Denise Gonzalez.[2]
Speaker:	( ).
Defense Lawyer:	Your Honor, Ed Martin, on behalf of Miss Gonzalez. We are here on a plea agreement which

is ent- been entered into by
Miss Gonzalez, uh Mr. Benton,
and myself. And we have, she
has signed and uh read the plea
agreement and has signed it. I
present that to the court now.

In the opening, the judge "calls the case" by identifying the case number, the name of the defendant, and usually the nature of the proceeding (i.e., that it is a change of plea), although this is not done here. Then the prosecuting county attorney and the defense attorney introduce/identify themselves by name. It is also typical for the defense attorney to hand the judge the plea agreement, signed by the defendant and the two lawyers, that has resulted from plea bargaining, as is done here. The judge has the defendant's case file on the bench with him. In this way the procedure begins with the grounding of the verbal exchange in its unique and individual specifics.

Up to this point the participant structure of the procedure has been one in which the judge and the lawyers are the relevant speakers. As we move to the substance of the procedure, it is understood that the interaction between judge and defendant predominates. Quite often before this shift occurs, one or more of these three participants attempts to engage in anticipatory repair of what is to come—that is, to anticipate sources of confusion and unclarity and to provide the information that will prevent the need for repair at a later time. Although this does not occur in the plea we are considering here, it does occur in the other three transcripts in appendix F.

Social Background Questions   (*lines 14–33*)

Judge: Thank you, Mr. Martin. [10
secs] For the record, you are
Denise Marie Gonzalez?

Defendant: Yes, sir.

Judge: How old are you? They call you
Neese? How old are you?

Defendant: Eighteen.

Judge: Where do you live?

Defendant: One oh seven (   ) (Hart).

Judge: How long have you lived in
Tucson, Neese?

Defendant: Eighteen years.

Judge: What education have you had? [4
secs] 'S how much edu-schooling
have you had?

Defendant: Uhm [2 secs] Seven. [2 secs]

Judge: Uhm do you read and understand
English?

Defendant: Yes, sir.

Not all the judges ask social background questions of this sort, and nothing in the written law requires it, but the majority of the judges do ask such questions. The judges see such questions as allowing them to determine from the defendant's answers and the defendant's demeanor whether he or she is capable of understanding what is to happen in the rest of the procedure. Also, they see such questions as additional prefatory material personalizing and individualizing the procedure, an issue I return to in the following chapter.

Plea Agreement Comprehension Questions   (*lines 34–53*)

> Judge: Did you read this agreement that Mr. Martin just handed me over carefully?
>
> Defendant: Yes, sir.
>
> Judge: Uhm I assume that you did because your signature appears on the back page opposite today's date. Did you in fact sign this agreement?
>
> Defendant: Yes, sir.
>
> Judge: And you did read it over before you signed it?
>
> Defendant: Yes, sir.
>
> Judge: Do you understand what this agreement says?
>
> Defendant: Yes, sir.
>
> Judge: Is there anything in here that you don't agree to?
>
> Defendant: No, sir.

Rule 17.4.c explicitly requires that defendants be asked if they understand and agree with the written plea agreement, and all the judges ask such questions. The answers to such questions can provide evidence that the defendant "knew" certain information that was in the plea agreement. All these judges do, however, provide all the information in the plea agreement again verbally, creating redundancy and repetition in the way they index and meet the requirement of the written law.

Nature of Charge   (*lines 54–60*)

> Judge: If I understand it right, uh Neese, you propose to enter a plea of guilty to the charge of robbery, uh is that your understanding?
>
> Defendant: Yes, sir.

Rule 17.2a specifies that the defendant must be informed of the nature of the charge. This is an unusually abbreviated way of informing: the judges typically identify the statute under which the person is being charged when they name the charge. Only one judge regularly described what the charge/crime actually involved. It appears that this part of Rule 17 has come to be interpreted as requiring that the defendant understand what he,[3] or in this case she, is charged with, rather than that he understand the nature of the charge. This is the first point where written substantive criminal law in the form of criminal codes is indexed, so that due process procedural law and substantive criminal law begin to intersect and continue to do so through the procedure.

Conditions of Plea Agreement and Sentencing Possibilities   (*lines 61–144*)

Judge: And in exchange for that uh plea, the state is going to uh uh dismiss the charge that's presently against you, which is armed robbery.

Defendant: Yes,   /sir/.

Judge: /You/ understand that? Do you realize that if I accept this plea that uh you face uh possible uh imprisonment-

Repair

Defense Lawyer: *Your Honor, may I interrupt here, this plea agreement is also posited upon the fact that Miss Gonzalez will receive probation.*

Judge: *Uhm [4 secs] Assuming that you received a probated sentence, and then violated the probation, it's a maximum of five years.*

Defense Lawyer: *No, it's a minimum of five, (I think) it's /five years   /.*

Judge: */Minimum of / five.*

Defense Lawyer: *It's not a hard five. This /is (   ) /-*

Judge: */Five to/ life? I can't remember the /sen / tence.*

Defense Lawyer: */Yes /.*

Judge: All right. [2 secs] Uh- Neese- the possible punishment, I understand that you've agreed to uh a plea that stipulates that you'll receive probation, is that your understanding?

Defendant: Yes, sir.

Judge: But I want you to understand
        that- uh if I go- first of all,
        that provision isn't binding on
        me. If I decided after I were
        to receive uh probation report
        that uh I couldn't go along
        with it, then I would permit you
        to withdraw your plea. Uh you
        understand that? Assume that I
        decide I can go along with it,
        uh noting right off the bat
        your age, uh and did put you on
        probation, there would be a
        number of terms and conditions
        attached to your probation, uh
        first of all, obviously, that
        you're violating the law. 'N
        there might be others that I
        don't know anything about cause
        I don't know anything about you.
        Uh if you were to violate that
        probation, *then* your probation
        could be revoked, and you could
        then be sent to prison. You
        understand that?

Defendant: Yes, sir.

Judge: And if you were sent to prison,
        uh the termwould be uh five
        years uh at a minimum. And how
        much of that five years you'd
        have to serve, I- uh minimum, I
        can't really tell you now. But
        it could be a substantial
        period of time, now are you
        aware of that? [2 secs] Did
        Mr. Martin discuss that with
        you?

Defendant: Yes, sir. [4 secs]

Judge: So in effect, you- I take it
        your understanding and entering
        into this plea agreement is that
        you will receive probation and
        you expect to abide by the terms
        and conditions of probation that
        the court would impose. Is
        that right?

Defendant: Yes, sir.

In this particular plea, the judge merges the information about sentencing possibilities and conditions of the plea agreement, going back and forth between them. This is not unusual, but if there *are* specific conditions, and this is not always the case, it is more common for them to be kept separate, though both are required by Rule 17.2. b, and often these two topical coherencies are not even contiguous or adjacent to one another in the sequential structure of the plea.

Notice that in the material in italics, the defense lawyer interrupts to "repair" the work the judge is doing by pointing out that probation is a condition of the guilty plea—that is, the defendant can only receive probation as a sentence and cannot be sentenced to jail or prison. He then repairs the judge's work again by correcting the sentencing information the judge is giving—that is, if probation were violated, the prison sentence would be a minimum of 5 years, not a maximum of 5 years. This material illustrates the repair of a topical coherency while it is still ongoing. From the transcript, it appears that the judge never clarifies this issue.

It is common for lawyers to participate in the repair of both sentencing possibilities and conditions of the plea agreement in this way. The repair reflects not only the importance of this information but also the difficulty for judges in memorizing the sentencing possibilities for every statute in the book, the failure of relevant information to appear or appear clearly on many plea agreements so that the judge is unable to readily read it off, and the duty of the lawyers as officers of the court to help the judge make the plea good.

Constitutional Rights   (*lines 145–240*)

Judge: Do you understand, Neese, that
you don't have to do this? You
have a right to go to trial on
the charges that are presently
ag- against you? [2 secs]

Defendant: Ye/s sir/.

Judge: /Uh/ and that if the state
failed to prove its case against
you at trial, uh that uh the
jury would be required to return
a verdict of not guilty?

Defendant: Yes, sir.

Judge: You understand there won't be
any trial if I accept this
plea?

Defendant: Yes, sir.

Judge: Uhm it says on page two and I
need to be sure for the record
that you understand all of the
rights that you're giving up,
uh'n what I was just uh
referring to uh specifically is
that you have a right to a jury

trial in this matter. Do you
know that?

Defendant: Yes, sir.

Judge: Do you understand that if you
can't afford a lawyer that the
court will appoint a lawyer to
defend you and to represent you,
uh both before the trial and at
trial?

Defendant: Yes, sir.

Judge: And do you realize that you have
the right to face uh cross-
examine, and confront the
witnesses that the state would
have to call to prove your guilt
in this matter?

Defendant: Yes, sir.

Judge: Uhm you would have the right to
present witnesses and evidence
in your defense, and to compel
the attendance of witnesses uh
if they wouldn't agree to appear
voluntarily?

Defendant: Yes, sir.

Judge: You have the right to have the
court tell the jury- instruct
the jury that uh you are to be
presumed innocent and that the
presumption of innocence uh
stays with you at all stages of
the trial uh until uh a jury
was satisfied under the law that
the state had borne the burden
which it has of proving your
guilt beyond a reasonable doubt.
Do you understand that?

Defendant: Yes, sir.

Judge: I believe uh that you'd be
entitled to a twelve-person
jury, and that each member of
the jury individually would have
to be satisfied that the state
had borne the burden of proving
your guilt beyond a reasonable
doubt. Do you realize that?

Defendant: Yes, sir.

> Judge: And you could either remain
> silent and rely on the
> presumption of innocence and not
> take the risk of incriminating
> yourself, or you could choose to
> testify in your defense if you
> wished. That's an option that
> you won't have either if I
> accept this plea. Do you
> realize that?
>
> Defendant: Yes, sir.
>
> Judge: Do you fully understand that the
> reason you're giving up all
> those rights if I accept this
> plea is that that will end the
> question of your your guilt or
> uh- non-guilt, and there won't
> be any trial, and then the
> question uh is uh is the
> sentence. That's all that's
> left. Do you understand that?
>
> Defendant: Yes, sir.
>
> Judge: OK. After all that, is it still
> your desire that I accept this
> plea?
>
> Defendant: Yes, sir. [11 secs]

All the judges review the defendant's constitutional rights in this way, although some judges give a more abbreviated version of these rights than others and elicit fewer comprehension assents from the defendant. And there is striking agreement across judges on what these rights are. Because the rights are stated in the plea agreement, which the judge refers to, this part of the procedure, like the statement of the conditions of the plea agreement, is highly redundant.

Repair of Condition of Plea Agreement   (*lines 241–287*)

> Judge: *What attached notice uh is*
> */referred to (   )/?*
>
> Defense Lawyer: */Your Honor, if there's/ a*
> *notice in the file, we've filed*
> *this case (   ) before you was*
> *involving the juvenile /(   )*
> *presided over/.*
>
> Judge: */Oh, yes, yes, yes, yes/ yes,*
> *yes. [17 secs] All right, I d- I*
> *thought I had remembered this*
> *case. All right, do you*
> *understand that as a part of*
> *this agreement uh you must*

<blockquote>
<table>
<tr><td></td><td>testify truthfully uh if there
is uh a trial or an
adjudication proceeding
involving Johnny (Luna)?</td></tr>
<tr><td>Defendant:</td><td>Yes, sir.</td></tr>
<tr><td>Judge:</td><td>And that if you fail to uh uhm
to do that, that uh this
agreement isn't gonna be
binding on the state. You
understand that?</td></tr>
<tr><td>Defendant:</td><td>Yes, sir.</td></tr>
<tr><td>Defense Lawyer:</td><td>Your Honor, I think the record
should indicate that she has
already done that.</td></tr>
<tr><td>Judge:</td><td>Oh, you have. /All right/.</td></tr>
<tr><td>Defense Lawyer:</td><td>   /Yes, Your
Honor/.</td></tr>
<tr><td>Judge:</td><td>Is there any question in the
state's mind that uh uh
/defendant has/-</td></tr>
<tr><td>County Attorney:</td><td>/No, your Hon/or. That (   )
piece has been taken care of.
[2 secs]</td></tr>
<tr><td>Judge:</td><td>All right. As I understand it,
Neese, in effect you've been
promised probation, in exchange
for your plea in this matter.
But, I think now you understand
that even if you get probation,
uhm that if you violate it you
could still go to prison. Now
you understand that?</td></tr>
<tr><td>Defendant:</td><td>Yes, sir.</td></tr>
</table>
</blockquote>

The material that follows the constitutional rights in this plea constitutes further repair of the conditions of the plea agreement, this time initiated by the judge, who has just now noticed additional written material attached to the plea agreement. This repair comes between two standard topics (constitutional rights and coercion questions) which are themselves not interrupted by repair material.

Coercion Questions   (lines 288–311)

<blockquote>
<table>
<tr><td>Judge:</td><td>Did anybody else- did anybody
make any other promises than
just that to you?</td></tr>
<tr><td>Defendant:</td><td>No, /sir/.</td></tr>
<tr><td>Judge:</td><td>   /In / exchange for your plea?
Did anybody use any force</td></tr>
</table>
</blockquote>

>   against you, or make any threats
>   against you
>
> Defendant: /No, sir/.
>
> Judge: /to get/ you to change your
>   plea? I have to be satisfied
>   that this is something you're
>   doing voluntarily. Uh is it?
>
> Defendant: Yes, sir?
>
> Judge: Have you discussed it fully and
>   carefully with Mr. Martin?
>
> Defendant: Yes, sir.
>
> Judge: D' you think he's giving you
>   good advice?
>
> Defendant: Yes, sir.
>
> Judge: You satisfied with his
>   representation?
>
> Defendant: Yes, sir.

All the judges ask questions that address whether or not the defendant was coerced into pleading guilty by threats, promises, or force, although usually they ask fewer questions than are in evidence here. Sometimes questions regarding satisfaction with the lawyer are either absent or separated from those regarding coercion in the sequential structure of a plea. As we can see from these questions, a relatively small portion of the procedure is therefore devoted to the concern with coercion.

Factual Basis   (*lines 312–337*)

> Judge: Okay. Tell me what happened on
>   June sixth, 1978, I seem to
>   remember a little bit from a
>   juvenile proceeding, but uh I
>   wanna hear it from you.
>
> Defendant: Well, we went to my friend's
>   house and uh he told me to uhm
>   go down to uh Mantigo's, so I
>   went and he told me to wait for
>   him (uh) a couple of blocks
>   down, so I waited for him. And
>   I drove him around for awhile,
>   and waited for him, then he
>   came.
>
> Judge: Y- you knew he was gonna rob the
>   place?
>
> Defendant: Yes, sir.
>
> Judge: And you were gonna help him get
>   away?
>
> Defendant: Yes, sir.

Judge: (All right). [2 secs] I'm
satisfied both because of the
defendant's statements and what
I recall of the juvenile matter
that there is a factual basis.

The factual basis is the part of the procedure in which the judge establishes that there are facts, which if believed by fact finders (e.g., a jury) in a trial, would be sufficient to convict the defendant of the charge to which he is pleading guilty. Is there evidence that the defendant really did what he is pleading guilty to? There is a sense in which this is the part of the procedure that substitutes for a trial. It is also the main part of the substance of the procedure addressing Rule 17 that requires the judge to deal with the specific individual circumstances that got the defendant into trouble.

Here, as in other parts of the procedure, the judge is redundant in indexing Rule 17 in that he both elicits information from the defendant during the procedure, or in other words gets her to confess on record, and refers to information he acquired on another occasion in a juvenile hearing which is part of the extended written record.

Invitation to Repair   (*lines 338–342*)

Judge: Do either of you have a problem
with the record?

Defense Lawyer: No, Your Honor, I don't.

County Attorney: No, Your Honor.

This inquiry by the judge, close to the end of the substantive part of the procedure, creates a repair slot, an opportunity for the lawyers to suggest any other changes they feel are needed before the judge makes his findings. As previously noted, several of the judges offer such an opportunity as part of their script. Lawyers often introduce repair activity at this particular juncture or after the findings, whether or not they are invited to, as we can see in the other examples in appendix F, suggesting that they view this juncture as particularly appropriate for such activity, just as they do the beginning of the substantive part of the procedure. In part this is because when judge and defendant have dealt with everything Rule 17 requires between them, there is again a return to a more encompassing participant structure in which the lawyers are implicitly included.

Findings   (*lines 343–356*)

Judge: Based on the record, the court
finds that there has been an
intelligent, voluntary,
understanding uh entry of a plea
by the defendant of guilty to
the charge of robbery, committed
on or about June sixth, 1978, in
violation of ARS 13-641 and 13-
643 A, as amended. That there

is a factual basis for the plea,
and the plea is accepted and
entered in the record.

The findings are the performative part of the procedure. They make it legally binding. Without this statement, the plea is invalid because there is no evidence in the
record that the judge has made the determinations required by Rule 17. It is crucial,
therefore, that the findings only come after everything required by Rule 17 has been
done because logically the judge cannot otherwise make such findings.

Closing   (*lines 357–433*)

Defense Lawyer:	Your Honor, may we waive time for sentencing because uh Miss Gonzalez's presently working. She has to take time off from work. Uh- the stipulated sentence has been agreed to. Uh- the state is familiar with who she is, there's no previous background of criminal record, uh- she's eighteen years old, the mother of a child. She needs to work /and-/
Judge:	/Mr. / Martin, I have no question in my mind, cause it's come back to me a little bit that I'm gonna go along with that provision, but I think there is uh uh definite benefit for the defendant in going through the pre-sentence process, as well as uh furnishing the court with information I don't know what particular terms and conditions uh uhm I might wish to impose uh I have no reason to believe that there'd be any ones in particular, but of course the probation office has uh a lot of discretion about that.
Defense Lawyer:	Fine.
Judge:	And I think at this point I'm gonna order that a pre-sentence investigation and report be made. What uh what hours do you work, Neese?
Defendant:	Uhm from eight to two-thirty.

Judge:	All right, if I were to uh provide this time for sentencing at four o'clock in the afternoon, uh uh is there any reason you can't- that's going to inconvenience you?
Defendant:	No, sir.
Judge:	Alright. It's ordered that uh a pre-sentence investigation and report be made by the adult probation office of the court. That uh sentencing in this matter [2 sec] uh be Friday, September twenty-ninth at four P.M. Have to-rearrange your weekend plans, Mr. Martin.
Defense Lawyer:	Your Honor, I'm always there.
Judge:	In division 0000. That's four o'clock in the afternoon, Neese. I want you to cooperate with the adult probabion office in the making of that report.
Defendant:	Okay.
Judge:	Uhm it's to both your advantage and to mine that they get accurate information. I must advise you if you don't appear on uh uh [2 secs] September twenty-ninth at four o'clock, that uh I might very well vacate this plea agreement and issue a bench warrant for your arrest. Do you understand that?
Defendant:	Yes, sir.
Judge:	Okay. Conditions of release remain in effect.
Defense Lawyer:	Thank you. I'll take over, Your Honor. [3 secs]
County Attorney:	May we be excused, Your honor?

Although it is unusual for a lawyer to request immediate sentencing of a defendant, it is always the case that the judge closes the procedure by setting a time for the sentencing and usually the case that he orders a pre-sentencing investigation by the probation department, with the final ending elements being quite brief, as here.

A Comparison of Genres of Due Process, Written and Spoken

The preceding two sections illustrate how Rule 17 is indexed in the internal structure of the substance of the spoken plea through the sequencing of topics, each of which meets a distinct demand of Rule 17. But there is another genre of written law, the appellate case law interpreting Rule 17, that is also important in that it too constrains how the spoken procedure is done.

When a legislature passes procedural rules such as Rule 17, it is understood that the following will occur: trial court judges implement the rule in the way they take pleas from defendants. Some of those implementations are challenged by lawyers as not being true to the intent of the legislation passed. These lawyers can appeal to appellate courts to invalidate the procedure of a specific defendant that they felt was done incorrectly. In this case, they can ask that a guilty plea be overturned by the court on the grounds that the requirements of Rule 17 were not met. Appellate courts do not consider any such request they view as frivolous. But if they think the appealing lawyer has a serious and plausible criticism, they consider the appeal. Whatever the appellate court decides then becomes law. This means the authority of *case law* supersedes or takes precedence over the authority of the *procedural rule*. Taking the new case law into consideration, the trial court judges then try again to handle the procedure as this new written law dictates, and this process can be cycled through indefinitely.

When Rule 17 is compared with case law that evaluates actual judges' instantiations of the rule, the broadest and most relevant difference is that what the procedural rule requires be done in the procedure, case law does not. Rather, case law demands that there be evidence in the written record of the case as a whole that the requirements of Rule 17 were met. Relatedly, case law does not require the judge to have met the requirements if there is evidence in the record that someone else, usually the defendant's lawyer, met them.

If we look again at Rule 17, it clearly specifies that the judge carry out its dictates in interaction with the defendant during the procedure:

Rule 17.2 . . . the court [meaning the judge] shall address the defendant personally in open court, informing him . . .

Rule 17.3 . . . the court shall address the defendant personally in open court and determine . . .

Rule 17.4 . . . the court, which shall address the defendant personally and determine . . .

In general terms, whereas Rule 17 required that the *judge* personally *inform* the defendant of the consequences of pleading guilty and *determine* that he understands the information, as well as that he has not been coerced into pleading guilty and that there is a factual basis for the plea, summaries of case law included in the Arizona Revised Statutes as of 1978–1979 show that the judge was not personally required to provide the defendant with the relevant information in or during the procedure. Nor was it necessary that the judge determine during the procedure that the defendant understood the consequences of pleading guilty and was doing so freely or even that there was sufficient evidence that the defendant in question had committed the crime to which he was pleading guilty.

Instead, case law required that *the judge determine from the extended record for the case as a whole that there was evidence the defendant had been informed of and understood the consequences of pleading guilty and was doing so freely.*

The cases appealed under Rules 17.2 and 17.3 generally complain that the judge failed to elicit a factual basis or failed to inform the defendant of some piece of information that this section required him to inform the defendant of: the nature of the charge, the sentencing possibilities, constitutional rights, or the right to plead not guilty. Appellate courts generally hold that knowledge of the consequences of pleading guilty need not come from the judge during the procedure.

> Defendant's knowledge of the consequences of pleading guilty need not be imparted to him solely by the trial judge; his knowledge may come from many sources, and all that is required is that there be something in the record from which it can be logically found on appeal that the defendant did, in fact, have the required knowledge. State v. Gutierrez (1973) 20 Ariz. App. 337, 512 P. 2nd 869. (Ariz. Rev. Stat., R. Crim. P., p. 96)

If there is no such evidence in the record, the case will be remanded to the trial court for an evidentiary hearing with the defendant to determine whether he understood the consequences of pleading guilty, thus creating the evidence where it does not exist.

In other words, the judge did not have to be the one to make the defendant knowing and voluntary, and it did not have to happen during the guilty plea itself. The defendant could have become knowing and displayed his knowingness and voluntariness in an earlier procedure from which a court reporter's transcript had become part of the record. The defendant's signature on the plea agreement or his or his lawyer's avowal during the guilty plea that he had discussed these matters with his client were, according to this case law, other possible sources of evidence for the judge to use in determining the defendant's relevant state of mind.

It is also clear in the case law that the responsibility for making sure the defendant has the information necessary to plead guilty knowingly and voluntarily is not limited to the judge but is shared with the prosecutor and the defense attorney.

> Both prosecuting and defense counsel are under duty to call to attention of trial judge at time guilty plea is entered any omissions that trial judge may have made because of trial court's failure to follow rules of criminal procedure. State v. Rodriguez (1975) 112 Ariz. 193, 540 P.2d 665. (Ariz. Rev. Stat., R. Crim. P., p. 103)

Thus, the two genres of written law, the procedural rule and the case law, differ in their interpretation of what the judge must do to secure the due process rights of the criminal defendant. There is, then, genre-specific ideological diversity within the written law.

All the judges do more than case law requires, as should be evident from the actual guilty plea examined earlier. There are at least two general reasons why the judges do more. Some judges personally believe that they should adhere to a higher standard than that set by case law. Case law clearly sets a minimum standard. Case law conveys the definite impression that appellate courts work hard to save the necks of judges who just are not doing a good job, and occasionally they are unable to save those necks. Case law does not praise the worthwhile or propose the ideal. It excludes the unacceptable.

Judges are also concerned that their decisions not be overturned by an appellate court. As noted earlier, an appellate court does not write opinions on cases unless it thinks the appellant has an argument worth taking seriously, even if it rejects that argument in its opinions. And the argument rejected today may become more plausible tomorrow in the same or a higher court of appeals. This means that losing positions—for example, that the judge *should* tell the defendant his constitutional rights and not just ask the defendant whether he has read them in the plea agreement—are considered to have merit and may be the winning positions at a later date. Lawyers who raise issues that are *heard*, even if denied, in this way push the due process standards above the case law standard that is called the law. Given that these relations between winning and losing issues exist in case law, and that trial court judges do not want to be overturned by appellate courts, it is risky for trial court judges to adhere to the case law standard rather than to a more demanding and protective standard.

It is clear that the judges do more than *case law* requires of them, but it may be less obvious that they do less than the *procedural rule* (Rule 17) asks of them. Most judges do not explicitly tell defendants that they have a right to plead not guilty (Rule 17.2d), and although Rule 17.2a directs them to explain the nature of the charge to defendants, most of the time the judges simply name the crime and the statute that describes the crime and do not explain what it entails to the defendant. It is the case law which gives the judges this leeway.[4]

But neither the procedural rule nor case law fully explains why the judges handle guilty pleas as they do. Neither case law nor the procedural rule specifically discusses the idea that some topics should be given more attention than others. But as a group, the judges clearly give the most elaborate care and attention to spelling out the conditions of the plea agreement and the sentencing possibilities and the least attention to the nature of the charge and to the possibility that the defendant was coerced into pleading guilty.

The spoken genre of due process law, the guilty plea, shows the influence of both written genres of due process law, but it mirrors neither, and in the elaboration of some topics and the abbreviation of others, the spoken genre is relatively autonomous of both written genres. Thus, just as the written genres of law differ from each other in their view of what must be done to guarantee defendants' constitutional rights in the guilty plea, the spoken genre is also distinct in its interpretation of due process protections, suggesting the genre-based nature of ideological diversity within the legal system.

Conclusion

The purpose of this chapter is to explore some aspects of the nature of the dominant legal interpretive perspective through examination of intertextual relations within written law and between written and spoken law. In chapter 1, I discussed the way in which law is seen within a Marxist tradition to be a form or expression of state ideological hegemony. In my view, law as a form of cultural hegemony is less monolithic than the term *hegemony* suggests and also less taken for granted and implicit than in some uses and meanings of hegemony. But our understanding of the nature of ideological diversity in law is not well developed: Marxists see ideological diversity dualistically, as oppositionally organized into relations of domination and subordination. Critical legal scholars typically equate law with written law, whereas students of the language of law usually look at either the written or the spoken, but not at the relations between the two, as I do here.

When judges organize the sequential structure of the procedure into topical coherencies that index and create an intertextual relationship with the written law, they reproduce the ideological dominance of the legal interpretive perspective. They submit to it and they impose it on others. And this occurs repeatedly in different instances of hearing guilty pleas. This intertextual relation is hidden from those who are not party to legal interpretive practices by its very nature—that is, by both the inaccessibility of the written law and by the inaccessibility of the training that has instructed lawyers in how to relate the written to the spoken legal practices (Philips 1982). This is consistent with Marxist ideas about how dominant ideologies maintain their hold through a kind of mystification of what they actually entail. Thus the outsider, the nonpractitioner, can retain an impression of the monolithic nature of law when drawn into legal proceedings and be unaware of the actual intertextual gaps that exist between genres of law because of the opaqueness of the interpretive and intertextual practices. I tried to take away some of this opaqueness and in so doing reveal some of the nature of ideological diversity in the written law and across written and spoken law and some of its configuration.

Rule 17 and case law that interprets it take somewhat different positions on what is procedurally required in hearing guilty pleas. Rule 17 is geared toward getting judges to determine knowingness and voluntariness of guilty pleas during the procedure itself. Case law on Rule 17, however, generally tends to find it adequate that there be evidence in the extended written record of the case somewhere, not necessarily in the procedure itself, that the knowingness and voluntariness of the defendant's plea was secured. So the different forms of written law express different ideological positions within the dominant legal interpretive tradition on due process procedural law.

The spoken law in turn reveals the influence of both Rule 17 and case law interpreting Rule 17. But the spoken law is not merely a reflection of the written law. It has an interpretive and practical life of its own through the agents of its implementation, the judges. It shares with both forms of written procedural law the active construction of ideological stances by legal practitioners.

Underlying this ideological diversity among written and spoken forms of law is legally institutionalized ideological conflict carried out through appellate challenges to trial court practices and trial court responses to appellate decisions. But this conflict, like the ideological diversity itself, is obscured and unavailable to the outsider in the actual courtroom practices.

In this chapter I argue that the judges' spoken guilty pleas suggest the influence of both Rule 17, which asks that the judges determine knowingness and voluntariness in the guilty plea procedure, and case law, which requires only that there be evidence of the defendant's knowingness and voluntariness in the record of the case as a whole. But in the next chapter I argue that within the group, some judges are more procedure-oriented in the way they conduct guilty plea procedures, whereas other judges are more record-oriented in the way they hear guilty pleas.

4

Two Ideological Stances
in Taking Guilty Pleas

In chapter 3 I showed how the judges index elements of the written procedural rule, Rule 17, that governs Arizona guilty pleas, and in so doing adhere to the written law. The guilty plea procedure can be thought of as a sequence of topics, discrete discourse units, each of which indexes a different aspect of Rule 17. At the same time, written case law from Arizona appellate courts that interprets Rule 17 influenced the way the judges with whom I worked hear guilty pleas. Case law interpreting Rule 17 only requires the judges to make sure during the guilty plea that there is evidence in the written record of the defendant's case that the plea is knowing and voluntary. Rule 17 itself, on the other hand, states that knowingness and voluntariness must be established through interaction with defendants themsekves. As I also explained in Chapter 3, all the judges create a string of topics that index different parts of Rule 17. All do more than case law requires of them and less than Rule 17 asks of them. In their spoken procedures, then, the judges reflect the influence of more than one genre of written law but no slavish adherence to either of the genres on which I focus, so we begin to get a sense of the interpretive agency of the judges as social actors.

In chapter 4, I take a rather different approach to the same spoken guilty pleas initially analyzed in chapter 3. As chapter 3 suggests, the judges constitute an interpretive community in that they have a good deal in common in the way they hear guilty pleas. But in this chapter I show how within this community, there are systematic differences among the judges in the way they take the plea and in the way they talk about why they take the pleas as they do. I characterize these differences as record-oriented versus procedure-oriented strategies.

In chapter 3, I explained that the procedural rule governing the guilty plea, Rule 17, requires the judge to determine *in the procedure* that a defendant is pleading guilty knowingly and voluntarily. Some judges explained their interactional strategies in taking guilty pleas as due to their intent to personally establish the defendants' know-ingness and voluntariness during the procedure. For this reason I refer to these judges as *procedure oriented*. In contrast, case law interpreting Rule 17 only required that there be evidence in the written record covering the entire history of the case that the defendant was pleading guilty knowingly and voluntarily, and did not require that knowingness and voluntariness be determined by the judge during the procedure. Some judges explained their interactional strategies in taking guilty pleas as due to their concern to make a good record of the case that could not be overturned by an appellate court. Also consistent with case law on Rule 17, these judges saw themselves as sharing responsibility for making sure defendants were pleading guilty knowingly and voluntarily with others whose contributions to that responsibility were evident in the overall written record of each case. For these reasons I refer to this group of judges as *record oriented*. In this way, we can see that the variation in the spoken law is related to the variation in the written law.

I demonstrate how judges who use procedure-oriented strategies vary the proce-dure from instance to instance at every level of discourse more than record-oriented judges do. They do so because they believe that to make the defendant "knowing" and therefore voluntary, they should tailor the procedure to the individual for more effective communication of the information he needs to know. Record-oriented judges, in contrast, do not feel that defendants require such tailoring to understand what is being said to them. Moreover, the record-oriented judges are concerned about stan-dardizing their procedure. They want to make sure they do everything the written law requires them to every time they hear a plea so that their pleas will not be overturned by an appellate court.

Procedure-oriented judges' pleas are also more elaborate than record-oriented judges' pleas. This is because procedure-oriented judges give more information to defendants and, by asking them more questions, get more information from defen-dants. From their point of view, this is how they involve the defendant more in the procedure and thus make the defendant more knowing. Again, record-oriented judges do not feel all this is necessary for defendants to "know" they are waiving their due process rights to a trial by pleading guilty. And the record-oriented judges believe that if they involve the defendant unnecessarily, they risk spoiling the procedure because the defendant may say something that is not consistent with what must be said for the procedure to be legally valid.

Thus, as should be evident, this chapter further develops the theme introduced in chapter 3 that legal ideology is dominant in judges' interpretive practices—dominant in their conscious awareness or practical consciousness of what they are doing and how they make sense of what they are doing. But this chapter moves beyond chap-ter 3 in asserting that legal ideology is not the only kind of ideology being enacted through the strategies judges use in hearing pleas. We can also see these judges as enacting liberal and conservative political ideologies. Procedure-oriented strategies and the reasons judges give for using them suggest a liberal concept of the role of the state in relation to the individual. Procedure-oriented judges subscribe to the view that the defendants need the judges' help in obtaining due process and the judges willingly assume the role of personal protector of the individual's rights in their capacity as representatives of the state. Record-oriented strategies and the reasons judges give for using them suggest a conservative role for the state in relation to the individual. The record-oriented judges do not see the defendants as needing their personal protection, and to some extent they eschew the role of protector in their capacity as representatives of the state. When record-oriented judges look to the written record of the case for evidence that the defendant was informed of his due process rights, they are looking for evidence that others (i.e., lawyers or even police) informed the defendant of these rights, and as they do so they are also sharing their responsibility to the defendant with others rather than taking it entirely onto themselves as the procedure-oriented judges do.

The same judicial behavior, then, can mean more than one thing. It can be ideologically polysemous. It can have both legal and political meanings and significance, in spite of the judges' denial, detailed in chapter 2, that there should be or is anything of a politically ideological nature about what they do in the courtroom.

Chapter 4 is lengthy and I develop the arguments that sustain these generalizations in the following way: I speak in more detail about the nature of the data on which my analysis is based. Then, after summarizing the key ways in which the presence versus absence of variation in discourse structure and elaboration versus abbreviation of the plea are manifest in the data, I provide detailed documentation of the differences between procedure- and record-oriented judges' strategies. I illustrate these differences with excerpts from the transcripts of four pleas in appendix F (Four Changes of Plea)—two from a record-oriented judge and two from a procedure-oriented judge. Following this qualitative analysis of the two strategies, I discuss quantitative measures and reflections of the elaboration and abbreviation of the plea that characterize procedure-oriented and record-oriented strategies, respectively. I then talk about how we can see these strategies in political ideological as well as legal ideological terms. Finally, I look at my analysis in light of Marxist ideas about ideology and discuss how this analysis offers new views on such Marxist issues as the nature of ideological diversity, oppositional relations among diverse ideologies, ideological consciousness, and the critique of ideology.

The Database Revisited

In this chapter and those that follow, I base the analysis of judges' interpretive perspectives on three kinds of data and on relations among those forms of data. The three kinds of data include (1) transcriptions of tape recordings of 44 guilty pleas, or changes of plea, from the nine judges in the study; (2) notes from posttaping interviews with the individual judges in their chambers; and (3) transcriptions of tape recordings of career history interviews with each judge.

Transcripts of Guilty Pleas

The guilty plea is treated here as a speech genre, as it was in chapter 3. It has a clear beginning and end. Like other procedures in the sequence of criminal procedures through which defendants and their cases move, it has a specific legal performative function. Like genres that have been studied in verbal art performances (Bauman 1986; Briggs 1988), this procedure has an underlying discourse format to which it must adhere for it to be recognizable as an instance of the procedure. And lawyers evaluate performances not in the esthetic terms relevant for verbal art but, rather, as the good or bad professional work of the judge.

I observed each judge twice before taping him. I usually followed observations and tapings with posttaping interviews, in which I asked the judges why they handled the procedures as they did.

Table 4.1, Changes of Plea, shows the number of taped pleas done by each judge and the average length of time it took each judge to do the plea. In the section on quantification, we see that this variation in time and number is related in part to the different ideological stances of the judges in the way they hear the plea. Table 4.2, Nature of Charges, shows the kinds of crimes each judge was dealing with. There are more charges than pleas (51 rather than 44) because some defendants are charged with more than one crime and some pleas have more than one defendant. The crimes are organized in table 4.2 in the same way that they are organized in the annual reports of the Superior Court of the State of Arizona, Pima County, which is prepared by the court administrator. The crimes pled to in my database occur in similar frequency to their occurrence in those reports: charges of burglary, theft, and drug crimes account for more than half of the cases processed. Certain crimes that occur do not appear in my database, notably murder, kidnapping, and rape. This is because such crimes are not frequent and defendants typically do not plead guilty to such crimes. Instead, such cases go to trial because the County Attorney's Office is reluctant to plea bargain in a way that would permit those accused of such serious crimes to plead guilty to a lesser charge; thus, the defendant has nothing to lose by going to trial.

Notes from Posttaping Interviews

Although readers should view the transcriptions of the pleas as the core database, interviews with the judges in their chambers after observations and tapings figure prominently in this chapter because they are the source of the judges' explanations as

TABLE 4.1 Changes of Plea

Judge	No. of Pleas in Database	Average No. of Minutes/Plea	Time Range of Pleas in Minutes	Charges			
				Felonies	Open	Misdemeanor	Total
1	2	13	11–15	1		1	2
2	2	33	24–42	1		1	2
3	6	15	10–22	5	1	1	7
4	7	8	5–15	6	2	1	9
5	5	18	13–24	4	1	1	6
6	5	13	8–23	4	2	1	7
7	4	13	10–15	1	1	1	4
8	6	10	5–13	5	1	1	7
9	7	5	4–7	2	3	2	7
Total	44			29	11	11	51

Note: The number of *charges* differs from the number of *pleas* because some defendants are charged with more than one crime and some pleas have more than one defendant.

TABLE 4.2 Nature of Charges

Charge	Judge									Total
	1	2	3	4	5	6	7	8	9	
Assault				1	1	1	1			4
Burglary			2	2	1	1	1	1	4	12
Drugs		2	1	2	1			3	1	10
Fleeing law enforcement						1				1
Forgery						1				1
Fraud				1				1		2
Robbery			1	1	1			1		4
Theft	1		3	2	2	3			1	12
Traffic violation							2		1	3
Trespass (a misdemeanor category only)	1							1		2
Total	2	2	7	9	6	7	4	7	7	51

to why they handled the procedure as they did. The amount of time each judge spent with me varied considerably, and their influence on my understanding of the way the spoken law involves their interpretation of the written law varied accordingly. Here they offered their views on how to handle pleas to ensure that the defendant was pleading guilty knowingly and voluntarily.

In the following discussion, we come to understand judges' ideological stances by relating the transcribed pleas and the posttaping interviews to each other. Thus, there is an intertextual dimension to the analysis, as there was in chapter 3, and as in real life. Generally the actions in the plea procedure are never understood in and of themselves by parties to the procedure but rather in relation to other interactions experienced by parties, although these other interactions would not typically include the interviews of a research project.

The nature of the analysis of the intertextuality here depends on ideology being manifest in the two kinds of data quite differently. In the pleas themselves, the judges' interpretation of the written due process law on knowingness and voluntariness is implicit, but for the majority of judges their interpretation is nevertheless coherent, ramifying consistently throughout the procedure in their interactional strategies. In the interview data, the content of what the judges say makes their ideological stances (i.e., their interpretations of the governing due process law) explicit, but these interpretations emerge in a fragmentary and partial way as if the judges do not usually talk about why they handle the procedures as they do. From the judges' point of view, their talk *about* their own practices explains their talk *in* practice in the courtroom. My own representations of their views of why they do what they do lend more coherence to those views than they had as they emerged in the interviews.

Career History Interviews

The career history interviews are the third source of data in this chapter's discussion of diversity in ideological stances. Some of the judges talked about why they do what they do when hearing guilty pleas in this tape-recorded interview as well as in the posttaping interviews which were not recorded. These data, already drawn on heavily in chapter 2 (Trial Court Judges as Nonideological), are used to display the judges' own words so that readers can see how the judges themselves talk about what they do and why they do it.

Procedure- and Record-Oriented Strategies

As already noted in the introduction to this chapter, procedure- and record-oriented judges differ in two general respects in the way they hear guilty pleas. Procedure-oriented judges vary the way they hear the pleas from defendant to defendant much more than record-oriented judges, and their pleas are longer or more elaborate. The greater variation is reflected at every level of discourse structure, a variation captured through reference to the topical discourse units presented in chapter 3: (1) procedure-oriented judges vary the actual sequential order of their topics; (2) within a given topic they vary whether or not they include the same elements each time, and they vary the topic-internal ordering of those elements more; (3) they vary the actual specific wording of those elements more.

The greater elaboration of pleas by procedure-oriented judges is also most clearly understood as a manipulation of the topics presented in chapter 3. Not all topics are expanded more by procedure-oriented judges. Only three topics are a central part of the two contrasting strategies—social background questions, constitutional rights, and the factual basis for the guilty plea—but these are enough to make a significant difference. The procedure-oriented judges ask the defendants questions about their social background near the beginning of the procedure. The record-oriented judges simply do not ask such questions. Thus, some judges include an entire topic that others do not. Although all the judges tell the defendants what their constitutional rights are, procedure-oriented judges give more elaborate explanations of these rights than others. In addition, procedure-oriented judges repeatedly ask the defendants if they understand these rights, a process I refer to as comprehension checks, whereas record-oriented judges check comprehension fewer times. The third topic, the factual basis, is the part of the procedure in which the judge has to determine whether there is in fact evidence that the defendant committed the crime with which he or she is charged. The preferred procedure-oriented strategy for doing this is to get defendants to narrate what they did, and the judges recognize there is a "confessional" dimension to this strategy. Strategies for getting this information that I characterize as record-oriented all have in common getting the defendant to assent to someone else's version of what happened.

Table 4.3, Procedure-Oriented and Record-Oriented Strategies, displays which judges use the specific strategies associated with procedure-oriented judges. In this table the judges are listed from most procedure-oriented at the top to most record-oriented at the bottom. This pattern represents a reordering and regrouping of the judges compared with earlier tables in this chapter, which ordered them from 1 to 9, the order in which they came onto the bench (see chapter 2). This new ordering suggests that interpretations of due process cross-cut modes of judicial selection and length of time on the bench.

TABLE 4.3 Procedure-Oriented and Record-Oriented Strategies

Strategy by Judge	Significant Overall Variation	Elaboration of Constitutional Rights	Multiple Comprehension Checks of Rights	Social Background Questions	Elicitation of Confession— Factual Basis
Procedure Oriented ↑					
Judge 2	x	x	x	x	x
Judge 7	x	x		x	x
Judge 8	x		x	x	x
Judge 5		x	x	x	x
Judge 6			x	x	x
Judge 1			x		x
Judge 3				x	
Judge 4					
Judge 9			x		
↓ Record Oriented					

x = An x indicates the judge's guilty pleas include the relevant feature. For example, Judge 7 elaborates information about constitutional rights, but Judge 8 does not.

Table 4.3 presents the nine judges as on a continuum from most to least procedure-oriented. However, the judges can also be grouped. When I contrast them as groups in the discussion to follow, I usually set up a general contrast between the top six judges as procedure-oriented and the bottom three judges as record-oriented. This is because, as the table indicates, the bottom three judges do almost nothing to involve the defendant in the procedure, whereas all the top six judges make a significant effort to involve the defendant. This means, of course, that the majority of judges in my group are procedure-oriented. However, as becomes clearer in later discussion, for some purposes it is revealing to conceptualize the three judges at each end of the continuum as most clearly expressing contrasting strategies, while the three judges in the middle reveal a mixed (or even muddled) approach to due process issues. Relatedly, the four transcripts of pleas in appendix F (Four Changes of Plea), from which I draw excerpts to highlight the contrast between procedure-oriented and record-oriented strategies in this chapter, come from judges in the top group of three (Judge 8) and the bottom group of three (Judge 4), respectively.

I turn now to a more detailed examination of the contrast between procedure-oriented and record-oriented strategies for securing defendants' due process rights in the guilty plea.

Overall Variation in the Guilty Plea

The judges in this study all see themselves as having developed their own personal script for the procedure from various sources, including the written law, and their experiences as lawyers, which sometimes involved their seeing other judges handle the same procedure. In other words, each judge consciously worked out a personal way to do the procedure, deciding what to include and an order in which to raise various topics. The main reason given for the development of a personal routinized script, which entailed a commitment on some level to doing the procedure the same way every time it was done, is that this is a way to ensure that the requirements of the written law governing the plea are met. These judges identified their scripts as their own personal interpretations of the procedural due process law governing the procedure. I, however, see socially systematic and culturally shared organized diversity in these interpretations.

Although all the judges see themselves as having developed a personal script for doing the change of plea, the general conception of this script is not identical for all the judges. Procedure-oriented judges see their scripts as inherently variable. Here Judge 5 explains his image of his script:

(1) If I had to draw an analogy, it would be like: I need to get from here to San Francisco and I'm going to drive a certain route. And I want to make sure I stop here, here and here. But what I *talk* about on the way may not be too important. How I describe what I see may not be too important. It may be important as to my listeners. But I *do* know that I have to get from here to there and I've got to make these stops along the way. And so I think you have to have, you know, the framework but not necessarily a particular choice of words to move from one part to the next part. (Judge 5, Career History Interview, p. 66)

Record-oriented judges, in contrast, *aspire* to a fixed script.

(2) I have developed my own style, if you will, of taking a change of plea and I have changed it on very very few occasions. (Judge 9, Change of Plea Interview, p. 11).[1]

All the judges acknowledge that variation is necessary and that there is a need to be flexible, but for the record-oriented judges, a change in the way they handle the procedure is the exception, not the rule:

(3) The only time I've changed it was when I wasn't sure in my own mind that the defendant understood what I was saying to him. You know because of the illiteracy or the language that called for ([an interpreter]) or something like that. (Judge 9, Change of Plea Interview, p. 11)

These views are consistent with the much greater variability from case to case in the way procedure-oriented judges hear the plea. As already noted, this variability is evident in every aspect of language structuring in the pleas and is difficult to quantify.

First, the procedure-oriented judges vary the actual sequential ordering of topics more than record-oriented judges. In chapter 3, I discussed the sequence of topics that appeared most frequently in the database:

  I. Opening
 II. Substance of Procedure
    [Social Background Questions]
    Nature of Charge
    Plea Agreement Comprehension Questions
    Conditions of Plea Agreement
    Sentencing Possibilities
    Constitutional Rights

        Coercion Questions
        Factual Basis
        Findings
III. Closing

Most of these topics appear in every plea, although individual judges differ in their ordering of these topics. A comparison of the four plea transcripts in appendix F indicates that although Judge 4's (record-oriented) topics are in the same almost identical sequence in his two pleas, Judge 8's (procedure-oriented) are not. Here I oversimplify by eliminating representation and discussion of various repairs to the procedures to focus attention on sequential ordering.

Judge 4's topic sequences in the two pleas look like this:

Robbery	*Prescription Falsification*
Opening	Opening
Nature of Charge	Nature of Charge
	Conditions of Plea Agreement (partial)
Plea Agreement Comprehension Questions	Plea Agreement Comprehension Questions
Constitutional Rights	Constitutional Rights
Coercion Questions	Coercion Questions
Conditions of Plea Agreement	Conditions of Plea Agreement and
Sentencing Possibilities	Sentencing Possibilities (merged)
Factual Basis	Factual Basis
Findings	Findings
Formal Plea (few do this)	Formal Plea
Closing	Closing

Judge 8's topic sequences in the two pleas look like this:

Robbery	*Prescription Falsification*
Opening	Opening
Social Background Questions	Nature of Charge
Plea Agreement Comprehension Questions	Conditions of Plea Agreement
Nature of Charge	Plea Agreement Comprehension Questions
Conditions of Plea Agreement and Sentencing Possibilities (merged)	Social Background Questions
Constitutional Rights	Constitutional Rights
Coercion Question	Coercion Questions
Factual Basis	Sentencing Possibilities
Findings	Factual Basis
Closing	Findings
	Closing

Overall, then, the sequential structure of topics is less predictable for the pleas of this procedure-oriented judge than it is for the record-oriented judge.

    Second, although all the judges to some extent vary the elements included in a topic and their ordering, procedure-oriented judges reveal considerably more variation in this area.

Third, the pleas of the procedure-oriented judges show greater variability at the level of specific wording of particular elements within a topic. Both topic-internal and sentence-internal variability can be illustrated by comparing procedure-oriented Judge 8's two different versions of coercion questions in his two pleas from appendix F. In the prescription falsification case, there is no question about any promises made to the defendant, whereas in the robbery case there is. The order of the questions is also different, with questions about the lawyer coming at the beginning in the first example, and at the end in the second example. Finally, the actual wording of the questions changes. I have highlighted the two versions of the question about force to facilitate comparison at the level of wording.

Prescription Falsification   (*lines 193–221*)

> Judge: Have you discussed this matter
> carefully with Mr. Ripkin?

> Defendant: Yes, sir.

> Judge: Do you feel that he's given you
> good advice?

> Defendant: Yes, sir.

> Judge: Are you satisfied with his
> representation to this point?

> Defendant: Yes, sir.

> Judge: *Has anyone uh used any force or*
> *made any threats against you?*
> *To get you to change your plea*
> *(in this matter).*

> Defendant: No, sir.

> Judge: Uh has anyone made any promises
> uh of benefit or reward uh in
> some fashion to get you to
> change your plea?

> Defendant: No, sir.

> Judge: (   ) That being the case,
> then, I uh uh must assume that
> your willingness to plead guilty
> is uh something that you're
> doing voluntarily and uh after
> thinking about it, exercising
> your free will. Is that
> correct?

> Defendant: Yes, sir.

Robbery   (*lines 288–311*)

> Judge: Did anybody else- did anybody
> make any other promises than
> just that to you?

> Defendant: No, /sir/.

Judge:	/In/ exchange for your plea? *Did anybody use any force against you, or make any threats against you*
Defendant:	/No, sir/.
Judge:	*/to get/ you to change your plea?* I have to be satisfied that this is something you're doing voluntarily. Uh is it?
Defendant:	Yes, sir?
Judge:	Have you discussed it fully and carefully with Mr. Martin?
Defendant:	Yes, sir.
Judge:	D' you think he's giving you good advice?
Defendant:	Yes, sir.
Judge:	You satisfied with his representation?
Defendant:	Yes, sir.

What is the motivation for the procedure-oriented judges' commitment to and realization of variability in the way they handle the procedure? Several of these judges articulated a basic commitment to "tailoring" the plea to the individual defendant. They seem to value tailoring both as a way of expressing attention to and concern for the individual and as a means of improving communication.

Judge 5 talked about the value he attaches to tailoring sentences to individual defendants.

(4) I did a lot of sentences in that year that we had the criminal bench. And whether that creates some mental callouses or not, I don't know. I suspect it does. And I at one point near the end of that year said, "I just cannot do any more sentences. I've run out of any creativity, any objectivity, any uh *tailoring* of sentencing capacity. I just don't have it. The well is dry. I've got to get out of this. Because I see that I'm doing it mechanically and that's wrong." Each case is different and you have to look at it that way. (Judge 5, Career History Interview, p. 51)

Several judges expressed similar ideas regarding the plea. For example, Judge 8 talked about how he has changed the way he hears pleas since he came on the bench.

(5) I think as time goes by I'm becoming a little more efficient, but I still like to look at people when I'm talking to them—and depends on what the case is. You know, I suppose in some ways it's a luxury to be able to do what you want to do. We can't. We have too many cases and we've got to get rid of them as quick as we can, like it or not. (Judge 8, Career History Interview, p. 56)

Here, Judges 5 and 8 juxtapose treating people as individuals with providing efficient or speedy justice. Though Judge 5 and Judge 8 are among the three most varying judges, both still express regret that they must standardize more than they wish to get cases through court.

Although procedure-oriented judges may have intrinsically valued treating each defendant as an individual, our discussions made it clear that their main reason for varying the procedure was to make sure the defendant understood what was going on, so that the due process requirement of knowingness and voluntariness would be met. Judge 5 makes the connection between the judges' variation and the defendants' understanding explicit.

(6) I think about the listener, the person to whom I'm speaking. And I guess I learned that that's essential to communication when I was a salesman. You're not going to sell anything unless the person heard what you said and assimilated it and understood it. You might as well just be talking to a wall. And if I don't get feedback that suggests that people are understanding and are going with me, I will modify, until I start to get feedback. . . . Some people are so concerned with what they are saying and whether they're saying it in the right way and whether they're being quote unquote judicial at the time and things of that kind that they miss whether they're communicating at all, and the function is communication. (Judge 5, Career History Interview, pp. 58, 60–61)

In the next section it becomes evident that these judges rely on social background questions to tell them whether and how they must tailor the procedure to the individual to make sure the defendant knows what he is doing.

Record-oriented judges simply do not express the degree of concern with these issues articulated by the procedure-oriented judges. Their view is that they can handle the procedure the same way with most defendants and be understood, although for the exceptions to that general rule, they do modify their standard plea in the interest of making sure the defendant understands what he is doing.

I turn now to the way the procedure-oriented judges and record-oriented judges differed in the degree to which they included or elaborated on the three topics of social background questions, constitutional rights, and factual basis.

Social Background Questions

Judges ask social background questions near the beginning of the procedure, usually just after the opening of the procedure. The six procedure-oriented judges who ask these questions varied in the number of questions they ask, ranging from three to five such questions in the database as a whole. All these six judges always asked defendants what their age and level of education were. The following excerpt illustrates the questions Judge 8 asked in his robbery case, already discussed in chapter 3. These are questions Judge 4 does not ask.

Robbery   (lines 15–33)

> Judge: Thank you, Mr. Martin. [10 secs] For the record, you are Denise Marie Gonzalez?
>
> Defendant: Yes, sir.
>
> Judge: How old are you? They call you Neese? How old are you?
>
> Defendant: Eighteen.

Judge: Where do you live?

Defendant: One oh seven (   ) (Hart).

Judge: How long have you lived in Tucson, Neese?

Defendant: Eighteen years.

Judge: What education have you had? [4 secs] 'S how much edu-schooling have you had?

Defendant: Uhm [2 secs] Seven. [2 secs]

Judge: Uhm do you read and understand English?

Defendant: Yes, sir.

When I asked the procedure-oriented judges why they asked such questions, generally, they agreed that these social background questions provide them with information that enables them to tailor the procedure to the individual—the purpose of the variation discussed in the preceding section. The defendant's responses to social background questions would enable the judge to determine whether the defendant was "able" at all to plead guilty knowingly and voluntarily, or to determine what it was necessary to do in the procedure to make this particular defendant knowing and voluntary. That was why the judges asked these questions at the beginning of the procedure. They set the stage for what would follow.

The information to which the judges attached the greatest importance, spontaneously offered repeatedly as an example by them, was the level of education the defendant had attained. The judges held this to be the key indicator of whether the defendant could read and understand the plea agreement and of whether the defendant could understand the information the judge intended to give him.

In my career history interview with Judge 5, we drifted into why he did things the way he did and he brought up his own question about schooling:

(7) Okay. I do it [i.e., ask a question about schooling] because I want to know how . . . I want a fact in there that would suggest intelligence. First of all. He or she was at least competent enough to finish high school or get their GED and read and write and understand the English language so that there's a factual basis for suggesting that they understood what they read. Okay? Now, I suspect, if I left that out, did not make that inquiry, if I use the magic words at the end, "knowingly, intelligently and voluntarily enters a plea," the court might say this: "That's what the judge found. There must have been something from the demeanor and appearance of the defendant at the time that suggested that he was intelligently making this plea though we can't find anything in the record. . . . See here's his magic words at the end. So he must have found that." And they would perhaps put aside that argument on appeal on that basis. So the magic words can have significance at times to that extent, even though there won't be anything in the actual record of the proceedings to suggest intelligence. And there's a lot of that that goes on. (Judge 5, Career History Interview, pp. 68–69)

In other words, although an appellate court would not require the judge to have specific evidence in his court proceeding that a defendant was intelligent or educated enough to be "knowing," this judge wants that evidence to be there and gets it by asking a question about schooling.

If the number of years of schooling was low, a judge might use simpler language or go over the information more slowly and carefully, or at least that was his intent. Judge 2 specifically told me that of the two pleas he did in my taped database, both for possession of marijuana, one was longer than the other (42 minutes versus 24 minutes) because of the difference in the education of the defendants. In one case the defendant had not completed high school. In the other case the defendant had had some college education.

The judges' attention to educational level is consistent with the importance Americans attach to education. Americans frequently explain negatively evaluated behavior by an actor's lack of education. Because level of education is closely related to concepts of class and race, which we know we are not supposed to blame for negative behavior, attributions involving education can be understood to function sometimes as "code" for attributions associated with class and race. In other words, inferences based on level of education are suspect as standing in for class and race stereotyping. And when judges make inferences about what it means that a defendant has a particular educational level, they may be voicing acceptable versions of racial and class stereotyping. However, educational level may *really* predict a defendant's ability to understand the procedure.

As Judge 5's comments suggest, the judges made a distinction between the actual answers to the questions and the defendant's demeanor while answering. When the judges were pressed about what aspects of demeanor would give them insight into the defendant's ability to understand, their answers made it clear that they were not thinking of dress and hairstyle or cleanliness and neatness but, rather, the nonverbal behavior associated with speaking. More than one judge specifically mentioned pausing. For example, if a defendant paused before he answered a question, the judge could take that as evidence that the defendant did not understand the question.

As already noted, it was the express intent of at least some of the procedure-oriented judges to link the variation discussed in the preceding section to the responses to the social background questions discussed here—that is, for the answers to those questions to enable the judge to tailor the procedure to the specific defendant. But I did not find socially systematic variation in the degree of elaboration of the change of plea based on the defendants' answers to social background questions. For example, the level of education of the defendant does not allow us to predict the degree of elaboration of constitutional rights.[2] It is still possible, however, that both the social background questions and the variation from instance to instance of the procedure, even if not causally linked, give the procedure-oriented judges a different presentation of self than the record-oriented judges and lend the procedure a subtly different overall feel than that of the record-oriented judges, one that suggests more of a personal concern for the individual.

Even if the differences in behavior that we have considered so far do not give the procedure a different feel (and I cannot say that they do on the basis of my own experience), they do reflect an important difference in ideological stance: they display the intent, even if it is an intent not fully realized, of these procedure-oriented judges to handle the procedure differently each time in ways influenced by characteristics of the defendant before them.

This is an intent the record-oriented judges clearly do not share. When I asked these judges why they did not ask defendants questions about their social background, their answers varied, but the judges all had little interest in the issue and simply saw social background questions as largely unnecessary.

As noted earlier, the more record-oriented judges also look with disfavor on involving the defendant in the procedure because it potentially creates problems with the establishment of a "good" record that would not be overturned by an appellate court. Although it seems that few problems could be raised by asking the defendant social background questions, doing so *did* set the precedent for the defendant's involvement. And in spite of the seeming innocuousness of the questions, the responses *were* unpredictable. Judge 8's prescription falsification case illustrates this unpredictability. In the following excerpt, the simple question, "Where do you live?," leads the judge and the defendant into the "trouble" of a side sequence of several exchanges that although not threatening to the procedure, does lengthen it and requires the attention of the judge to get back into the standard sequence.

Prescription Falsification   (lines 59–100)

Judge: Uh how old are you?

Defendant: Thirty-four.

Judge: Where do you live? Where is your home?

Defendant: Uh my hometown is (   ). That's where my wife and family [2 secs] /are right now./

Judge: /All right./ How long have you been in Tucson?

Defendant: Totally, about one year, but just before last Christmas, we moved back to (   ).

Judge: Uh these incidents uh apparently relate to- Well, one of them relates to an incident that occurred last August of seventy-seven, and the second one uh (   ) prescription drug charge to uh an incident on July eighteen, 1977. Were you in Tucson at that time?

Defendant: Right. That's from uh December of last year almost the whole year I lived in Tucson. I worked for (that company).

Judge: What kind of work (do) you do?

Defendant: Uh (that's the) supervisor, clerk. (Ordinarily I was) a clerk and became a supervisor.

Judge: /Uh what/-

Defendant: /Most of/ my jobs have been administrative type things.

Judge: Where, specifically, were you working here in Tucson?

Defendant: For U-Totem stores. [2 secs]

Judge: Uh you do read and understand the English language.

Defendant: Yes, I do.

Judge: How much education have you had, Mr. Appleton?

Defendant: Two years (   ).

This is the type of exchange the record-oriented judges would rather avoid, and they can avoid such exchanges by not asking the questions in the first place. Thus, both behaviorally and ideologically, an issue that is elaborated on for the procedure-oriented judges is abbreviated for the record-oriented judges.

Constitutional Rights

All the judges inform the defendants of their constitutional rights. None of them "have to," according to the case law discussed in chapter 3, because all the case law requires is that there be evidence in the record that defendants were informed of their constitutional rights, and such evidence is ample. The constitutional rights are spelled out in the written plea agreement and when defendants sign the plea agreement, they are verifying that they have read its contents. Defendants are then asked during the procedure if they have read and signed the plea agreement, which the judge also holds in his hand and checks for a signature during the procedure. Sometimes defendants are also asked if they have discussed the plea agreement with their lawyers and if they understand it. There is on this issue, then, great redundancy in the record providing evidence that defendants know and understand the constitutional rights they are waiving by pleading guilty. Nevertheless, in every instance of this procedure in my database, all the judges informed the defendants of their rights and asked if they understood them.

Even so, procedure-oriented judges engaged in more elaborate exchanges with defendants than did record-oriented judges to inform them of these rights and make sure they understood what they were giving up. In the following two transcript excerpts, I present the abbreviated version of the rights from Judge 4 and then the elaborate version of the rights from Judge 8 from their prescription falsification cases. These two excerpts of constitutional rights illustrate the two main ways in which the procedure- and record-oriented judges differ in how they handle the constitutional rights. First, procedure-oriented judges do more comprehension checks. In other words, they more frequently ask defendants if they understand what they have just been told, essentially breaking down the information into smaller chunks with one check for each right identified, whereas record-oriented judges ask if defendants understand groups of rights. Here Judge 8 elicits evidence of understanding seven times to Judge 4's three times.

Second, procedure-oriented judges say more about what the rights are. I think this is generally evident in the excerpts to follow, but I highlighted the information about the right to an attorney in each judge's delivery to make direct comparison as easy as possible. Judge 8 treats this right as two subrights, one to an attorney during a trial and the other to an attorney in pretrial proceedings, whereas Judge 4 mentions only the trial. In other respects Judge 8 does not so much add any new information as create redundancy.

Judge 4: Prescription Falsification   (*lines 70–105*)

> Judge: Do you understand that uh- you
> are entitled to a trial by jury
> on the charges that are filed
> against you in this case?
>
> Defendant: Yes, Your Honor.
>
> Judge: And that by entering a plea of
> guilty at this time, you're
> giving up and waiving your right
> to a trial by jury?
>
> Defendant: Yes, Your Honor.
>
> Judge: D'ya understand that you do have
> the following specific jury-
> trial rights which you are
> giving up, and that is the right
> to confront the witnesses who
> have made the charges against
> you, and to cross-examine those
> witnesses, the right to present
> evidence and to call witnesses
> in your own defense, to require
> the state to compel those
> witnesses to appear and testify,
> *the right to be represented by*
> *an attorney appointed free of*
> *charge at the trial of*
> *proceedings,* the right to remain
> silent, to refuse to be a
> witness against yourself, and to
> be presumed innocent until
> proven guilty beyond a
> reasonable doubt. Do you
> understand that you're giving up
> all of those- uh jury trial
> rights by pleading guilty?
>
> Defendant: Yes, Your Honor.

Judge 8: Prescription Falsification   (*lines 119–192*)

> Judge: All right. Specifically, you do
> not have to enter into this

Judge: agreement at all uh and if you *do* enter into it, you give up certain valuable constitutional rights. Uh as matters now stand, you have uh entered pleas of not guilty in each of these three files, and you have an absolute right to uh a jury trial in each of the files and (on) each of the charges in those files. Do you understand that?

Defendant: Yes, I do.

Judge: Uh at any such trial you'd have *the right to the assistance of a court-appointed attorney if you could not afford uh a lawyer to represent you, and of course that assistance would be available to you uh at pretrial proceedings as well as a trial. (You) give that right up.* (Do you) understand that? You'd also have the right to uh face and confront and to cross-examine the witnesses that the state would have to call to prove your guilt. That right would be lost to you as well. (Do) you understand that?

Defendant: Yes, I do.

Judge: Uh you'd have the right to compel the attendance of witnesses in your defense, if uh they would not appear voluntarily. (You) understand that?

Defendant: Yes, sir.

Judge: You'd have the right to have the court instruct the jury uh that you are to be presumed innocent until the state had borne the burden which it has of proving your guilt beyond a reasonable doubt. Are you aware of that?

Defendant: Yes, sir.

Judge: Uh you also have the right, of course, not to incriminate

> yourself. You could either
> take the stand and testify
> yourself or uh remain silent and
> rely on the presumption of
> innocence uh. That's a decision
> that you would make uh together
> with your lawyer. And *that*
> right you would also give up.
> You understand that?

Defendant: Yes, sir.

> Judge: In other words uh you give up
> all those rights because there
> isn't gonna be a trial if I
> accept these pleas uh this plea
> uh. That will dispose of the
> issue of your uh your guilt uh
> and the state's ability to *prove*
> your guilt. And all that would
> remain then would be uh for me
> to decide what disposition to
> make (of that). You understand
> that?

Defendant: Yes, sir. [3 secs]

Although I did not focus my discussion with the judges on their treatment of the constitutional rights, their general comments on why they handled the procedure as they did show how their interactional strategies in this topic relate to their ideological stances. Here the procedure-oriented judges assume personal responsibility for making sure the defendants know and understand their rights in the procedure itself. They are not willing to assume, even when the defendant says he read and understood the plea agreement and reviewed it with his lawyer, that this is really the case. Generally, they also feel that by eliciting evidence of understanding from the defendant, the defendant becomes more firmly committed to the plea. The defendant's repeated express understanding of each right makes it more difficult for him to back out later, to claim later that he did not know his rights or did not understand them, or to deny that his plea was "voluntary."

In contrast, the record-oriented judges are willing to rely in part on the record of the procedure as a whole to reveal the defendant's knowledge of his constitutional rights. They are also willing to share their responsibility for making sure the defendant is knowing with the defendant's lawyer and the defendant himself, to act as if they believe the defendant when he says he read and understood the plea agreement and discussed it with his attorney.

The Factual Basis

In many ways the most conspicuous difference between procedure-oriented and record-oriented judges is the way in which they handle the factual basis topic. As I explained in chapter 3, the judge must make sure in the factual basis that there is evidence for each element of the crime the defendant has committed as its elements are statutorily defined. In general, all the judges agreed that the factual basis must come from the defendants themselves, for it to be true that they were pleading guilty knowingly and voluntarily. The judges also generally agreed that involving the defendant in establishing this factual basis was risky because of the possibility that he would say something not consistent with a legally valid factual basis for his crime, either out of ignorance of the law or because he did not want to admit guilt. There is, then, an inherent tension in the factual basis: on the one hand, the defendant must be involved for the procedure to be legally valid; on the other hand the defendant's involvement threatens the legal validity of the procedure. The judges with procedure- and record-oriented ideological stances resolved this tension differently through ways of conceptualizing and enacting what it means to involve the defendant. Not surprisingly, the procedure-oriented judges sought to involve the defendant more, whereas the record-oriented judges sought to limit the defendant's involvement.

The procedure-oriented judges usually began the factual basis with an open-ended question, basically asking, "What happened?," or, "What did you do that makes you think you are guilty of this crime?" In this way, these judges tried to elicit an account or a narrative from the defendants themselves. Often this approach did not work because the defendant was not very forthcoming. And even when the defendant was, the judge usually wanted to clarify aspects of the events at issue. So open-ended beginnings are usually followed by a mixture of many yes–no questions that invite a very narrow response and more open-ended "Wh" questions.

Judge 8's factual bases can be used to illustrate this approach. In the first factual basis from the prescription falsification transcript the defendant is unusually forthcoming. He rambles on and on. Note that the judge asks him to identify the drug he is taking, a fact that must be specified as an element of the crime. And his own lawyer comes in (see arrows to left of relevant text) to guide him to specify what he thinks the judge needs to hear. This defendant was already serving time when he committed this new crime but was released during the day to the custody of a drug counseling program (Project Create) where he worked.

Prescription Falsification   (*lines 456–572*)

> Judge: Tell me about the uh
> incident this summer, July
> eighteenth uh involving
> apparently some Valium.
> What happened there?
> Defendant: Well, I was at the annex
> (at Project Create). I was
> hardship, you know, and I'd
> go out to (Project Create)
> and work, counsel, and
> stuff. And uh I'd spend my
> nights and weekends at the
> annex as a condition of
> third-party release. While

lifting weights one night
at the annex- it was a
Friday night- I hurt my
back a bit (   )
(recurrent) back problems
for fifteen or sixteen
years. And uh all they
gave me was aspirin and
Tylenol and I was- it was
pretty- pretty bad and (the
head PO just said) to go
lay in the bunk for awhile
or something. They tried
to call the medic, but the
medical care, you know, at
the annex (in) Pima County
jail isn't up to par, so I
waited from Friday night
until Sunday afternoon to
get to see the jailhouse
doctor (at- at the main
jail) and when I saw him,
this Dr. Schatz, he's he's
he has my uh record of
(all) the time I've been in
custody of- of Pima County
sheriff's department. But
he wanted uh- he was gonna
put me in traction. He
didn't do that. He gave me
a double doses of Tylenol
with uh codeine in it (or)
Valiums. He said, "Don't
go to Project Create for a
week. Just stay in your
bunk (for a while)." That
wasn't real effective. I
was used to uh taking
stronger medication and
stuff like that. It helped
somewhat. I remembered I
had an old prescription
from (General) Pharmacy in
Tucson. It was a
prescription I'd brought to
Tucson, or my doctor from
Wisconsin had sent out
here, with-

→   Judge: *Was that for Valium?*
     Defendant: It was for Valium, and it

had three refills on it.
(But uh) I only filled it
one time for one hundred
and twenty ten milligram
Valium. And uh I thought,
well, rather 'n go see a
doctor here, or go out on
(the) streets and buy those
drugs, you know, I'd just
go see if I could get it
refilled. But in the
meantime uh the effect of
the codeine (happened).
(It was uh a little like)
banging on the head. I'd
never- in all honesty, I've
taken- [2–3 secs]

→   Defense Lawyer: (*Just tell him about the*
prescription [*7 secs*]
That's what he wants to
find out.)

Defendant: Oh, wow. Um Okay. I wanted
to see if I could refill
that prescription. And
it's uh- [2 secs] It was
no longer the statu- uh the
time (limit had) run (out).

Judge: More than a year old?

Defendant: More than a- well no- yeh,
it was. I guess it was
about fourteen months or
so- fifteen months. (So)
basically that's it.

Judge: Didja actually as a result
of that uh obtain any
Valium, or- or simply
attempt to and /apparently
uh/

Defendant: /Just an attempt./

Judge: the druggist uh uh must
have re- reported that
attempt to the
authorities?

Defendant: The druggist called back to
Wisconsin to see if uh-
that was if it could be
refilled and stuff and uh
wasn't all (   ). In the
meantime uh [2 secs] I uh
called (Gerald's) Pharmacy

and impersonated someone
from the doctor's office.

Judge: I see.

Defendant: And the DPS came and, as a
result. /(   )/

Judge: When /you uh/ took that
move, I take it you knew
that was against the law.

Defendant: Uh well now we can get into
the (huhnh huhnh).

Judge: Well, does it surprise you
that that is a violation?

Defendant: No, it doesn't surprise me
that it was a violation.

Judge: I think there's a
sufficient factual basis uh
gentlemen. Do either of
you have any problems? [3
secs]

Defense Lawyer: None, Your Honor.

In Judge 8's robbery factual basis, the defendant is more typically reserved, but here the judge does not question as much as he usually does and makes reference to earlier proceedings in which this same defendant was brought before the court on the same charge:

Robbery   *(lines 312–337)*

Judge: Okay. Tell me what happened on
June sixth, 1978, I seem to
remember a little bit from a
juvenile proceeding, but uh I
wanna hear it from you.

Defendant: Well, we went to my friend's
house and uh he told me to uhm
go down to uh Mantigo's, so I
went and he told me to wait for
him (uh) a couple of blocks
down, so I waited for him. And
I drove him around for awhile,
and waited for him, then he
came.

Judge: Y- you knew he was gonna rob the
place?

Defendant: Yes, sir.

Judge: And you were gonna help him get
away?

Defendant: Yes, sir.

Judge: (All right). [2 secs] I'm
satisfied both because of the

defendant's statements and what
I recall of the juvenile matter
that there is a factual basis.

The procedure-oriented judges want to involve defendants in this way to make sure they are pleading knowingly and voluntarily. If *the defendant* confesses, he is more likely to *know* he is pleading guilty and know what he is pleading guilty to. If *the defendant* confesses, the judge has evidence that he was pleading guilty voluntarily, it is argued. And the defendant is less likely later to deny that he understood what he was doing.[3]

The record-oriented judges show more diversity in their strategies for establishing a factual basis in part because they are less concerned that a factual account come from the defendant. One common strategy is for the judge to ask the defendant several yes–no questions, one each for each statutory element of the crime, as in "Did you possess the marijuana? Did you know you possessed it? Was it a usable amount?"

A second common strategy is to present a brief summary of the facts to the defendant and then ask the defendant if he agrees that this is what happened, again a yes–no question. The judge may summarize the facts because he can find them repeatedly stated in the written record. (One judge in my group was known for getting the factual basis from the grand jury transcript.) He may also ask one of the lawyers to do it, or one of the lawyers may particularly want to, for any of several reasons, most of them involving not trusting the defendant to do it without somehow messing it up.

Judge 4 uses the second strategy in the robbery transcript to follow. He summarizes the facts, then asks the defendant if he agrees.

Robbery   (*lines 194–222*)

Judge:	Further admitting by pleading guilty to crime of attempted armed robbery, a class three felony, with two prior convictions that [2 secs] on the twenty-sixth day,
Judge:	*does the first uh degree burglary offense still require nighttime?*
Defense Lawyer:	*No.*
County Attorney:	*No, Your Honor.*
Judge:	*All right. Are you admitting by pleading guilty to attempted armed robbery uh [2 secs]* Mr. Southcutt on December the twenty-sixth, uh 1978, uh you committed to- you attempted to commit the crime of robbery, that is, you attempted to take property uh from uh the person or under the control of Martha O'Malley uh while you were armed

with a deadly weapon, to wit a
gun and that uh y- you attempted
to- rob uh Ms. O'Malley by
force or fear?

Defendant: I attempted to it.

Judge: You attempted to it.

This is characteristic of this judge's approach in my database. In the prescription falsification example, however, Judge 4 invites the participation of the defense lawyer who defers to the county attorney, a departure from his more typical approach, suggesting something unusual about this case that cannot be gleaned from the procedure itself.

Prescription Falsification   (*lines 209–247*)

Judge: What's the factual basis, Mr.
Sawyer, please?

Defense Lawyer: Judge, I think we will just
agree with what the county
attorney will tell the court.

Judge: All right. [5 secs]

County Attorney: (   ), Your Honor. [27 secs]
The uh factual basis in this
case, Your Honor, uh Mr. Farmer
obtained a prescription for
Tylenol number four uh which
falls under the prescription
and dangerous drug statute. And
uh the prescription was for the
amount of uh fifteen tablets,
the prescription was altered to
twenty-five tablets when
presented to the pharmacy. Uh-
Mr. Farmer has been charged
under the statute for altering
the prescription from fifteen to
twenty-five tablets of Tylenol
number four.

Judge: Mr. Farmer, by entering a plea
of guilty, are you admitting
that on January second, 1979,
you did- alter a prescription
for Tylenol number four by
increasing the uh number of the
uh capsules, and presenting uh
that uh to a pharmacy in uh
Pima County, Arizona, with the
intent to obtain the altered
number of uh pills.

Defendant: Yes, sir.

Judge: You're admitting that that's true?

Defendant: Yes.

Note that even though the judge allows this summary, he still restates the facts in his own terms in seeking the defendant's involvement.

When I asked them why they did not involve the defendant more, the record-oriented judges said they felt it was not necessary. In the one taped interview (as opposed to my usual procedure of taking notes), I talked to Judge 9 about why he did not try to involve the defendant more in the factual basis. This judge prefers to get the factual basis by asking the defendant one yes–no question for each element of the charge.

(8) PHILIPS: Well one argument that I have heard is that you want the defendant to describe a set of events because you actually want the defendant to feel that somehow he's gone through some kind of confession or . . .

JUDGE 9: Well see I, you know I don't feel that way. Let me tell you why. See, you know, adult probation officers are the same way. They feel that any time a guy gets convicted that they've got to either . . . they've got to bare their soul to them, all right? Or if they don't bare their soul to them that somehow they're worse than somebody else that comes in and bares their soul, you know? Well, I may have a black robe but I don't have a white collar around me. You know, I'm not a priest, I'm a judge. And as far as I'm concerned, some of these defendants, for whatever reason, and they could have a variety of reasons, don't really want to stand out there in open court or with the pre-sentence report and say, you know, detail, "This is what I did." So I, you know, I just don't put them to it. I don't feel it's necessary. As long as I get from them the elements of the crime to establish the factual basis, that's all I need. I don't expect the defendant, never have and never will, to sit out there and tell me his motive for it, the reason he did it, how he did it and, you know, step by step. I don't think it's necessary. A lot of defendants for a variety of reasons, you know, don't want to do that and even though they know they're guilty and they're pleading guilty. You know, my mother was sitting in the back of the court room and I was charged with uh you know sexual assault or something like that, I don't think that I'd want to stand up there and say in front of my family exactly what I did and how I did it and you know it isn't necessary. You know, why do it to them? (Judge 9, Change of Plea Interview, pp. 19–20)

Thus, at least this judge, who was the only one to express this view so vehemently, is reluctant to humiliate the defendant in public, a humiliation that others may feel is an appropriate rather than inappropriate part of the defendant's punishment. This excerpt suggests that rather than lacking concern for the individual, Judge 9 was showing his concern for the individual in a different way than the procedure-oriented judges, who tried to involve the defendants. He respects the defendant's privacy rather than showing interest in him, in a manner reminiscent of Brown and Levinson's (1987) distinction between negative and positive politeness. However, this same judge acknowledged that relatives of criminal defendants had taken him to task on more than one occasion for seeming mechanical, cold, and indifferent in his manner, so his concern was not recognized as such.

Judge 9 also articulated the concern shared by other record-oriented judges that involving the defendant would spoil the procedure. In the following excerpt he was responding in general to my comment as we looked at a transcript of one of his pleas that he did not ask many open-ended questions. Because most such questions occur in the factual basis, it is relevant here:

(9) Let me tell you something. I take a Change of Plea, okay? The state and the defendant agreed on it. [2 secs] I feel my role as a judge at the time of the Change of Plea is to make sure that I take the Change of Plea in conformance with the Rules of Criminal Procedure and, you know, the case law as set down by the Supreme Court. I don't feel my job is to go out there and destroy a Plea Agreement that's been entered into by, you know, the State and by the defendant. If I can avoid destroying a Plea Agreement I won't do it. And the easiest way *not* to destroy a plea agreement is to not ask quote unquote what you call open-ended questions, where you get the response that you need for the plea agreement to be binding. (Judge 9, Change of Plea Interview, p. 15)

In sum, all the judges involve the defendant, but whereas for procedure-oriented judges this means getting the defendant to fulsomely confess if possible, for record-oriented judges it means getting the defendant to assent to someone else's framing of the issues. However, the judges made it clear that although their predominant strategies were the ones they personally favored, they did change strategies as the need arose to get the factual basis—those who preferred yes–no questions would move to open-ended questions when they had difficulties and those who preferred open-ended questions moved to yes–no questions if what they were doing did not work. Overall, the greater number of questions asked by procedure-oriented judges stands out more clearly than the type of question.

There is a certain irony in the configuration of behavior and ideology in the variability among the factual bases. The record-oriented judges ask what sociolinguists view as more coercive questions because yes–no questions limit the possible range of answers allowed the respondent more than "Wh" questions do. But the more open-ended "Wh" questions of the procedure-oriented judges, which when answered are taken as evidence of "voluntariness," create the potentially more painful experience for the defendant.

Quantitative Reflections of Elaboration and Abbreviation

Thus far I discussed the contrast between the elaborating interactional strategy of the procedure-oriented judges and the abbreviating interactional strategy of the record-oriented judges both descriptively and qualitatively. But the ways in which this difference is reflected in language use can be captured quantitatively as well (see table 4.4, Quantitative Reflections of Elaboration and Abbreviation of the Guilty Plea).

The clearest reflection of this strategic difference shows up in the third column of table 4.4 (Average Number of Responses Elicited from Defendant). This column takes the number of responses by the defendant to questions from the judge for each plea for a given judge, adds them together, then averages them by the number of pleas done by that judge. Responses by the defendant rather than questions from the judge were calculated so that repetitions of the same question when a defendant did not initially

TABLE 4.4 Quantitative Reflections of Elaboration and Abbreviation of the Guilty Plea

Strategy by Judge	No. of Pleas	Average Time of Plea (min.)	Average No. of Responses Elicited from Defendant	Percentage of "wh" Questions (Relative to Yes–No Questions)
Procedure Oriented				
↑				
Judge 2	2	33	95	4
Judge 7	4	13	27	12
Judge 8	6	10	41	12
Judge 5	5	18	60	8
Judge 6	5	13	33	9
Judge 1	2	13	33	9
Judge 3	6	15	21	8
Judge 4	7	8	16	5
Judge 9	7	5	16	1
↓				
Record Oriented				

respond would not inflate the number of questions asked. Because in some cases a response from the defendant was inaudible, the numbers are if anything lower than the actual number of questions responded to.

As we can see from this column, the average number of responses ranges from 16 to 95, a considerable range. For the three most procedure-oriented judges, the collective average is 54; for the three most record-oriented judges, the collective average number of responses is 18. This means there are roughly three times as many instances of defendant involvement in the procedure at the procedure-oriented end of the continuum as there are at the record-oriented end of the continuum.

The fourth column, Percentage of "Wh" Questions, shows the percentage of questions that use a "Wh" word (who, what, where, when, or why) rather than a yes–no form of question. Thus, of Judge 2's average of 95 questions, 4% or approximately 4 questions, will be "Wh" questions; the remaining 91 questions will be yes–no questions. This percentage reflects the combination of social background questions, such as "How many years of schooling do you have?," which are in practice no more open-ended than yes–no questions, and questions in the factual basis, such as "Then what happened?," which are very open-ended. This is another way of measuring the judge's effort to involve the defendant.

All efforts to involve the defendant entail more risk to the procedure than not involving the defendant because any time the defendant speaks he may say something that pushes the procedure off track or threatens the legal validity of the procedure, which in turn requires more effort on the part of the judge to make the procedure good. But I think the percentage of "Wh" questions is a better reflection of the willingness of a judge to take that risk than the overall frequency of responses because, as argued elsewhere (Philips 1987a), such questions are associated with more egalitarian and less controlling and controlled relationships and modes of interaction than yes–no questions. They signal to the defendant a slight relinquishing of control on the part of the judge and a willingness to allow the defendant more agency in constructing the legal reality being negotiated than the use of yes–no questions.

The percentage of "Wh" questions asked by judges ranges from 1% to 12% of all questions asked. For the three judges at the procedure-oriented end of the continuum, the collective average of "Wh" questions is 9%, whereas at the record-oriented end of the continuum, the collective average of "Wh" questions for those three judges is 6%. Here, then, the frequencies of "Wh" questions suggest that record-oriented judges are less prone than procedure-oriented judges to giving up a little control and risking a struggle to make the procedure good.

Column 2 of table 4.4, Average Time of Plea (Min.), shows that the extent to which a judge elaborates on the plea affects the overall amount of time the plea takes. The average length of time the plea takes varies from 5 minutes to 33 minutes. The three most procedure-oriented judges by qualitative measures collectively average 18 minutes per plea, whereas the three most record-oriented judges collectively average 9 minutes a plea, or half the time.

Table 4.5 (Pleas Scheduled in Court Calendar Sample) offers evidence that those judges who take less time to hear the pleas hear more pleas (i.e., carry a heavier workload of pleas and therefore also a heavier load of sentencings than the judges who take more time). Column 2 displays the percentage of pleas scheduled for each judge over the total number of days I was present in the Pima County Superior Court. Each day I was in court I obtained a copy of the daily court calendar. This schedule lists all the procedures for each judge's court that are to take place that day. Because procedures are often canceled at the last minute, this schedule does not show the pleas actually heard on those days but, rather, the pleas scheduled to be heard by the judges. The percentages in this column show the proportion of the pleas scheduled for each judge in my group (rather than the proportion for all judges on the bench at that time), so that we compare only the judges within my sample.

TABLE 4.5 Pleas Scheduled in Court Calendar Sample

Strategy by judge	No. of Pleas Scheduled	Percentage of Total for the Group	Percentage of Pleas Done by Groups of Three
Procedure Oriented			
↑			
Judge 2	12	5	
Judge 7	37	14	25
Judge 8	15	6	
Judge 5	32	12	
Judge 6	27	14	33
Judge 7	19	7	
Judge 3	38	15	
Judge 4	29	11	41
Judge 9	38	15	
↓			
Record Oriented			
Total	257	99	99

Thus, of the pleas assigned to this group, Judge 2 was scheduled for only 5% of them whereas Judge 9 was scheduled for 15% for the sum total of days I obtained the schedule. Column 3 shows that the three most record-oriented judges together were assigned 42% of the pleas, whereas the three most procedure-oriented judges were assigned only 25% of the pleas.

In general, then, the procedure- and record-oriented judges hear guilty pleas in a somewhat different way. Procedure-oriented judges hear fewer pleas but give more time to each plea. Record-oriented judges hear more pleas but give each plea and each defendant less time.

Recapitulation

At this point it may be useful to review the differences between record- and procedure-oriented judges. Record-oriented judges take an ideological stance that is closer to the minimal requirements of the case law governing this procedure discussed in chapter 3. They are most concerned with making a good record. Their individual routines show little variation from instance to instance of handling their procedure, and it is their intention to handle the procedure exactly the same way each time unless special circumstances call for special measures. Their main reason for not varying the procedure is to make sure they get everything said that must be said to establish a record that cannot be overturned by an appellate court. Variation makes it more likely that something legally necessary for a "good" plea will be left out. Relatedly, record-oriented judges do not elaborate on the plea but aim to say the least possible (which also helps with getting it right every time) and to involve the defendant as little as possible. Involving the defendant threatens the legal viability of the procedure. The record-oriented judges do not see a need to give the defendant extensive constitutional rights information, to elicit frequent comprehension checks from him, or to elicit social background or factual basis information from the defendant. These judges believe that the procedure they conduct is not the only activity through which the defendant's knowingness and voluntariness in pleading guilty are established. Therefore, there is no need for the judges to give extensive attention to this matter in the plea. Relatedly, these judges see the lawyers and the defendant as sharing responsibility with them for making the defendant knowing and voluntary in his plea, another reason not to give this due process issue extensive attention in hearing guilty pleas.

Procedure-oriented judges, in contrast, meet the due process requirements of the guilty plea in a manner more consistent with Rule 17, which sets a more demanding standard than case law, as discussed in chapter 3. They say that they are primarily concerned with determining for themselves through the procedure that the defendant is pleading guilty knowingly and voluntarily, rather than with making a good record that cannot be overturned by an appellate court. The routines these judges develop are inherently more variable. It is their intent to tailor the procedure to the individual defendant and to use the information they get from asking the defendant social background questions to achieve that tailoring. They give the defendant more constitutional rights information and get more factual basis information from the defendant than is true of the record-oriented judges. They see this greater exchange of information as their way of making the defendant knowing and voluntary in his guilty plea. These judges see it as their personal responsibility to ensure that the defendant is knowing and voluntary and they see the change of plea procedure as the activity in which they are to carry out this responsibility. It is not enough that there be evidence from the written record or testimony from lawyers and the defendant that his due process rights have been met; they must make sure for themselves.

Through different interactional strategies, then, the judges realize in discourse practice different ideological stances—different interpretations of the written procedural law governing the guilty plea. From their point of view, they are enacting different individual interpretations of the written law. However, as I try to demonstrate, I see their interpretations not as individual but rather as shared, as culturally transmitted and socially organized ideological diversity. The judges who handle the procedure in similar ways give similar reasons for handling the procedure those ways.

There is some evidence, albeit slim, that the socially systematic interpretive differences among judges on the Pima County Superior Court Bench are evident in other parts of the country as well. Two other court studies discuss a contrast between legal practitioners who approach criminal cases in a way that *particularizes* each case and those who *universalize* their treatment of criminal cases and defendants, a difference that sounds very much like the difference between procedure-oriented and record-oriented judges' tailoring versus standardizing of the guilty plea. Levin (1977) describes how Pittsburgh judges particularize their treatment of criminal defendants, whereas Minneapolis judges universalize their treatment of criminal defendants. And Maynard (1984) describes how in the plea bargaining process in a California city, prosecutors representing the County Attorney's Office tried to standardize their approaches to cases, whereas public defenders aimed to particularize each case. Packer's (1974) idea that the two separate value systems of "crime control" and "due process" compete for priority in the criminal process, the former entailing more standardizing and the latter more individualizing treatment of defendants, is also relevant here.

The concerns that Judge 5 and Judge 7 expressed earlier in this chapter about their tendency to standardize their procedures over time for the sake of efficiency, and the reproaches to Judge 9 that his standardization in treatment of criminal defendants made him seem indifferent to their plight, invoke a widespread cultural tension in the United States between attention to and respect for the uniqueness of each individual and a desire for bureaucratic social processes that are efficient in their use of time and money. Americans may care about whether their judges are efficient versus concerned (i.e., this difference may "really matter"), but because public discourses about the judiciary are presently dominated by the organized bar's emphasis on the legal professional qualifications of judges, this concern is not reached in those discourses.

Liberal and Conservative Political Ideological Stances

As previously argued, when the judges offered explanations for their behavior in the plea, they cast these explanations in legal interpretive terms—that is, as having to do with the realization of due process requirements and with their exercise of the judicial discretion allowed them in meeting the requirements of the written law. Judicial discretion is generally not seen as ideologically laden in the U.S. political sense of ideology as "conservative" or "liberal." As discussed in chapter 2, trial court judges are not supposed to allow their political ideologies to affect their behavior, and these judges say they adhere to that standard. They see themselves as trying and largely succeeding in keeping their political ideologies from affecting their judicial behavior. It is apparent, however, that a procedure-oriented stance on due process enacts a politically liberal conceptualization of the role of the state in relation to the individual, whereas a record-oriented stance enacts a politically conservative conceptualization of the role of the state in relation to the individual, a point I now consider in greater detail.

The *conservative* view of the relationship between the individual and the state calls for as little intervention from the state in the lives of individuals as possible. There is a concern with and even fear of encroachment of the state on individual liberties. This view is also associated with the assumption that individuals are equally capable of taking care of themselves and should not need to be taken care of by the state, that it will even cripple them for independent action if the state protects them. Finally, some believe that protection of individuals by the state impinges on their dignity, that it is demeaning and insulting to treat people as if they need to be taken care of.

The contemporary version of U.S. *liberalism* calls for the state itself to take on the role of protector of human liberties, particularly on behalf of those who cannot do this for themselves, through no fault of their own but, rather, because they are power-less and exploited by those in power. All are *not* equally capable as individuals to do this for themselves. Some need more help than others. To render some people equal to others, the state must give them special protection and help.

Record-oriented judges essentially instantiate and espouse a conservative view of the relationship between the state and the individual in their approach to the guilty plea. They do not take the legal mandate that it is *their* responsibility to make sure a defendant pleads guilty only knowingly and voluntarily as seriously as do the procedure-oriented judges. They frequently refer to their assumption that the defendant knows what he is doing, and they distribute responsibility for knowingness and voluntariness among themselves, the defendants, and the lawyers. They also assume, in their standardization of the plea, that most of the individuals they confront as defendants are equally capable of comprehending what they are told. And by attributing this capacity to the defendants, they give them dignity.

Procedure-oriented judges instantiate a liberal view of the relationship between the state and the individual. They personally assume the responsibility for protecting defendants' due process rights that the state, through the written law, assigned to them. They embrace the view that it is their role to represent the state as protector and preserver of individuals' civil rights. They further assume that some individuals, because of their (class) background, need more help than others, more careful attention, simpler language, and more time from the state.

This means that whether the judges intend it or not, in their exercise of the judicial discretion that written law allows them, the judges not only enact *legal* ideological positions but also American *political* ideologies. They implement them in their legal practices. If they do this in procedures to which they give little time and thought, procedures like the guilty plea in which they are highly constrained by law and routinized in behavior, how much more must this be the case in areas of law that allow greater judicial discretion?

Abel (1979) and others argue that governmental liberal reforms intended to empower economically and politically disadvantaged groups, such as people's courts, instead extend or further the penetration of the state into these people's lives. The same argument can be made on a microstructural level regarding what I characterize as a liberal procedure-oriented approach to the guilty plea. The procedure-oriented approach, intended in principle to demonstrate a personal interest in and concern for each defendant, is unquestionably more invasive into the lives of defendants, albeit on a small scale. At the same time, it inevitably reveals the real personal struggles in those lives that lead people to become under the control of the state, struggles that the record-oriented pleas keep invisible.

Discussion: Conceptualizing Ideological Diversity

In chapter 1, I discussed the way that Marxist scholars who theorize ideological diversity conceptualize this diversity in oppositional terms—as involving a struggle between dominant and subordinate sectional interests that can be transformed by critique of the hidden interests of the dominant class. How does the foregoing discussion of ideological diversity within the ideologically dominant state alter Marxist understanding of the social ordering of ideology?

Critique of Ideology

This chapter reveals ideological stances that were otherwise hidden. I suggest, either implicitly or explicitly, several sources or causes of this hiddenness and develop analytical strategies for overcoming it. The legal ideological stances the judges take in hearing guilty pleas are implicit and hidden partly because of the intertextual and indexical nature of the construction of meaning in discourse. I have substantiated my claim that judges enact ideological stances in their judicial behavior by relating multiple instances of the judges doing these guilty pleas to each other. I could not recognize a judge's ideological stance by seeing him hear only one plea. Lawyers who participate in many guilty pleas probably readily recognize the variable strategies I document, but this recognition, like my own, depends on relating multiple instances of practice to one another. To the person who does not actively participate in multiple instances of such discourse, the possibility of directly apprehending these ideological stances may be remote. Some of this implicitness, then, derives from the indexical and intertextual nature of meaning in human interaction. Methodologically, the comparison and intertextual relating of multiple instances of the same activity helped me uncover the judges' ideological stances.

At the same time, it is clear from the discussion in this chapter that ideology is more implicit in some forms of discourse than it is in others. It is implicit in the guilty plea procedure itself, yet in my interviews with judges they were able to be explicit about why they heard the pleas as they did. This should heighten awareness generally that ideology is manifest in different forms of discourse in different ways. Most studies of ideology that rely on speech as data use interviews as their primary source of data (e.g., Willis 1977; Martin 1987; Kennedy & Davis 1993) and take the *content* of these interviews as the basis of their analysis. These studies are very worthwhile, and they have inspired me to analyze my data in the way that I have. But the neglect of socially oc-curring speech, or of actual practice more generally in such studies (Abu-Lughod 1985, who analyzes actual practice, provides an example of an exception), means that em-pirical contributions to the understanding of ideology are somewhat skewed and sig-nificantly underrepresent the implicit nature of ideology in many forms of discourse.

So far I have talked about how the hiddenness of multiple legal ideologies can be inherent in the nature of discourse itself. But another aspect of the hiddenness of ide-ology and ideological diversity is more local and has to do with the relationship between legal and political ideologies in the legal system: the judges' practical consciousness also obscures what they are doing.

The judges denied being aware of any political ideological dimension to their own courtroom behavior. In chapter 2 (The Myth of the Trial Court Judge as Nonideo-logical), I talked about how although it is considered appropriate within our legal system for appellate court appointments to be based in part on a judge's political ide-ology, this basis is frowned on at the trial court level. This position in itself reflects the insurgent take-over of judicial appointments by the organized bar and the decline in control over these appointments by political parties. Currently, the trial court judge-ship is defined as one in which there should be no influence of political ideologies in judicial behavior.

As discussed in detail in chapter 2, the judges in this study acknowledge having political ideological beliefs, but all expressed to me the intention and the desire not to allow their political ideologies to influence their behavior on the bench. And yet all of them also made it clear that some involvement in political party activity and relations with people active in political parties played a role in their becoming judges. Such activity was central to becoming a trial court judge. Over the generations, the amount of such activity necessary and appropriate to seeking a judgeship has declined, con-sistent with the decline of political party control over judgeships.

The judges in this study took the position, then, that it is somehow possible to *be* politically ideological (i.e., to have views) and also to participate in the political pro-cess, yet not enact one's ideological position in the courtroom. At least this is the position they all expressed to me. The judges' denial of ideological influence on their behavior (which is how *they* conceptualized it) must be recognized itself as an ideo-logical stance.

To explain their behavior, the judges invoke the legal ideological framework that defines what they are doing in the guilty plea as protecting individuals' constitutional due process rights. This legal framework basically says that what the judge is doing is for the defendant's own good to protect and take care of him. To put forth such an interpretation obscures the possibility of a political ideological interpretation in which the judge is understood to be in a position of power in relation to the defendant and as a representative of the state is imposing the authority of the state on the individual. A political ideological framework at least acknowledges that an exercise of power is taking place and that there are different ways to carry out that exercise. A political ideological interpretive framing of the judge's role in the guilty plea defines these dif-ferent ways of exercising power as motivated by different theories of government.

But to conceptualize the judges' behavior as motivated by political ideologies is not consistent with the legal framework in which the judge's concepts of justice and fairness are supposed to predominate and motivate his behavior. In this context, then, the judges treat legal and political ideologies as in conflict and allow the legal to dominate.

But although the judges present the legal interpretive framework as dominating their behavior, the ideological diversity within that tradition is also obscured. It is obscured by the judges' claims to have made individual, personal interpretations of the written law governing the procedure in the way they hear guilty pleas. As indicated earlier, the judges interpret their own actions as motivated by their personal interpretations of the law. They formulate a personal routine or script for handling the procedure by reading the statutes and case law interpreting the statutes and themselves come up with an interpretation of that body of law.

The key issue here is that the judges present what they are doing as individual and for the most part downplay the influence of the behavior and opinions of their colleagues, the other trial court judges on the bench. They do not articulate the existence of shared views, interpretive practices, or interactional strategies. They do not recognize or do not acknowledge a sociocultural dimension to what they are doing. Yet, as I try to make clear, members of each group (procedure-oriented vs. record-oriented) share the interactional strategies and the "reasons" given for such strategies that I present here with others in the group.

Ideology is in its nature sociocultural and shared. Ideas cannot *be* ideology unless they are shared. If they are "individual" rather than "social," then ideas are only manifestations of the "personality" of the judge. To acknowledge the possibility of a socially systematic dimension to the judges' interpretations opens up the possibility of political interpretive communities *within* the legal framework. Such recognition threatens the claims of lawyers to a universalistic scientific and moral epistemology and to direct apprehension of this epistemology by an individual mind rather than a sociocultural mind. Once again, if the legal framework is going to dominate interpretive activity, certain kinds of recognitions cannot be tolerated, so they are not acknowledged. In this case, shared systematic variation in interpretation of the law, and similar enactments of those interpretations through the deployment of particular interactional strategies, cannot be acknowledged by the judges. Such sociocultural interpretive diversity is not compatible with the individuality of interpretive agency that is posited and presupposed in the legal interpretive framework.

Oppositional Relations

The judges' condemnation of any political ideology in their own judicial behavior and their lack of acknowledgment that their interpretive practices are shared with others do not just obscure the ideological nature of what they are doing. These positions on the part of the judges also obscure the possibility that the ideological diversity I am discussing is organized oppositionally in any way.

Ideological struggle has, however, shaped the nature of the legal and political ideological frameworks that provide the "reasons" for judges' behavior in court *and* the relations between those ideological frameworks. But the dominant and subordinate sectional interests involved in struggle are not in the kind of oppositional relations Marxists typically envision. I refer here to the relations between political parties and the organized bar. In the ideological struggle for definition of judicial roles, the organized bar and its promulgation of legal ideology are ascendant, and political parties and their promulgation of political ideologies are descendant and suppressed. The success of the organized bar in defining the role of the trial court judge is a major factor in the suppression of political ideological discourse.

Marxist perspectives also would not encourage us to look for conflict *among* the judges or to consider it of interest because of their being in structurally identical positions as these positions are generally conceived. Scholars influenced by Marx look for social struggle where groups of people are in a dominant–subordinate relation, and the judges are not in such a relation to one another. Poulantzas (cited in Carnoy 1984), who argues that conflicts between the state and sectional interests outside it sometimes become internalized within the state, provides a relevant exception to this view of struggle in the Marxist tradition. This exception seems to be the case here, where the judges can be seen as enacting liberal and conservative ideologies that are quite overtly opposed in other contexts.

Because more judges are hearing the plea using a procedure-oriented approach than using a record-oriented approach, one could say that the liberal view is "winning" in this limited field of activity. But if we are seriously considering the impact of the different ideological stances on the hearing of guilty pleas, it may be more accurate to say that the judges at each end of the continuum from most record-oriented to most procedure-oriented affect legal activity somewhat differently. The procedure-oriented judges are giving each defendant more time and attention, whereas the record-oriented judges are dealing with more defendants so that their strategy is affecting a greater proportion of the population of the criminal defendants who come before the bench relative to the number of judges using this strategy. The record-oriented judges may be few in number, but they are carrying more defendants per person than the procedure-oriented judges.

Thus far I suggest that the ideologies articulated here are in an oppositional relationship, even though this possibility is not one invited by the judges' overtly expressed views or by Marxist discussions of ideological conflict. There is also another way in which the ideological diversity I document here is unlike that which Marxist discussions of ideological struggle more commonly address. Generally, when multiple ideological stances are articulated in analyses of ideological struggle (e.g., Willis 1977), one gets the impression, although this issue is not usually addressed, that the ideological stances are somehow similar in kind: equally conceptually detailed, equally coherent, equally elaborated on by people in speech and action. I do not find this in the ideological stances taken by the judges, either in their explanations of their due process reasons for hearing the plea as they do or in their actual behavior. In both their self-explanations and their courtroom behavior, the procedure-oriented judges are more fulsome and forthcoming than the record-oriented judges. The procedure-oriented judges are generally more "into" their own interpretive practices. They have much more to say and see more complexity and subtlety in what they are doing than do the record-oriented judges. So the record-oriented stance is much less elaborate than the procedure-oriented stance. This makes it clear that when multiple ideological stances are embedded in an area of practice, different amounts of activity can sustain them.

Consciousness

Some of the judges told me they consciously enact their interpretations of the written law within the legal interpretive framework. But all the judges denied knowingly enacting political ideologies or expressed the intent not to enact the ones they had. Yet, I have said that they are enacting political concepts of the role of the state in relation to the individual. Does this mean they are dupes and I am the knowing one, a familiar Marxist (and anthropological) position from which ideological critique and explication are done? It is difficult for me to assess their conscious intentions. Nevertheless, it may be useful to articulate the range of possible combinations of consciousness and lack of consciousness or awareness of the enactment of ideological stances on the part of judges. Such articulation can show how the judges may vary in their conscious awareness of their enactment of ideological stances in keeping with Comaroff's (1985) general suggestion that there are varying degrees of consciousness among people who are enacting ideological positions.

First, some judges may have simply adopted someone else's procedural routine or part of the routine, with little or no reflection about its legal and political ideological significance, or with the deliberate choice not to think about the legal or political implications of the way in which the procedure is handled. I suspect that this is the case for the judges who are in the middle range of overall elaboration of the guilty plea—that is, neither completely procedure-oriented nor completely record-oriented (as displayed in table 4.3, Procedure-Oriented and Record-Oriented Strategies). In interviews, these judges were either conflicted about how to handle the procedure or had no clear reasons why they handled it as they did beyond asserting that it was the product of their own interpretive activity. As Comaroff (1985) makes clear, one of the most important features of Bourdieu's (1977) concept of habitus is that ideology can be practiced yet never have gone through a state of conscious awareness. This possibility is illustrated by these judges, who enact ideological stances in the way they handle the procedure without apparently consciously intending to do so.

Second, the judges could consciously enact a legal stance but not consciously see any political ideological dimension to their courtroom behavior in hearing guilty pleas. This is in fact the way in which the majority of the judges presented themselves to me, as having legal but not political intentionality.

Third, the judges could deliberately and consciously enact both legal and political ideological stances but deny awareness of the political (conservative or liberal) dimension to me because of its perceived incompatibility with the legal focus on justice and fairness required of them if they are to continue to be judges. I think that such was the case for some of the judges.

Importantly, it does not follow that because a judge has an ideological consciousness about this procedure, the guilty plea, he will be ideologically conscious and intentional in the way he carries out other legal procedures. Such consciousness may be fragmentary and partial when it is there. I think some judges make a conscious choice to think in a more deliberate politically ideological interpretive way about some legal activities than about others. Because of the pressures on relatively ideologically aware people not to be politically ideological in the way they function as judges, they may feel they have to pick their battles regarding what issues and in what contexts they will take a stand ideologically in or through their actions.[4]

Most of these judges do not talk about the guilty plea as if it were a particularly important activity in which to bring their legal interpretive powers to bear. They are more aware of the political implications of their sentencing records than of their courtroom behavior. This awareness may be because of the great beam of light that social scientific research focuses on this aspect of judicial behavior. The judges who articulated the greatest awareness of the possibility of enacting political ideologies, Judge 2 and Judge 5 (who also had the longest procedures), expressed being troubled by some of the sentences they were required to hand down in certain kinds of criminal cases. For example, both believed that crimes that had no victim, such as smoking marijuana, should be sentenced with less harshness than the law required them to impose as judges. Both these judges voluntarily left the bench within a few years of the period of data collection for this study, in part I think because they found it difficult to resolve the conflict between their political ideologies and what they were required to do as judges. In this way, the most consciously ideological judges are eliminated from the system.

In general, then, we must posit varying degrees of ideological consciousness among the judges, with clear pressures in the trial court context that encourage legal interpretive consciousness and repress political ideological consciousness.

Ideological Polysemy

In this chapter, it is apparent that judges' courtroom behavior can be expressing both legal and political ideological interpretive perspectives. Thus, the same behavior can instantiate more than one ideological framework at the same time. For example, when a procedure-oriented judge asks the defendant social background questions, he is both interpreting the written law as calling for knowingness and voluntariness to be established in the procedure by him and assuming a liberal protective role as representative of the state in relation to the defendant.

I refer to the existence of more than one ideological framework that can be realized simultaneously through the same single social action as ideological polysemy. Polysemy traditionally refers to multiple meanings of a single word. Here I use it to refer to specifically ideological multiple meanings of wider discourse. The assumption of much late 20th-century work on language in context is that though a form may have potential multiple meanings (or functions), only one of those meanings is realized in any given instance of the use of the form in speech, with context overdetermining what is underdetermined in the abstract meaning of the form.[5] Here I argue that the discourse has multiple meanings at the same time but that these meanings differ in the degree of consciousness with which the judges as speakers recognize or acknowledge them. This point is raised again in the remaining chapters.

Most immediately, in chapter 5 (Judges' Ideologies of Courtroom Control), I develop this idea of polysemy by arguing that in addition to enacting legal and political ideologies, judges also enact ideologies of courtroom control. I show that judges' different ideas about courtroom control are consistent with their own distinctive strategies for taking guilty pleas. And I argue that although legal and political ideologies are more restricted in the social domains for which they are relevant, ideologies of control are pervasive in everyday life and connect how the judges think about what they do in the courtroom to how Americans more generally think about how to get people to do what they want them to do.

5

Judges' Ideologies of Courtroom Control

In chapter 4, I described how judges enact different ideological stances in the way they hear guilty pleas, realizing different interpretations of the written procedural law as they do so. Judges conceptualize their judicial behavior in hearing guilty pleas as their individual interpretations of the written law concerned with protecting defendants' due process rights. Thus, it is appropriate to characterize their conscious ideology as legal. However, although judges represent their thinking as consciously legal, their practices also realize political ideologies because different interpretations of the procedural law governing the procedure enact liberal and conservative positions regarding the role of the judge and therefore the state in relation to individual citizens. Judges in fact repudiate the enactment of political ideology in their courtroom behavior, expressing the belief and hope that it does not affect the way they hear guilty pleas. Their denial of the political disconnects it from the legal; thus, political and legal ideologies are not consciously or explicitly connected to one another in the judges' discourse with me and are in practice compartmentalized.

The fact that the same judicial behavior realizes or enacts more than one ideological framework means that social action in the courtroom is ideologically polysemic. It has more than one meaning and a choice between meanings is not guided or forced by the contexts in which the behavior in question occurs. This is contrary to the predominant form of functionalism espoused in linguistic anthropology in the second half of the 20th century (Hymes 1967) in which a form is conceptualized as multifunctional but as having only one of its possible functions realized in an instance and determined by the context in which it occurs.

In this chapter, I argue that there is yet a third ideological orientation or framework within which judges vary that is also realized in the discourse practice of taking guilty pleas; the ideological framework of COURTROOM CONTROL. According to the procedure-oriented judges with whom I worked, judges disagree among themselves about how to go about maintaining control over a courtroom and even about whether particular judges are in control. They see courtroom control as a matter of judicial style rather than a matter of interpretation of the law, but like due process ideologies, courtroom control ideologies are explicit. And I argue that procedure-oriented judges and record-oriented judges enact different courtroom control ideologies, just as they enact different due process ideologies.

In chapter 4 I showed how procedure-oriented judges involve defendants in establishing a factual basis for the guilty plea much more than record-oriented judges do. They run the risk of legally invalidating the plea when they do this. Record-oriented judges do not feel this risk is necessary to make sure defendants are knowingly and voluntarily waiving their due process rights to a trial, but procedure-oriented judges do. In this chapter, I show how when judges try to involve defendants in the factual basis, the defendants resist confessing in ways that threaten judges' control over the procedure, and more generally over the courtroom, a control the judges must struggle to maintain. Because record-oriented judges more often try to involve the defendant, they more often risk this loss of control. Successful courtroom control is one of the criteria on which the bar organization evaluates judges when they are being considered for retention of their judgeships (discussed in chapter 2). So, when the judges risk loss of control, they are risking their professional credibility, their reputations as good judges, and the respect of the lawyers who come before them.

Procedure-oriented judges are willing to take this risk, but it is not without its price. They see themselves as having an informal style of controlling the courtroom. They aspire to an informal style because they believe it will make the people who come before them more comfortable in the courtroom and more willing to participate in courtroom procedures (i.e., to talk). They view the judges whom they characterize as more formal as overly controlling and as intimidating people in a way that reduces their participation. Some even feel that formality conveys a sense of superiority, and they believe it is wrong for a judge to act as if he thinks he is better than everyone else. Procedure-oriented judges are aware that they in turn are viewed as too casual and as prone to losing control over the courtroom by judges and lawyers who prefer a more formal style. This puts some procedure-oriented judges on the defensive. They are the ones who have to defend their approach, not the record-oriented judges. And they deny that they lose control over the courtroom.

When we compare the two kinds of ideologies that the judges explicitly articulate—that is the due process and courtroom control ideologies—they emerge as both similar and different in interesting ways. Most centrally, courtroom control ideologies are everyday ideologies: the ideas articulated in them are expressed in and about a wide range of U.S. contexts, particularly hierarchically organized bureaucratic contexts such as school classrooms and doctor–patient encounters. Due process ideologies, in contrast, are more restricted to domains in which legal ideologies are interpretively salient, like the courtroom. But both ultimately have in common an obscuring of the exercise of power by judges over defendants, an obscuring Marxists have suggested is a key characteristic of ideology.

In the discussion to follow, I give broad consideration to what I mean, in my local ethnographic context, by courtroom control and loss of control. I analyze an instance of loss of courtroom control in Judge 6's courtroom to highlight some of the key features of loss of control. Next I analyze defendants' resistance to confession in the factual basis as a more subtle threat to the judges' control over the courtroom and show how the judges maintain or regain their control through their responses to these threats. Then I describe the procedure-oriented judges' ideologies of courtroom control, revealing how these ideologies can explain why they involve the defendants in the factual bases as they do, in spite of the constant resistance of the defendants to this involvement. Finally, I discuss the broader implications of these ideologies of courtroom control for our understanding of the nature of ideological diversity in judges' courtroom practices.

Courtroom Control and Loss of Control

In this section I discuss what courtroom control and loss of control are and why the judges and the lawyers with whom they work consider whether or not they have control of their courtrooms so important. Discussions around the Pima County Superior Court took the concept of courtroom control for granted; thus, when court personnel gossiped about situations in which judges were said to have lost control of the courtroom, no one asked what was meant by such an assertion, although some cases were much clearer than others and involved more agreement about what had happened among those party to the situation. I also took for granted what it means to say that control has been lost and in retrospect feel the concept of "loss of control" is one I brought to the research project, which was modified rather than acquired through participation in courtroom activities. I acquired this concept, like most of us, through early socialization experiences: seeing my parents lose control over their own children, experiencing loss of control over my younger siblings, and witnessing teachers, particularly substitute teachers, lose control over their classrooms, possibly contributing myself to their loss of control. Thus I knew too that people who lose control can be diminished by the experience by "losing the respect" of those over whom they lost control. For me, too, control and loss of control have a taken-for-granted quality, but it is not difficult to become explicit about some basic features of these phenomena as Americans understand them.

Courtroom control centrally refers to the judge's ability literally to exert command from a distance over the actions of the physical bodies of those in his courtroom without recourse to physical coercion. This command is carried out through speech and largely involves control over the speech of others. An example of a taped courtroom procedure in which the judge clearly lost control over the courtroom both illustrates loss of control and displays some of the key features of control.

In this procedure the defendant appeared before Judge 6 to be sentenced for a crime to which he pled guilty. He had been in the county jail for about 2 months, and while I was sitting in the courtroom waiting for procedures to begin he was brought into the room by sheriff's deputies in hand and leg cuffs and seated at a table facing the judge's bench. When this defendant pled guilty in an earlier procedure, the conditions of his plea agreement were that if he pled guilty, he would receive no more jail time than what he would have already served by the time he was sentenced, and that he would be put on probation. So he came to the court from the jail fully expecting to be a free man at any moment.

However, unknown to the defendant, even as he was on his way to the court, the judge was in his chambers informing the deputy county attorney and the public defender that he had changed his mind about the conditions to which he had earlier agreed and was no longer willing to free the defendant. The judge is within *his* rights to do this. That is why during the guilty plea, judges say something like, "*If* I agree to accept the conditions of this plea agreement, then you could receive the following possible sentence." I do not know what crime the defendant was charged with because it was not central to my project at the time and was not mentioned during the procedure or in my notes from my posttaping interview with the judge. But the judge did tell me that he had decided that the nature of the charge coupled with the defendant's past record made the crime more serious than he first realized. Some lawyers and judges would say that this judge's last-minute change of heart might not have happened had this judge paid enough attention to the written record of the case at an earlier time.

At any rate, the defendant learned for the first time that the judge had changed his mind after he was seated in the courtroom next to his lawyer, who then began to talk with him in a low voice. Soon the defendant started yelling at his lawyer and did so intermittently for about 20 minutes. At one point the defendant tried to hobble out of the courtroom (recall he was chained) but was stopped by sheriff's deputies, who brought him back to his chair. When the judge came into the courtroom he immediately started the sentencing involving this defendant, at which point I turned on my tape recorder. (See appendix G, Refusal of Plea Agreement in Aborted Sentencing Transcript, for the complete procedure.)

1	Judge:	Uh CR 00000 state of Arizona
2		versus Harry Dolan. This is the
3		time set for sentencing. Uh
4		present um-
5	Lawyer:	Todd True on behalf of ( ).
6	Lawyer:	Paul Coffman ( ).
7	Judge:	(Show) the defendant in custody.
8		Uh as I informed you gentlemen
9		in chambers, I have reviewed the
10		uh defendant's record and I
11		cannot go along with the plea
12		agreement with you. If I were
13		to sentence him I would sentence
14		him to the (uh) state prison and
15		certainly give him more than uh
16		time served. The plea
17		agreement provides that the
18		defendant may withdraw his plea uh.
19	Defendant:	I don't wanna withdraw my plea.
20	Judge:	All right (let) the record show
21		that the defendant has withdrawn

22		his plea and the court orders
23		that the matter be set for trial
24		um-
25	Defendant:	I don't wanna withdraw my plea!
26		{louder than last time;
27		basically a shout; he shouts the
28		rest of the time}.
29	Judge:	You don't wanna withd/raw your
30		plea?/
31	Defense Lawyer:	/Be quiet/ please. [2 secs]
32		Your Honor, I would request that
33		you withdraw his plea. If my
34		client doesn't want to, I don't
35		know what I can do about it.
36	Defendant:	Well I can't get probation, I
37		can't get ROR (if) I go to
38		trial. Uh I want to get this
39		taken care of right now. I'm in
40		twenty-four lockup for eight
41		weeks. I'm entitled to some
42		rights.

As the procedure progressed, the defendant's antagonism escalated:

115	Defendant:	/( )I've been/ in lockup
116		for two months, twenty-four-hour
117		lockup.
118	Judge:	I will uh I will re /tain-/
119	Defendant:	/In/ a little
120		cell this big. Twenty-four-hour
121		lockup.
122	Judge:	I will retain the May
123		seventeenth trial date and I
124		will uh order a Rule 11
125		examination.
126	Defendant:	I'm not taking no Rule 11.
127	Judge:	Who who do you want?
128	Defense Lawyer:	Your Honor, Dr. Madagan
129	Defendant:	Fuck this shit.

Shortly after this exchange the defendant tried to walk out again and the sheriff's deputies took hold of him and escorted him from the room. We see here how fine the line is between the hegemony and the coercion of the state (Gramsci 1971).

These excerpts make it possible to identify and refer to some of the features central to the perception that there was loss of control in the courtroom. The most general and common loss illustrated here is the judge's loss of control over the floor, control over who speaks when about what. In the second excerpt the defendant inter-rupts the judge (lines 118–119). In the first excerpt the defendant speaks when, from a legal point of view, the lawyer should be speaking for him (lines 20, 26). Although arguably the lawyer has lost control over his client, this loss is experienced as the judge's loss as well as the lawyer's. In the first excerpt the defense lawyer also interrupts the judge (line 32) by addressing the defendant.[1]

Other common diacritica of loss of control exemplified in this case are yelling (yell-ing by anyone signals loss of control) and physical movement from position by the defendant. Yelling is considered a loss of control over a speaker's emotions and an expression of anger, itself a specific form of loss of control as these aspects of commu-nicative behavior are conceptualized culturally. Once again, however, the defendant's loss of control is still seen as the judge's having lost control of the courtroom. The second factor, movement from position by the defendant, is regularly and predict-ably interpreted as a potential or actual threat to the judge's physical well-being by those working for the court, even though in other circumstances it would not be.

Courtroom control, then, ultimately refers to the judge's ability literally to exert command from a distance over the actions of the physical bodies of those in his court-room without recourse to physical coercion.

An important dimension of the judge's ability to sustain the cooperation of those in the courtroom is the defendant's submission to and cooperation in the legal pro-cedural framework imposed by the courts. This defendant refuses that cooperation. When given the opportunity to withdraw his plea in the first excerpt, he refuses, even as his lawyer tries to agree with the judge, thus destroying any illusion that the lawyer is representing his client's wishes. In the second excerpt the defendant refuses a Rule 11 examination which would consider his mental competency to stand trial. The judge and the lawyer ignore him and proceed to pick a doctor to perform the exam, again belying any attributions of free agency to this criminal defendant and undermining claims to legitimacy of the legal system based in part on such attributions.

Both lawyers and judges consider courtroom control very important. Although there is no agreement among the judges regarding how to think about courtroom control, as I discuss in more detail later, none of them want to be involved in the kind of incident just documented. Judges know they must pay attention to this issue of control for several key reasons. First, a loss of control can threaten them physically, so they must maintain control on some level for their own self-preservation.

Second, loss of control can destroy the legal validity of a procedure. Words can be uttered that are inconsistent with the legal reality being constructed. For example, in the material just quoted, it is difficult for the judge to accept the defendant's with-drawal of a plea, the legal act the judge is trying to accomplish, when the defendant is saying on the record that he does not want to withdraw it. If a procedure's legal valid-ity is destroyed, everyone's time and money is wasted, including that of the taxpayers who reelect the judges.

Third, loss of control can affect the ability of judges to achieve what at least some judges desire in the way of giving the public a sense of satisfaction, involvement in, and comfortable use of the legal system, which these judges view as belonging not just to them but to all of us.

Fourth, the judges' reputation with the legal community and the public, and thus their ability to get reelected, depends in part on their ability to control the courtroom. As discussed in chapter 2, before each election in which voters vote whether to retain judges, the State Bar of Arizona polls the lawyers who appear before the judges regarding their judicial qualities. Courtroom control or discipline is one quality considered. The local newspaper then publishes the results of such polls before the election. In addition, articles based on this poll plus interviews with lawyers appear in the editorial pages of the newspaper with recommendations to voters on whether to retain individual judges. In these articles, as well as in the polls themselves, courtroom discipline regularly figures as an aspect of their performance worthy of mention. Thus, regardless of how judges feel personally about the issue of courtroom control, their own ability to control a courtroom, and what others think about that ability, they must give the issue their attention and will be drawn into taking positions on it because it is so directly linked to their ability to keep their jobs.[2]

In the next section I show how when judges establish a factual basis for a guilty plea, defendants resist confessing to having committed the crimes with which they are charged, even though they are pleading guilty. Such resistance threatens judges' control of the courtroom, even though this resistance is mild compared to the kind of resistance I just documented here. Thus, I establish a connection between the judges' concern with controlling the courtroom and the way they hear guilty pleas.

Resistance to Confession in the Factual Basis

Regardless of the extent to which the judges in this study were procedure-oriented or record-oriented in the way they established a factual basis for a guilty plea, the defendants regularly resisted having the information elicited from them in the way the judges wanted. They often either did not respond to questions they were asked or responded in a way that from the judge's point of view did not contribute to or make progress in getting a factual basis on the record that was legally binding. At the same time, the procedure-oriented judges' efforts to elicit factual circumstances from the defendant caused them to be met more often with resistance than were the record-oriented judges.

Three kinds of resistance from defendants regularly occur in this database. First is *denial.* Defendants often directly deny some element of a crime for which there must be evidence, if the factual basis is to be legally good. This is the kind of resistance that must be dealt with and turned around or reversed if the judge is to find that there is a factual basis for the plea. Second is *obscurity.* Defendants often give responses to questions that are uninterpretable or obscure so that they really do not make sense and do not contribute to a relevant court record. This is probably deliberate some of the time but not all the time. Third is *mitigation.* Defendants frequently contribute information to the factual basis that appears intended to remove blame from themselves, and in some cases to put it onto others, or to present their actions in a light that shows them to have intentions of a positive, blameless, or simply human kind, which in other circumstances might have positive consequences and be viewed favorably. This is the most common kind of information given by defendants that does not contribute to establishing a factual basis in the sense that the judges must establish one to meet the law. Each of these is dealt with in turn in more detail.

Denial

As I have already suggested, *denial* is the kind of resistance from a defendant that most threatens the legality of a factual basis. Generally speaking, there is little evidence that defendants who deny what the judge wants them to admit are knowingly focusing on a particular element critical to the statutory definition of the crime the way the judge is. Rather, on the face of it, such denial is often embedded in a string of denials—that is, "no" answers to questions that would have to be given "yes" answers (or less commonly "yes" answers to questions that should be answered "no")—in order for the procedure to move forward and the record to be good. The following example illustrates this. It comes from a charge of petty theft that involved the defendant's finding a credit card and making no attempt to return it. What is crucial from a legal point of view is that there be evidence that there was a way the defendant could have returned it but did not for his act to be considered "theft." The defendant is refusing to acknowledge that he was aware of a way to return the card.

> Judge 6:   And uh [8 sec] did you make any
> efforts at all uh to uh-notify
> the owner that uh you had his
> card?
>
> Defendant: No, I didn't.
>
> Judge 6:   All right. And uh [6 sec] there
> was the name of a bank on the
> card, was there not?
>
> Defendant: Uhn ah not that I know of.
>
> Judge 6:   Any address on the card, or any
> place that a bank or someone
> that you could uh call about the
> uh /fact that you had it?/
>
> Defendant: /I really didn't examine it/
> that well.
>
> Judge 6:   All right, but the but uh can we
> uh can we agree that those cards
> do have some-
>
> County Attorney: Judge the the card does have the
> Visa bank number on it. I
> believe that uh the ray way I
> was able to trace it (   ) and
> get the records was simply to
> call the number. So so (I)
> called Visa.
>
> (Tape E, Side 2, p. 29)

This example illustrates one of the key ways in which judges deal with denial. One of the lawyers steps in and provides the factual evidence the judge is seeking. This happens fairly often. As noted in chapter 3, it is the lawyer's duty, as an officer of the court, to do what he perceives necessary to make the procedure good, and record-oriented judges specifically say that they depend on the defendant's lawyer to go over issues with the defendant that they do not themselves necessarily address in court. Lawyers come in uninvited with the procedure-oriented judges in this way more often when there is denial than when there is either obscurity or mitigation, presumably because denial is more threatening to the legal bindingness of the procedure.

Bear in mind that when the lawyers do this, the judge can be seen as having lost control over the procedure. The three judges with whom lawyers came in in this way most frequently in my data were also the three judges with the poorest bar poll ratings on the criterion of courtroom control.

Having a lawyer provide evidence is not the only response to denial of elements of a charge. The following example illustrates the response of the judge to denial that I think of as "nailing it down." Here the judge simply asks question after question in the critical area or areas of denial until he has enough admissions among the denials to satisfy himself. The charge here is robbery, which involves among other things the taking of a person's goods without his consent and violence or intimidation by the perpetrator against the victim in a face-to-face encounter. In this case the defendant robbed a clerk in a store.

> Judge 5: And what did you do- on the ninth of January that makes you think you're guilty of this crime? [2 sec] Did you take some property or money from him?
>
> Defendant: No, I received the money from him.
>
> Judge 5: Okay. Then how was it that he gave it to you?
>
> Defendant: I asked him for it.
>
> Judge 5: Did you ask him for it in such a way that- that there wasn't much choice on his part?
>
> Defendant: I asked him for it in- in a derogatory tone.
>
> Judge 5: Did you h- have a show of uh some weapon or force?
>
> Defendant: I had my hand in my pocket.
>
> Judge 5: Did you suggest to him you had some weapon there?
>
> Defendant: How would you say "suggest"?
>
> Judge 5: However- way you thought you might have conveyed that to him.

Did you try to indicate to him
in some way that you had a
weapon?

Defendant: I thrust- I thrusted my hand in
my pocket.

Judge 5: Like i you were-

Defendant: Forward (yes).

Judge 5: As if you were holding a gun?
[2 sec]

Defendant: Yeah. [2 sec]

Judge 5: And- uhm- at that time you-
said to him, "I want your
money" or words to that effect?

Defendant: 'N I asked for his money.

Judge 5: /All right/

Defendant: /He asked/ me if he could help
me, and I says, "Yes, you can
give me your s you can give me
some money."

Judge 5: Okay. And at that time you you
thrust your finger forward in
your pocket which suggested you
might have a weapon. [2 sec]

Defendant: Yes.

Judge 5: Lemme ask you this, Mr. Mellon.
Do you think he would have given
you the money [2 sec] if you
hadn't done that? [2 sec]

Defendant: I don't know. [5 sec]

Judge 5: How much did you receive from
him?

Defendant: Uh- I never counted it.

Judge 5: And what did you do after you
got it, did you- run or jump in
a car or what?

Defendant: No I walked.

Judge 5: All right. Did you tell him not
to call the police or something
of /that/ kind?

Defendant: /No./ [3 sec]

Judge 5: The money that was given to you
was not given in- as a gift or
anything was it? In your mind?

Defendant: No, it wasn't my money.

Judge 5: Pardon?

Defendant: No, it wasn't my money.

Judge 5: It wasn't your money?

Defendant: No.

Judge 5: And he wasn't giving it to you
because he liked you or you were
a nice guy?

Defendant: No, it wasn't a gift.

Judge 5: All right.

(Tape 6, Side 2, pp. 4–6)

In this unusual and lengthy example, the judge simply goes over the same ground until he elicits the admissions he is seeking from the defendant. One common strategy that we see in this example is the exclusion of possible lawful circumstances for the act in question through negative questions/assertions that the defendant also denies—that is, here the money the defendant says he "received" (rather than took) was not a gift, was not because the victim liked him, and was not because he was "a nice guy."

This example also illustrates a common problem in factual bases: poor fit between factual circumstances and the charge to which the person is pleading guilty, and the defendant's unwillingness to accommodate the court by acknowledging facts that fit the crime to which he is pleading but that do not very well describe what he did. Statutory descriptions of crimes really are written to match up with common circumstances or behavioral acts judged to be crimes. Some acts that we want to call crimes are atypical and uncommon. This is true in the previous example, where there was no *real* physical threat to the victim yet the factual circumstances do fall within the statutory description of the crime. Certainly the perpetrator intimidated the victim and this intimidation made the victim give up his money.

Lack of typicality, however, also stems from the plea bargaining process. As a result of plea bargaining, the initial charge is sometimes dropped and the defendant pleads guilty to a less serious charge, or what is referred to as a lesser included charge. The resulting lack of fit between facts and charge often figures in defendants' denials, as in the following examples. In the first example that follows the defendant was originally charged with sale of marijuana. A number of people were arrested by the police when they entered a house with a large amount of marijuana in it. Those in the house were charged with possession of marijuana for sale. But this particular defendant was outside in a car, which had a baggie of marijuana in the glove compartment. So they charged him with what they could, simple possession of marijuana.

Judge 2: /Okay. November twenty-four,/

Defendant: /({whispers to lawyer?})/

Judge 2: 1977, you did-
have in your possession-
marijuana. Right?

Defendant: Yes (sir).

Judge 2: And and you at least you had a
substance that you could see and
feel and touch and you thought
it was marijuana. Right?

Defendant: Uh- /yes./

Judge 2: Well. /Okay/ there were other
peo/ple/ involved.

Defendant: /Yeah/. W no eh uh I w I was
gonna say it was in the it was
in the vehicle.

Judge 2: Okay. All right. It was in your
vehicle.

Defendant: Uhh/hh/.

Judge 2:   /In/ *a* /vehicle/.

Defendant: /It was/ in *a* vehicle.

Judge 2: And you were in that
/vehicle too?/

Defendant: /I was in the/ vehicle /there ./

Judge 2:   /Okay./
All right. Okay. Then- it could
be said that /that/

Defendant: /(   )/

Judge 2: it's /in your/

Defendant: /(   )/

Judge 2: possession and you're not
denying it.

Defendant: Right.

(Tape C, Side 2, pp. 17–18)

Again, the judge must nail it down. Here the defendant can deny possession, a key element of the crime, because apparently the marijuana was not in *his* car, but ultimately he does not.

The next example involves a combination of unusual lack of fit in a case pled down from child molestation to aggravated assault. The defendant is a woman and the assault is considered aggravated because the victim was a child.

Judge 6: All right, on or about the
thirteen day of February
1979 um- Miss
Bennett, did you um- um [3 sec]
uh strike or otherwise assault
um uh Rowena Nelson?

Defendant: Yes, sir.

Judge 6: And uh at that time um how old
was Rowena?

Defendant: I'm not sure of the age um.

Judge 6:   S she under fifteen /years/

Defendant: /Yes, sir./

Judge 6:   of age? Uh under ten?

Defendant: Yes, sir.

Judge 6:   Okay. Um- did you hit her with
                 your hand or what?

Defendant?:   (   )

County Attorney: (Plea) t touching with the
                 intent to injure or provoke.

Judge 6:   Uh /did you-/

Defendant's Lawyer: /Or insult./

Judge 6:   Did you touch her with intent to
                 injure or provoke her?

Defendant: To insult.

Judge 6:   Pardon?

Defendant: To insult /(   )/

Judge 6:   /To/ insult? All right.
                 Okay. Uh what did you do?

Defendant: I touched her in a uh pubic
                 area.

Judge 6:   Rgh. Okay. [2 sec] Are you
                 her mother?

Defendant: Am 'er mother- *her* mother?

Judge 6:   Yeah.

Defendant: No, sir.

Judge 6:   Mkay. Um. [4 sec] I I I take
                 this w w w I take it this was
                 not done um in any um- um [2
                 sec] well- you were not acting
                 as a nurse or you weren't
                 dressing the child or anything
                 of that nature when you touched
                 her there.

Defendant: (   ) sir.

Judge 6:   Um- okay.

(Tape L, Side 1, pp. 50–52)

Denial, then, can stem from both general resistance on the part of the defendant and from a more particular resistance to admitting to something that is not really exactly the case because of a poor fit between facts and the statute under which the defendant is pleading guilty.

Obscurity

Obscurity, or obscure responses to judges' questions, also presents problems for at-
taining a legally sound factual basis for a plea of guilty, but it is not as threatening to
the legal validity of the procedure as denial. The examples of obscurity in my database all constitute relatively long responses in a narrative form to an open-ended request from the judge to tell him what happened. They are, then, in discourse form,
similar to the factual basis narratives that particularly record-oriented judges themselves produce, and similar to the narratives they elicit from defendants' lawyers. On
the face of it they appear to be relatively cooperative responses of the sort the judge
really wants. But they differ from narratives by officers of the court in that they are
referentially obscure rather than referentially explicit, as in the following examples.
The first example is from a theft case. Note the items in italics.

>   Judge 1: All right. Tell me what happened
>   then on November first
>   concerning this property. [2
>   sec]
>
>   Defendant: We were at *his* house in uh early
>   in early in the day 'n-and
>   then h *he* left with some other f
>   you know friends and-
>
>   Judge 1: His house, we're speaking of
>   who?
>
>   Defendant: Uhm, *where* I got the bag. [4
>   sec]
>
>   Judge 1: A man's house? You /don't/ know
>   his name?
>
>   Defendant: /Yes./
>
>   Yes, David Marner.
>
>   (Tape G, Side 1, pp. 21–22)

    The next example is from a charge of first-degree conspiracy to violate marijuana
laws. It involves an interpreter who translated between the Spanish of the defendant
and the English of the other participants. The rendering here leaves out the interpretive process, so the defendant's words are actually the interpreter's English translation of his Spanish.

>   Judge 8: Tell me what happened uh Mr.
>   Carreras. I understand this
>   relates to uh an incident that
>   occurred on June first, nineteen
>   seventy-eight. And that you
>   were involved with some other
>   people named uh Manuel Lado,
>   Martin Micos, Pedro Valenzuela.
>   And Vincent Gonzalez. Uh tell
>   me what, what you did.

> Defendant: Uh I was (talking) to *them* about
> *that thing.* And we talked and
> and I *did that thing.*
>
> Judge 8: Well, when you say you did it,
> did you uh arrange to uh make a
> sale and participate in a sale
> of uh two hundred over two
> hundred kilos of marijuana?
>
> Defendant: Yes.
>
> Judge 8: You knew that that was against
> the law at that time?
>
> Defendant: Yes.

(Tape A, Side 2, pp. 25–27)

What I have called referential obscurity can be traced to several rather straightforward sources. From a linguistic perspective, what is most generally involved is the use of terms that have no clear referent, either in prior text or in the ongoing nonverbal context. In other words, as highlighted in the previous two examples, pronouns referring to persons are used before they are identified by a proper name or full noun that could be tied to a name in the written record, the proverb "do" is used when no full verb to identify the relevant activity was used, and demonstratives such as "that" along with dummy noun forms such as "thing" are also used without creating the context to allow the hearer to tie them to concrete objects and actions.

The response of the judge to such accounts is to make them explicit, to give them referential concreteness, either by forcing it from the defendant by explicitly asking for the identity of referents, as in Judge 1's example, or by providing it himself, as in Judge 8's example. A lawyer may also provide the referential explicitness. Although referential obscurity is not procedure threatening in the way denial is, apparently it must be overcome for the judge to be satisfied that he made a good record because it is almost never allowed to stand unexplicated.

Mitigations

Mitigations by defendants, or accounts that appear intended to cast what the defendant has done in a less negative light, have a rather different status than the two other forms of defendant resistance to confessing discussed thus far. They have no equivalent by which they must be replaced—there is no refusal to admit that must be replaced by an admission, and there is no obscure account that must be replaced by an explicit account. Rather, from the point of view of the legal purpose of the factual basis, they are simply unnecessary, which helps explain why judges treat them essentially as if they were nonexistent. They are not irrelevant to the case as a whole, however. They are important in probation investigations and play a significant role in determining within a possible sentence range what actual sentence the defendant receives, mild or harsh, although this does not necessarily mean that the information the defendants bring out qualifies as a mitigation for sentencing purposes from a legal point of view.

Regardless of how the written law conceptualizes the factual basis and the change of plea, and regardless of what the defendant has learned from his lawyer about its legally defined purpose, it is apparent that defendants associate mitigation with admissions of guilt because many offer mitigations with their admissions. In addition, it is also clear that ideas about how to lessen blameworthiness are culturally shared because many defendants bring forward similar kinds of information in similar microcontexts. Here I consider a few of the more common mitigations.

Drinking and drunkenness are frequently mentioned as part of the complex of activities in which a crime was committed. In the next example, the defendant at first says he does not know what he was doing at all.

> Judge 1:   Now uh I have to also make the
>   finding that there's a fact
>   basis upon which you could be
>   found guilty of this charge. So
>   you'll have to tell me what
>   happened on- sixteenth day of
>   November 1978. What did you do
>   concerning this p property
>   located at forty-six hundred
>   West Twenty-third Avenue? In
>   Tucson.
>
> Defendant: Well at that time, Your Honor, I
>   don't, I don't know too much
>   cause I was drunk at the time.
>   [3 sec] /(   )/
>
> Judge 1:   /Uh do you/ remember
>   going in there? [3 sec]
>
> Defendant: (Partially, yeah), I do.
>
>   (Tape F, Side 1, pp. 19–20)

Some mitigations, not surprisingly, are, in a conventional way, tied to particular types of crimes. As we saw in the transcript excerpts in chapter 4, people charged with falsifying prescriptions report having pain that was difficult to bear with only the drugs available to them without such falsification. Crimes involving money repeatedly entailed two types of mitigations: needing money and rightfully being owed the money.

In the next two examples, defendants who took things explain that they needed money. The first example, of a charge of grand theft, is from a record-oriented judge, showing that record-oriented strategies do not automatically preclude the kinds of troubles these judges are trying to avoid.

> Judge 3:   Well according to the testimony
>   of the witness that appeared
>   before the Grand Jury uh you uh
>   were in the store when it was
>   open and you loaded these
>   cigarettes into a box and then
>   into a shopping cart and took

them out of the store. Is that
/what hap/pened?

Defendant: /Yes, sir./

Judge 3: And what did you intend to do,
sell the cigarettes?

Defendant: Yes, sir.

Judge 3: Keep the money?

Defendant: (No). I was—w w in need of
money, you know. And I was
waiting to go to school, and I
was just broke, I was uh in need
of money.

Judge 3: All right. Well, the Court finds
there's a factual basis for the
defendant's plea.

(Tape C, Side 1, pp. 55–56)

The next example is from a charge of obtaining property by means of a false or fraudulent pretense—falsifying the amount of money orders—the case with the most loquacious defendant in my database.

Judge 8: Did it occur to you at that time
that that was uh a violation of
law?

Defendant: Oh, I was well aware that it was
a violation of the law. But uh
you know it's- I held those
(money cards) for that period of
time although I was you know
somewhat uh broke and stuff and
could have used the money and
taken the cash in the till.

(Tape A, Side 1, p. 10)

Actually, this defendant is saying that he held off his crime for a while in spite of needing money, a rather more complex use of this mitigation than the last example demonstrated.

In the next example, the record-oriented judge reiterates the defendant's mitigation, offered in an earlier attempt to handle this change of plea that was not recorded. This defendant is charged with attempted second-degree burglary and attempted theft.

Judge 4: Mr. Carter I I asked you if uh
[3 sec] in pleading guilty to
the crime of attempted burglary
in CR 00000, second degree, a
class four felony- if you were
admitting that [2 sec] on March
the- second uh 1979, you [2
sec] attempted to uh enter- uh

> [2 sec] a residential structure
> belonging to- Marvin Gordon- uh
> located at 6121 North North
> Archilla in Pima County,
> Arizona. [2 sec] With the
> intent to commit a theft. [2
> sec] I believe uh you told the
> Court that you had done [2 sec]
> a substantial amount of work for
> Mr. Gordon at that location [2
> sec] improving his premises- I
> take it carpentry work and so
> forth, is that correct?

Defendant: Yes, sir.

Judge 4: That uh he had not paid you the
> amount uh that uh was due to
> you. That you uh entered uh
> that residence uh with the
> intent to [2 sec] take his
> property and uh to withhold it
> uh with the intent to return it
> uh to him only upon payment to
> you of the money that uh he
> owed you. Is that what you
> told me?

Defendant: Yes, (sir).

(Tape F, Side 1, pp. 33–34)

Although this type of mitigation is typically tied up with some kind of stealing, and with some concept of recompense, it can be seen as an instance of a more general mitigation of the wronged person acting against the person who wronged him to right that wrong.

A final category of mitigation is the account that presents the defendant as having been drawn into crime by others, whether innocently or knowingly. This can be seen as a shifting of blame or responsibility from oneself to another. There are several cases in this database in which a person charged with theft or burglary was a lookout or driver for the person who did the actual act, and one might expect such mitigations from them, but that is not where they are in this database. Still, this mitigation does seem characteristic of the accessory role. The first example comes from a charge of second-degree trafficking in stolen property:

Defendant: Okay wel- well at the end when
> uh um my little brother got
> involved again and I didn't know
> about and I wanted to protect
> him and I hid anything that he
> had any contact with. And I did
> hide it.

(Tape J, Side 1, p. 24)

In the next example the account comes from the defendant's lawyer, who has stepped in where the judge is trying to elicit the factual basis from the defendant on a misdemeanor case of reckless driving. This case involved a translator whose translation to the defendant is not represented here. Once again, bear in mind that the mitigation comes originally from the defendant.

> Defendant's Lawyer: The defendant and the co-
> defendant uh- went to a house
> that was staked out by the
> Tucson Police Department.
> Apparently the co-defendant had
> burglarized the house. And uh
> secreted some property outside
> of the house. The co-defendant
> then asked the defendant for a
> ride to pick up the property.
> Mr. Ryan did not know that the
> property was stolen. Uh he gave
> the co-defendant the ride to the
> house- The police officers uh
> at the time that he arrived at
> the house, confronted the
> defendant the the defendant
> became uh afraid and uh he
> began to drive away from the uh
> that location in his truck. Uh
> I think the evidence would show
> that he drove away at a very
> high rate of speed, that he went
> through at least two- three stop
> signs uh one on a major
> thoroughfare, one (into) Tucso
> Tucson Boulevard, and uh was
> stopped approximately three or
> four miles away from the point
> where this uh chase first
> began.
>
> (Tape E, Side 1, pp. 12–13)

In these examples the first defendant is defined as knowing and the second defendant as innocent. When defendants claim to be innocent of knowledge that might implicate them, the judges in my database never challenge them.

The final example of being drawn in by others is one in which the defendant reports to the judge that he was drawn into free admission of possession of marijuana by a friendly policeman.

> Defendant: Uh, sir when the officers were
> in our house, and uh an n we
> were they were like joking
> around with us and all, and they

> were pretty friendly and uh we
> openly admitted to it when he
> asked me uh I- he said, "I
> found this in your drawer. Do
> you- uh is it yours?," and I
> said, "Yes." It was a small
> quantity.

(Tape C, Side 1, pp. 7–8)

What are we to make, then, of these mitigations? It appears that the urge, at least in this American society, to exculpate ourselves even as we confess is almost irresistible. These defendants absolutely do not engage in self reproach, self-abnegation, or verbal self-flagellation. Nor do the judges push them in this direction. As Judge 3's example on pages 102–103 suggests, the judges usually do not respond to these mitigations in the way they do to denials. They do not try to get defendants to take back their mitigations by saying, for example, "But you realize being drunk is no excuse," in the way that they counter the denials. In general, there is little evidence in what the judges say that they have even heard these mitigations.

As already noted, although all the judges encounter the kinds of resistance documented here, the procedure-oriented judges deal with such resistance much more often. They make the choice to deal with resistance by deciding that involving the defendant is more important than avoiding the struggle to make the procedure good that involvement brings on. These judges do not see themselves as losing control, but others see some of them in this way. So their reputations can be undermined as a result of their strategies in a way that is much less likely to happen with the record-oriented judges. This is why control is more of an issue for procedure-oriented judges, it is why they elaborate this issue ideologically and the reason the issue is emotionally charged for them, as the next section demonstrates.

Judges' Ideologies of Control

I noted previously that I see myself as having come to the courts with cultural concepts of control that were both presupposed in and underwent change during my experiences in courtrooms and judges' chambers. Courtroom control was not an analytical focus of the research, but it came up so often in my conversations with judges that I began to pay more attention to it as an issue for them and eventually began to bring it up myself. However, I was never as self-conscious about courtroom control as a topic as I was about many other topics, nor as systematic in the way I approached it when gathering information. By the time I did the career history interviews from which I draw heavily to capture the judges' perspectives on courtroom control, I was actively co-constructing views on courtroom control with them in a way that I was not capable of doing when I asked them why they handled the procedure as they did and they gave me due process reasons for their behavior. This difference in my contribution to the dialogue I had with the judges is due in part to the culturally pervasive sharedness of ideologies of control in American society, in contrast to the nonsharedness of legal interpretive perspectives.

In my career history interviews, the issue of courtroom control came up with the five most procedure-oriented judges but not with the four most record-oriented judges. In three of these five interviews, the judges raised the issue of courtroom control. In the other two I brought the issue up. However, the judges with whom I raised the issue had raised it themselves in earlier posttaping interviews. In all these interviews, the subject came up during the last part of the interview, section E (see appendix B, Career History Interview), which I told the judges was the part most central to my own interests, and the part in which we considered from several vantage points the way that their social backgrounds affected their judicial behavior.

All these procedure-oriented judges (Judges 2, 5, 6, 7, and 8) made a conceptual distinction with regard to their own courtroom behavior between legal and nonlegal aspects of that behavior, as if the two could easily be distinguished. At the time, I too readily accepted the distinction. For some the distinction was more explicit than others. Demeanor, itself a legal as well as an everyday concept, was one term fairly often invoked to identify the putatively nonlegal.

(1) PHILIPS: This last section is a more
general section where I'm asking
you about the relationship
between your background and
your judicial behavior. . . .

   JUDGE 6: Well are we talking about the
demeanor or the thrust of their
ruling?

(Judge 6, Career History Interview, pp. 31–32)

(2) I mean I know that Judge Morrow can have, for example, can have a kind of imposing imperial demeanor which puts off. And I doubt that he has that much in the way of lawyers coming to him seeking some input or advice for that reason, among others perhaps. (Judge 5, Career History Interview, p. 16)

Although I expressly conceptualized the relationship I was looking into here as a social one, two of the judges volunteered the opinion that the extralegal variation in judges' behavior on the bench was a matter of personality, even though in this same section of the interview they readily attributed some of the same behavior to social background:

(3) And I think a lot of it depends upon your personality. . . . People feel comfortable calling me Joe as opposed to Judge and I don't know why that is. (Judge 5, Career History Interview, p. 15)

(4) I guess a lot of it depends on, not so particularly on the judge's background, but on the type of person he is. If he's very introverted I suppose he'd tend to be very austere in the courtroom. Reserved. If he's outgoing, generally speaking, then I suppose he would have a warmer, friendlier atmosphere in the courtroom. (Judge 6, Career History Interview, p. 34)

Within this realm of what were characterized as extralegal aspects of behavior, the most striking finding that emerges from examination of the interview transcripts is that these *procedure-oriented judges all made connections between formality, courtroom control, and ways of talking*.[3] Typically, these concepts became linked through their adjacency in the sequential structure of discussion of variation in judges' courtroom behavior, and for all the concept of formality was the salient one, so that discussions of formality were sometimes really discussions of courtroom control and formality could be said to be a code word for control. The following excerpts illustrate these key properties of judges' ways of talking about courtroom control.

(5) But I try very hard not to let anybody get the impression, rightfully at least, that I'm talking down to them. Whether it's a lawyer or litigant or juror. And I don't know, I'm not particularly conscious of it, but it's something I think is important. And I suppose I'm maybe more informal than some, (   ) that's not to say that there aren't plenty of times when I'm darn glad I have a black robe on and all the things I have to protect me, cause it's hard to control the courtroom. (Judge 8, Career History Interview, pp. 58–59)

(6) . . . but particularly jurors, they walk into a courtroom in many instances never having been there before, not knowing what to expect. There's a lot of mumbo jumbo legal talk going on. I think it's important and I try to make an effort, particularly when I'm empaneling a jury, to set them at ease. You know, I'll try to crack a funny once in a while just to relax them and get them talking. And I think they function better if they feel relaxed and comfortable in the situation they find themselves in, and I hope I accomplish that. Some people may say that I'm much too informal, but on the other hand it's all right to be informal as long as you don't lose control of the situation, and there's one thing that the judge has to do, that is maintain control of what goes on in the courtroom. (Judge 6, Career History Interview, pp. 35–36)

(7) But during that courtroom scene the judge who tried that case wouldn't even let the lawyers get out of their seat. You know, like John Trask, he's mellow and older, but he was in his heyday then. And he got up and the judge says, "What are you doing up?" He says, "Well, I was going to get a drink of water, Your Honor." And he says, "Well you ask me if you want a drink of water." He says, "May I have a drink of water, Your Honor?" "No." You know, things like that. Now I don't see any <u>need</u> of that. And I don't, I don't <u>practice</u> that. And I think a lot of this real rigid formality in the courtroom is a coverup for insecurity on the part of the judge. On the other hand, if the judge wants to run his courtroom that way, I say, "That's your business. I don't run mine that way." And I've never had any, I've never had any getting out of hand in my courtroom. (Judge 2, Career History Interview, pp. 56–57)

In making these connections between degree of formality, degree of courtroom control, and manner of speaking, these judges express the view that more formality helps one keep control of the courtroom but less formality helps make others, particularly the lay public, more comfortable and less reticent to speak in courtroom proceedings. Some of the judges explicitly express the goal of the judge as being to strike a balance so that the informality is enough to make people feel comfortable but not so much as to cause the courtroom (by which we really mean the people, of course) to get out of control, and not so little as to shut people out.

(8) I don't know why Ed {another judge} is unable to get that balance. Maybe it'll come in time. He seems to have to go <u>very</u> strongly the other way before he gets the response

that he wants in the way of quiet in the courtroom or whatever it may be. And I don't know if at some point he'll adjust some of his informality so that he can begin to get that balance, but there is some of that that you have to I think take into account. Maybe he will. (Judge 5, Career History Interview, p. 17)

(9) And I have a feeling that too many judges and too many lawyers try to make it an upper-crust club-type thing. They're, it's so extremely formal to the extent that they take the court system away from the litigants. (Judge 2, Career History Interview, p. 47)

There was, then, a significant amount of sharedness among the judges who talked about these issues in the ways that they conceptualized them. Whereas these judges professed not to know what any other judge did procedurally, they readily spoke in ways that acknowledged that they knew their own reputations with regard to control of the courtroom and the others' reputations as well. That they knew of each other's reputations is attested to by the frequency in the transcript quotations already cited here with which they told stories about themselves and one another.

Interestingly enough, each of the three judges in my study with the poorest evaluations on the issue of courtroom control in at least one bar poll brought up this image of himself during my study and actively argued against the view that he had trouble controlling the courtroom. It became clear that none of them was particularly troubled by situations in which they were seen as losing control. They did not see themselves as losing control, and where they acknowledged things had happened that others would perceive as loss of control, such as yelling, they made it clear that they did not themselves feel threatened by it. All three of these judges had strongly stated positions in which they were opposed to imposing the increased formality that they felt would be necessary to satisfy other people's ideas about maintaining control:

(10) I don't like to intimidate people with words. I don't like to use my power as a judge to intimidate people. That's not my function. And I don't like to be considered anything but a technician basically. Maybe that's not the way an attitude of a judge should be, you know, that he is separate and apart from different people. (Judge 7, Career History Interview, p. 30)

(11) I don't know how you feel about it, I know if I were a layperson walking in a courtroom I would certainly feel frightened by the whole situation, particularly if the judge doesn't exude some warmth and it can be a very difficult situation. . . . You want the people to realize this is a court of law where a very serious purpose is trying to be served and that's justice for litigants. And on the other hand you want the jury and litigants to perform reasonably well without any artificial restraints imposed by feelings of, "Gee, this is kind of an alien situation I'm finding myself in." I know once I can get a good laugh out of the jury panel, they all seem to relax. And then they start coming forth with, you know, more candid answers to questions. (Judge 6, Career History Interview, pp. 37–38)

(12) I've had people call me a sonofabitch in the courtroom down at juvenile court. And I listen to them, when they get through I'd say, "Now is that all you got to say?" And I have never had an occasion when that took place but what when the case was over, they'd

come to me, usually crying, you know, "God I'm I'm sorry I said that. I don't know what possessed me." But I always felt like the juvenile courtroom was so emotional and we had people that were just beside themselves. And it's not a formal situation. If I had been really formal about that, I could have been locking people up everyday. And for what purpose? I got more mileage out of just letting them say what it was they wanted to say and then get their ultimate cooperation, which is what I was wanting you know. I want them to take their kid home and help us fight his battles, you know. That's my approach. (Judge 2, Career History Interview, pp. 58–59).

Again, there is a good deal of similarity in the ways these judges defend their position: each prefers greater informality because it is less intimidating and more likely to get the nonlawyers involved in the legal process. Each conveys the sense of his belief that the courts are for the people and that justice is better served through the lay public's involvement in court talk. The ultimate goal, of course, is to enlist the cooperative participation of others in the courtroom in a way that is not physically coerced, regardless of how it is done.

One final way in which the expressed ideological stance on courtroom control differed from those views judges expressed about the procedural reasons they had for hearing the pleas as they did was that there was an emotional intensity around courtroom control ideology that was not around due process ideology. This should be evident from the vehemence of some of the positions I quote, but the following example shows the use of swearing to convey strength of feeling:

(13) I have <u>never</u> held anybody in contempt in the courtroom. I've never had to. And as strong as I've ever been on that is, like I've had some people who've tried to act out sometimes and act naughty. I get to the limit where a lot of judges 'll scream at them and say, "You're in contempt. Three hundred dollar fine." My approach has been I'll say, "Now, look Mr. Jones, I'm going to tell you something. I've never held anybody in contempt yet. Never put anybody in jail for acting out in the courtroom. But I'm just waiting for the right case to come along. So don't tempt me." And they've never tempted me. And I've never had a problem with lawyers. I know that there's a great variance on how some judges handle it. Every time I hear that, like newspapers 'll say, "So-and-so judge really runs a tight reign in his courtroom," the first question I ask myself, "I wonder if he's worth a damn as a judge." (Judge 2, Career History Interview, p. 58)

The procedure-oriented judges, then, take an ideological stance on courtroom control that the record-oriented judges do not take. This stance links courtroom control to degree of formality, which in turn is manifest in particular ways of using language. The judges present themselves as manipulating degree of formality to achieve both control of the courtroom and the level of involvement, particularly from nonlawyer participants in courtroom interaction, that they feel is desirable to meet their idea of what a legal system is supposed to be doing.

In contrast to their explicit elaborations of legal procedural ideologies, discussed in chapter 4, here the judges acknowledge knowing what other judges do in the realm of control. They perpetuate this knowledge through the stories they tell about one another, which display some common assumptions, and feel comfortable evaluating one another's courtroom control. And there is an affective component to their talk, in contrast to more neutral (though not entirely so) discussions of why they handle the procedure as they do. Their stories and evaluations are still a long way from actual direct acknowledgments of specific experiences in which courtroom control was truly an issue. Moreover, their talk about the positive benefits of informality focuses on lawyers, juries, and litigants, not on the criminal defendants, who are considered the real physical threat to judges, as evidenced by the presence of sheriff's deputies only when criminal defendants are present. In other words, the judges deny that loss of control or fear of loss of control was ever a reality for them personally, and they focus their professed concern on a more positive control of speech of participants in court procedures (i.e., getting people to talk, not stopping them).

Most central to the general line of argument of this chapter, however, is that procedure-oriented judges' beliefs that those who come to court should be made to feel comfortable enough to participate (even if this means that the defendants' resistance to confession causes others to see their courtroom as out of control) are consistent with the strategies they use, documented in chapter 4, for involving the defendant in the factual basis.

Discussion

This chapter focused on judges' ideologies of courtroom control as an alternative interpretive framework for making sense of judges' courtroom language use during the guilty plea—alternative to the due process ideologies offered by the judges to explain their own behavior. This discussion illustrates that judges conceptualize and talk about their courtroom behavior in more than one way, represented in the discourses of this research project as separate or compartmentalized. In other words, due process and courtroom control talk are contextually separate in content and form, and in the content–form relationship, of speech examined in this book.

In this final section I compare the legal due process ideologies discussed in chapter 4 with the everyday courtroom control ideologies discussed in this chapter. I consider the implications of the differences and similarities between these two interpretive frameworks for our understanding of the nature of ideological diversity manifest in judicial practice. Consistent with Marxist views of ideology as concealing power relations, I find that neither interpretive framework really acknowledges the struggle that goes on in the courtroom as defendants resist being defined as criminals, even as they plead guilty to crimes.

Due process ideologies and courtroom control ideologies differ in several important respects. Due process ideologies are considered legal but not political, whereas courtroom control ideologies are considered neither legal nor political. The purportedly nonlegal nature of courtroom control talk frees judges to acknowledge diversity in behavior and attitudes because this area is expressly and explicitly defined as having no legal consequences for the defendants and as therefore not addressable within a legal framework.

Related to this difference, I find the state of knowledge judges profess and display about one another is very different for due process and courtroom control ideologies. As already noted, the judges claim not to know each other's due process beliefs and practices, but they acknowledge knowing about each other's ability to control a courtroom and contribute to the construction of such knowledge with each other in an open, affectively laden way.

Both legal and control interpretive frameworks are dominant discourses, but each in a different way. Legal due process ideology totally dominates the construction of reality in the courtroom: it cannot tolerate what is defined as incompatible with it. Only legal realities are relevant and nonexperts are treated as having no ability to judge what is real. But the spheres of activity dominated in this way by this interpretive framework are limited to the legal. In contrast, control ideologies are thought of as having a kind of unofficial status in their relevance to hearing guilty pleas. They are in the background in actual courtroom activity if it is going well and are not particularly coherent or complex. But control ideologies are more widespread than legal ideologies within our culture as interpretive frameworks that people think within and are particularly familiar to people working in hierarchically organized bureaucracies. For this reason, it is easier for a wider range of people to engage in discussion that invokes these perspectives. The existence and nature of each of these ideological framings (i.e., the due process and courtroom control frames) depends on the existence and nature of the other. They are interdependent. They also mutually obscure one another because the connections between them are not acknowledged.

Judges know their ability to control a courtroom is defined by the organized bar as a significant dimension of their being evaluated as good or bad judges by lawyers and the general public. Judges' roles are doubly public in that they perform in public in the courtroom and then the news media evaluate that performance. Voters who vote on whether to retain these judges learn about how lawyers evaluate the judges through the news. Because of this, procedure-oriented judges, who are the ones criticized for lack of control, are compelled to think about and have positions on their own courtroom control and that of other judges. Debates over what is good in the way of courtroom control also flourish, in part because, as already noted, they involve ideology that is widely shared across institutional complexes in this country. This ideology is part of the commonsense experience of most if not all people in this country, and so people have opinions about it who would not have opinions about the more narrowly experienced due process legal ideology central to chapter 4.

Loss of control, itself a cultural construct, has many dimensions. It can be experienced as definitive, as in the example at the beginning of this chapter, where the defendant actively rejected all the options the court was prepared to give him. It can also be experienced less definitively, as when defendants resist confessing in the factual basis. In the factual basis, the ways in which defendants resist confessing can be seen as threatening the judge's control over the procedure-specific legal reality it is his job to construct. Because procedure-oriented judges make more of an effort than record-oriented judges to involve the defendant as a speaker in the guilty plea, they more often conduct procedures in which defendants resist confessing. So, these judges are more at risk for developing reputations as judges who are unable to control the courtroom. They know this, but their strategy, at least in part, is to fight this reputation by elaborating on ideologies of control that justify their approach to being a judge rather than becoming more like the record-oriented judges. These procedure-oriented judges want active participants in their courtroom procedures and are prepared to sacrifice the appearance of control for the appearance of willing participation.

It is plausible to see all of the judges' due process strategies and procedural rationales for why they handle the procedure as they do (discussed in chapter 4, this volume) as responses to defendants' resistance to confession. Thus, a record-oriented procedural rationale that argues that it is not necessary to involve the defendant very much in the procedure can be seen as a justification for tightening up control of the interaction in a way that minimizes and routinizes defendants' involvement in the procedure. Similarly, a procedure-oriented rationale that one cannot be certain of voluntariness and knowingness without the defendant's voluntary/active participation in the guilty plea itself can justify compelling more defendant involvement and in so doing loosening control.

But the judges do not actually acknowledge any real ideological struggle between the defendant and the judge for control of the definition of reality in the courtroom: when defendants resist confessing, this resistance does not lead to any debate between judge and defendant in a common field of meaning. And yet the judges' different due process stances discussed in chapter 4 can still be seen as responses to the defendants' resistance. These stances are different ways of and rationales for exerting control over resistant defendants' speech actions in the guilty plea. So judges are affected by defendants' resistance, even if this is unacknowledged in any direct way in their discourse in and about the procedure. In this respect there is a dialectical process between the judge, who is in a position of dominance, and the defendant, who is in a position of subordination. But the ideological manifestations of the struggles between judges and defendants have a displaced quality. They become expressed in diverse due process interpretive stances among the judges, who do not directly confront one another's positions in these expressions. The judges' reactions to defendants' resistances are also expressed in their ideologies of control, which also never directly address defendants' resistances.

The crucial point here is that the defendants' resistance really *does* have an impact on the judges, in spite of their not alluding to it overtly in their talk about their own practices. From a certain point of view, the entire range of ideological diversity in both the written and the spoken law is a response to defendants' resistance and its threat to the legal validity of the guilty plea. The judges' due process response buries this opposition, obscuring even its existence, and certainly obscuring any fear of or concern over it on the part of legal practitioners. So, there are signs of struggle in this procedure, so to speak, but they have an ideologically opaque quality.

These signs of struggle are also routinized in that different defendants resist in similar ways and the judges predictably respond to them in similar ways. These resistances do not give one the feeling that a revolution is about to happen, whatever that takes.

If we hold up this example of ideological diversity and struggle against the Marxist tradition of conceptualizing ideology, we see some interesting ways in which the ideological diversity described here is and is not captured by analytical distinctions fundamental to that tradition.

Marx is still widely held to have seen a dominant class as promulgating ideologies that justify its own continued domination. A key feature of such ideologies is that they obscure the true interests of the dominated class and make it seem as if the current order is actually in the interest of the dominated. Legal due process ideology does this in some ways. Judges take the position that however they treat the defendant in the guilty plea, their purpose is to protect the defendant's constitutional rights; yet from another point of view, the judges are simply extending their personal control and the control of the state over the defendant. By conceptualizing courtroom control ideologies as nonlegal and as unconnected to due process ideologies, the judges further obscure the extent to which the perpetuation of control over the defendant is a primary concern.

Marx saw the perspective of subordinated groups both as mindless submission to the view of the dominant class and as potentially resistant to that ideology through critique of ideology. Many scholars across a range of disciplines have become fascinated with envisioning subordinated groups as actively resisting dominant ideologies. Williams's (1977) concepts of counter hegemony and alternative hegemony are particularly influential ways of theorizing the possibilities for resistance. These concepts build on Gramsci's (1971) idea that ideological domination or hegemony is never complete and is always being resisted. But even as interest in documenting ideological conflict emerged, the possibility that resistance accomplishes anything was questioned, first eloquently by Willis (1977) and then with more ambiguity by Comaroff (1985) and Kennedy and Davis (1993). Both Comaroff and Kennedy and Davis describe cultural activities that can be seen as resistant to a dominant cultural order but have not led to a triumphant overthrow of the condition of subordination and are not necessarily conceived as resistance in a Marxist sense by those engaged in the resistance.[4] Their position is consistent with Foucault's (1972, 1980): they seem to be saying that the final evaluation of the significance of these acts of resistance can never be made because the acts keep being reinterpreted as the cultures of which they are a part change. Acts of resistance do, however, have the potential to contribute to ultimately successful challenges to ideological orders.

Certainly the resistance of the criminal defendants to confessing in court has a similar tentative potential to significantly challenge the legal order and has had significant impact on the due process ideologies of judges, but in its routinization, it has the quality of a *frozen* dialectic, or an easily contained opposition.

More central to what one sees in the courtroom activities and in talk about them, however, is that Marxist visions of domination, subordination, and struggle are too simplistically dualistic. They too much assume symmetries between ideologies in conflict, as if ideological processes were like a debate. Analysis here particularly reveals asymmetry and nonequivalence between the ideologies that are in conflict, rather than the analogousness of opposites suggested by largely theoretical Marxist characterizations of ideological struggle. In chapter 4 I showed how procedure-oriented judges elaborate on their due process rationales more than record-oriented judges. In this chapter I showed that record-oriented judges did not raise the issue of courtroom control at all. Rather, procedure-oriented judges raise both their own courtroom control views and those of others to argue for their own point of view.

This project also suggests more ideological diversity than any dualism can capture—diversity that itself is central to the maintenance of ideological domination by particular sectional interests. The concept of ideological polysemy directs attention to this issue. Thus, the same courtroom practices can be understood to enact legal due process interpretations, political theories of the role of the state in relation to the individual, and everyday commonsense ideas about how to control people without shutting them up. Such polysemy allows for the plausible denial of particular intentions so that a judge can claim to have due process intentions or courtroom control intentions but not political ideological intentions. Ideological polysemy contributes to the entrenchment of dominant ideologies through the ambiguity with which it imbues social practices and in this way presents a real challenge to ideological critique.

6

·———·

Ideological Diversity
in Legal Discourses

Ideology in Discourse Revisited

At the beginning of this book, I talked about how the Marxist tradition offers a model of ideology as socially ordered and as grounded in society, even though this model is simplistic in its image of a dualistic opposition between dominant and subordinate ideologies. And I suggested that the oversimplicity of this model is due in part to its lack of empirical engagement, particularly engagement with actual ongoing social practices. Marxist approaches to ideology acknowledge a role for language as a manifestation of ideology, but this role is not well developed. However, there is now a literature that looks at resistance as symbolic interaction (Willis 1977; Scott 1990), pays increasing attention to ideological diversity in legal language use in courts (Merry 1990; Conley & O'Barr 1990; Matoesian 1993), and fosters an emerging awareness of the shaping influence of relations of domination and subordination in the constitution of ideologies in discourse practices. Linguistic anthropological approaches to situated language use in the traditions of the ethnography of communication and textual analysis (which show culture and ideology constituted in discourse) offer theoretical and methodological models for the empirical and practical grounding of ideology in language use. But here, attention to the significance of power and to the shaping influence of relations of domination and subordination was much less developed than in Marxist traditions generally and is only now emerging in the study of language within these traditions.

In this book I bring together the Marxist study of ideology in law and the linguistic anthropological study of the constitution of culture in discourse to characterize and shed light on the nature of ideological diversity in legal discourse practices.

116

Ideology in Spoken Legal Discourse: Enacting Ideological Stances

Central to the characterization of ideological diversity here is my argument that judges enact ideological stances in the way they take guilty pleas. In my interviews with judges we jointly constructed the variation in the sequential structuring of their courtroom discourse as primarily motivated by and instantiating different interpretations of the due process procedural law "governing" the guilty plea procedure. Due process thinking dominates judges' practical consciousness in and about the plea. This consciousness reflects the ideological domination of law as an interpretive framework in courtroom activities. However, the judges' behavior is ideologically polysemous: although legal thinking is dominant, political ideologies involving different views on the role of the state in relation to the individual and commonsensical ideologies about different styles of interactional control are also being realized in the same judicial behavior. Courtroom discourse, then, does not "mean" one thing; it is ideologically polysemous.

The dominance of legal ideology is manifest not only in what judges say about their own interpretive practices but also in their organization of the courtroom discourse that constitutes the guilty plea. All the judges organize their pleas into a sequence of topics, each of which indexes and meets the requirements of some part of the Arizona Rules of Criminal Procedure, Rule 17. In this way they display their adherence to the written law and the subordination of their own discourse practices to a legal interpretive perspective.

The ideological diversity realized through variation among the judges in the way they handle the procedure is characterized as record-oriented or procedure-oriented. Such characterizations reflect the fact that judges are thinking in terms of procedural due process requirements as being met by the written case record as a whole or by the immediate procedure when they explain why they hear the pleas as they do.

These two ideological stances are realized in different discourse treatments of the string of topics that constitutes the sequential structure of the plea. In discourse terms, these different treatments are manifest in differing amounts of overall variation in the way a judge handles the procedure, in the presence versus absence of whole topics, and in the elaboration or abbreviation of particular topics, most notably the factual basis. At the sentence-structure level, the two ideological stances are realized by different questioning strategies in terms of the number of questions the defendant is asked and the relative proportions of yes–no and "Wh" questions. From the point of view of the organization of interaction, the record-oriented and procedure-oriented strategies differ in the amount and nature of defendant verbal involvement in the procedure. Both the treatment of topics and the questioning strategies are aspects of the way defendants are involved and controlled by the judges in the procedure.

Ideological diversity, then, is centrally realized in this study through variation among the judges in the organization of the discourse constituting guilty pleas.

Ideology in Different Forms of Discourse

At the same time, when we look at the courtroom discourse of the guilty pleas in relation to the other forms of discourse that were analyzed here, it is also apparent that all three of the ideological frameworks invoked here—the due process legal framework, the role of the state political framework, and the courtroom control framework—are made manifest and realized in rather different ways. Ideology is constituted differently in different kinds of discourse, and so is ideological diversity.

In the written law examined in this book, the procedural rule and case law are viewed as forms of written legal discourse that differ in the way they manifest ideology and ideological diversity. Rule 17 is explicit regarding what must be done procedurally to meet due process rights in the guilty plea, and it expresses a single position that these rights must be secured during the guilty plea itself. Case law reveals and distinguishes multiple explicit oppositionally organized positions on and interpretations of Rule 17, so it is overtly systematically intertextual and interpretive. Yet ultimately case law is consistent in not requiring due process rights to be secured during the procedure but allowing instead simply for evidence somewhere in the written case record that those rights were protected. Within the written law, then, genres of law can create ideological boundaries so that one genre differs from another in its ideological stance, and genres can vary in the amount of internal ideological diversity they display.

The spoken procedure, the change of plea, is also a containing or boundary-creating genre in the constitution of ideological diversity within law. It is treated and experienced as something separate from, but relatable to, forms of written law. The spoken procedure then is conceptualized as bounded and separable from the written genres for the purpose of some interpretive practices. The spoken procedure is like written case law in its obvious display of both ideological commonality and diversity. Collectively, the judges display an interpretation of the written law that is neither that of Rule 17 nor that of case law but shows the influence of both. The ideological diversity among the judges can also be interpreted as some judges being more influenced by Rule 17 (the procedure-oriented judges) and some judges being more influenced by case law (the record-oriented judges).

Although the judges see themselves as individual interpreters of the law, they function in a climate in which the entire bench for the Pima County Superior Court is their local interpretive community. The socially systemic variation among the judges in the way they enact interpretive stances in their pleas makes it clear that they influence one another in the way they handle pleas. This means that the ongoing spoken discourse that constitutes court activity at any given point in time and past discourses in which judges participated are also sources of influence on the judges and the way they handle the procedure at that same point in time, just as written law is a source of influence.

The judges draw on the forms of written law and spoken law when they hear their pleas, and they link a given plea intertextually to both written law and spoken law. Thus when judges produce procedure-oriented pleas they are aligning themselves with other judges on the bench who also hear their pleas in a procedure-oriented way. It is limiting, however, to think of this intertextuality primarily as involving one text being intertextually connected to another text, although this is a part of what judges are doing, because of the multiplicity of interconnections among forms of legal discourse. Most notably, one sees not only the direct influence of Arizona Rules of Criminal Procedure, Rule 17 and case law in the spoken plea but also shared strategies among the judges in the way they hear the spoken plea that cannot be derived from the written law but must come from judges imitating each other's discourse-organizing strategies. Judges thus function practically within an interpretive field in which written and spoken forms of legal discourse are connected in a richly intertextual way that is fluid and constantly changing.

In actual courtroom practices, the ideological stances that are enacted through record and procedure discourse construction strategies are *implicit* in the way the judges handle the procedure and are not made metapragmatically explicit during the procedure. These stances are also coherent, at least at each end of the continuum from more record-oriented to more procedure-oriented judges, in that judges who are procedure-oriented in one way are procedure-oriented in other ways, so that there is a consistency throughout the procedure in the way topical coherencies do or do not involve the defendant.

As already noted, when judges talk about why they handle the procedure as they do, they present themselves as interpreting the written due process procedural law governing the plea, so they are explicit in this respect about making connections between written texts and their spoken pleas. What makes their stances implicit rather than explicit is that the way they are making these connections is hidden from the outsider nonlawyer. Whatever connections of this kind are being made are opaque to the outsider. The hiddenness stems in part from the hiddenness of the written law itself. The defendant usually does not see the written law, does not know what it is, and does not know how to find it. This hiddenness also stems from the interpretive practices taught in law school that are essentially in the heads of the judges. The ideological diversity in the judges' interpretive stances, then, is also opaque to the outsider.

So far I have talked about written forms of law and spoken law as manifesting ideology differently. The judges' representations of their ideological stances in their interviews with me differed from that of the other two forms of language use central to this project as well. In general, judges were more *explicit* about their ideological positions in interviews than in the pleas themselves, but their positions often came out in a fragmented and partial way. In part this seemed due to the emergent nature of the interviews themselves.

The judges explicitly invoked their due process ideologies in metadiscourse about their spoken pleas, so in the interviews legal ideology was still salient but more explicitly so than in the spoken procedure. But whereas the judges present both written and spoken law as only involving legal ideology, the other two general ideological frameworks—the political and everyday control ideologies—also came into play explicitly in the interviews. Most notably, of course, procedure-oriented judges readily articulated control ideologies that involved ideas about the role of language in creating more formal and controlling as opposed to less formal and less controlling interactions with members of the public. They also took positions on the strengths and weaknesses of these ways of using language. And they clearly defined their due process thinking as legal and their courtroom control thinking as nonlegal. Political ideologies, however, although oriented to as a topic in the interviews, primarily took the form of the denial and repudiation of such as an influence on courtroom practices for all the judges. Political ideology is the most implicit of the three kinds of ideology in all my forms of talk, even though it is quite explicit in other domains within American politics.

The various forms of talk drawn upon in this study, then, manifested ideology and ideological diversity in very different ways.

Dualism, Opposition, and Domination

Marxist approaches to ideology raise the issue of how hidden or implicit ideology is. And I suggested in the preceding section that whether and how ideas are hidden is complex, subtle, and different in different forms of discourse. Marx-influenced traditions also pursue the idea that ideological diversity is dualistically and oppositionally organized in relations between dominant and subordinate sectional interests within a society. As discussed in chapter 5, a great deal of social scientific attention focused recently on the nature of the resistance of subordinated groups to their domination, some of which involved characterization of their resistance as symbolic action with ideological dimensions to it. This study, however, is primarily concerned with the ideologies of people typically defined as in a position to implement the ideological hegemony of the state and as implementers of dominant ideologies. It should not be surprising then that the organization of ideological diversity in their experience does not necessarily conform to earlier representations of such organization.

It is difficult to separate the dualism in the practical consciousness of the judges from the dualism rhetorically imposed on the forms of talk used in this study, but it seems clear that judges' discourses include both nondualistic and dualistic orderings of ideological diversity. Important nondualistic orderings of ideological diversity already discussed include the polysemous nature of courtroom discourse so that it expresses legal, political, and everyday ideologies and the ordering and containment of ideological diversity in the multiple written and spoken forms of talk considered here.

Several salient dualisms in the analysis of ideological diversity are also presented in this book. I present all three of the ideological frameworks that can be seen as enacted in the judges' courtroom language use as having a dualistic organization. Thus, within the legal ideological framework procedure-oriented judges are at one end of a continuum and record-oriented judges at the other end of the continuum in the way due process rights are interpreted. In political ideological terms, I characterize the procedure-oriented judges as liberal in their enactment of the state's relationship to the individual and the record-oriented judges as conservative in their enactment of this same relationship. Finally, I indicate that procedure-oriented judges both enact and espouse an informal, less controlling style of courtroom management, whereas the record-oriented judges enact a more formal and controlling style of courtroom management. In this way the terms in each dualism are connected to the terms in the other dualisms.

But the sociocultural status of these dualisms varies regarding what they mean to the judges and to me. The judges (and the general public) recognize only the conservative–liberal distinction as a dualistic organization of ideological diversity, and they deny its relevance to and for the courtroom: the overriding view is that political ideologies are not to be enacted by trial court judges. The record- versus procedure-oriented distinction is a dualism *I* proposed for making sense of the relation between what judges do in court and what they say about their concerns to protect defendants' due process rights. Because judges see themselves as making individual interpretations of written law in the ways they hear the plea and do not readily recognize local social systematicity in what they are doing, they do not recognize this dualism either.

The contrast within the everyday ideologies of courtroom control between informal and formal judges is, unlike the dualisms of political and legal ideologies, quite overt. But the judges do not see this opposition as having political implications or as being connected to the political and legal ideologies, as I suggest it is.

Not surprisingly, then, courtroom control is the only one of these dualisms about which judges speak in a way that suggests openly oppositional relations. In regard to political and legal ideologies, there is no acknowledgment (to me anyway) that individual judges are even in camps or that some are aligned with one another. Only around the issue of courtroom control, defined by the judges as noncentral to their endeavor, do we encounter open intensity of feeling and a suggestion of significant disagreement.

I see acknowledgment of opposition among trial court judges as essentially disallowed in the domains of politics and law and allowed around commonsensical ideologies of courtroom control, even though I argue that these different ideological frameworks are intimately connected because they are enacted by the same behavior. This lack of recognition and acknowledgment of ideological diversity within courtroom practice contributes to a sense of state law as ideologically monolithic.

Because judges are in the same structural position(s) and are not seen as being in relations of domination and subordination to one another (for example, they cannot tell one another how to rule), it does not appear, even if the ideological dualisms are in relations of opposition, that one group of judges is dominant and the other subordinate. It is still possible to talk about one ideological stance being dominant over the other, but not in simple terms. In this study many more judges were procedure-oriented than record-oriented. Their ideology was dominant in the sense of its having a larger presence in the local court. In this much those of a liberal political persuasion could be said to be "winning" over those of a conservative persuasion in the spoken law in any ideological struggle between them. But the conservative record-oriented strategy prevailed in case law that governed the procedure at the time of the study. And the defensiveness of the procedure-oriented judges, some of whom are defined as out of control by bar polls and newspaper editorials, suggests the dominance in public spheres of record-oriented standards of control and formality. On the other hand, the procedure-oriented view "wins" in terms of the amount of talk devoted by the procedure-oriented judges to its promulgation.

As discussed in chapter 4, there is imbalance and nonequivalence in the dualism of record- and procedure-oriented strategies: the procedure-oriented stance is much more ideologically elaborate than the record-oriented stance. Strategically, the procedure-oriented stance involves an elaboration of topics that are not elaborated on in the record-oriented pleas. And in their interviews, the procedure-oriented judges had much more to say about why they heard the pleas as they did, seeing more meaning and significance in this issue than did the record-oriented judges. They also had more to say than the record-oriented judges about the significance of styles of courtroom control and why they used the style of courtroom management they did. So, which view is dominant depends on how we conceptualize dominance. From this it should be evident that dualistically organized ideological diversity can be complex in ways unanticipated by Marxist theory.

The judges in this study are conscious to varying degrees of the ideological dualisms and oppositions identified in legal, political, and everyday control ideologies. But it is striking that ideology and conflict are most acknowledged where they are considered peripheral. Ideological conflict is displaced from the political and legal into the everyday "nonlegal" discussion of courtroom control in a way that furthers the image of the law as ideologically monolithic.

Both legal and political interpretive frames inform judicial behavior, but I have not yet addressed how these interpretive frames themselves are oppositionally organized. As discussed in chapter 2, the literature on the history of the judicial selection process and my own data suggest that judicial selection was more dominated and controlled by Democratic and Republican parties and by political ideologies in the past but is now more dominated by organized bar legal ideologies. There was a process of ideological conflict and struggle not only over the control of judicial selection but also over the kind of ideological framework that would be allowed to dominate the practical consciousness of judges in their interpretive activity. Now, bar politics and legal ideology are in the ascendancy while party politics and political ideologies are in the background, though far from eliminated. The rhetoric of professionalism used by the organized bar to justify its influence over the judicial selection process obscures this contest as it has most of the other oppositions on which I focused. This contest is also obscured by the fact that we are accustomed to locating conflict between sectional interests of like kind (e.g., between classes or genders or political parties), whereas this conflict is between nonlike sectional interests—in this case political parties and professional organizations.

In general, then, there is a good deal of ideological diversity in legal discourse that is dualistic and oppositional in its social ordering yet is not acknowledged as such because the opposition is obscured and hidden by the nature and social orderings of the ideologies themselves.

As already noted, the dualisms and oppositions in this study do not for the most part involve clear relations of domination and subordination. The exception to this generalization is the opposition or resistance defendants present to judges when judges try to get them to confess to crimes. Here, I do not know the views of the defendants and the sources and bases of their opposition, albeit somewhat routinized as they emerge in the courtroom, are fragmented and opaque.

Although it might appear that the judges are unaffected by the defendants' resistance, I believe they are very much affected by it. They show the effects of defendant resistance in their preoccupation with courtroom control. And their procedure-oriented and record-oriented strategies for hearing pleas can be seen as different responses to this resistance. The ideological diversity enacted by the judges, then, is itself partly stimulated by and can be seen as an engagement with the defendants' resistance, showing how even resistance that does not articulate a clear ideological position can influence and shape the nature of ideological diversity in a local cultural scene.

Thus, it should be evident that the social ordering of ideological diversity in discourse is considerably more complex than has heretofore been recognized. The nature and ordering of ideological diversity documented here obscure the existence of such diversity and perpetuate the vision of law and state as ideologically monolithic.

Rethinking Law and the Trial Court Judge

As argued throughout this book, it is a mistake and a misrepresentation to think of trial court judges as nonideological, as mere implementers of law made by others. This misrepresentation begins with the equation of law with written law. We are perhaps overinfatuated with a vision of the nation as governed by the rule of law, by which we mean written codified law, equating the permanence of writing with the permanence of rule, a permanence more illusory than real. Even students of judicial behavior equate behavior with what is written (e.g., with the recorded sentences for crimes). But I argue that judges' speech in the courtroom is law too, that there is spoken law as well as written law. Moreover, although spoken law and written law clearly interconnect, spoken law has a life of its own, logic and rationales of its own that are separate from and cannot be found in written law.

Professional associations of lawyers, referred to as the organized bar, encourage the vision of trial court judges not as politicians but as practitioners of a profession, as mere conduits of written law. This vision of the trial court judge is in their interest because it justifies a greater role for the organized bar in the selection of trial court judges and a reduced role for political parties and the citizen electorate in the selection of judges. But judges' actions on the bench are far from informed only by professional legal interpretive practice grounded in law school and honed in legal practice hermetically sealed from the rest of cultural life in the United States. Spoken law enacts the political authority of the state, and judges enact diverse concepts of that state. Spoken law exerts direct control over defendants. Legal speech can even be thought of, in its materiality, as a form of physical control. And judges enact diverse theories of control that are familiar to all of us because those theories ramify across hierarchical relations throughout American society.

This study then challenges the organized bar's vision of the trial court judge and the nature of legal practice. The appellate judge and the trial court judge are less different than that vision suggests. Trial court judges are not just practicing a profession but practicing politics and exercising power. And law is neither a coherent nor a truly separate form of thought in American society.

APPENDIXES

Appendix A

•———•

Social Background Questionnaire

THE UNIVERSITY OF ARIZONA

TUCSON, ARIZONA 85721

DEPARTMENT OF ANTHROPOLOGY
BUILDING 30
(602) 626-2585

August 21, 1979

TO: Pima County Superior Court Judges in Study of Judges' Use
        of Language

FROM: Dr. Susan Philips

RE: Questionnaire on Judges' Social Background

The pages that follow this memo constitute a written questionnaire eliciting information on your social background.
This questionnaire is a companion to the career history
interview I have been tape recording with each of you in that
both are designed to yield information that can be related to
and compared with your actual courtroom use of language.

Once again let me assure you that your anonymity will be
preserved in any use made of your responses to the questions,
and that you should feel free to refuse to answer any or all
of the questions. Please do not put your name on the questionnaire. Each judge has been given a number, written in the
lower righthand corner of each page.

Feel free to add comments or clarifications to your responses in the margins on the last page. I have also included
a self-addressed envelope so that you can return the completed questionnaire to me more easily at your convenience.

Let me thank you in advance for this final contribution to my
project. You have all given most generously of your time.

Susan Philips

SP/dh

I. Your SOCIAL BACKGROUND

    A. Date of Birth _____

    B. Place of Birth _____

    C. Where and with whom have you lived for over a year?
       Please begin with most recent cities of residence and progress
       backward until birth.

CITY AND STATE	YEARS	OTHER MEMBERS OF HOUSEHOLD

    D. EDUCATION

       1. Undergraduate college(s) attended:

Name	Major subject	Years Attended	Degree
Name	Major subject	Years Attended	Degree

    E. RELIGION

       1. What is your religious preference, if any?
       2. Are you a member of a church?
          If so, what church?

    F. FAMILY

       1. MARITAL STATUS
          Never married [   ] Currently married for the first time [   ]
          Divorced [   ] Separated [   ] Widowed [   ] Remarried [   ]

2. If you are presently married, for how long have you been so?

_____

If you were previously married, for how long? _____

3. Present spouse:

   a. Date of birth _____
   b. Place of birth _____
   c. Number of years of school completed _____
   d. Major occupations of adulthood _____

   _____

4. Past spouse:

   a. Date of birth _____
   b. Place of birth _____
   c. Number of years of school completed _____
   d. Major occupations of adulthood _____

   _____

5. Children:

AGE	SEX	PRESENT ACTIVITIES (School, job)
a.		
b.		
c.		
d.		
e.		
f.		
g.		

G. MILITARY HISTORY

   1. Have you ever been a member of the armed forces or reserves?
   2. If so, which branch?
   3. During what years?
   4. What rank did you achieve?
   5. Were you involved with administration of the military courts
   in any way during this time? If so, in what capacity?

II. YOUR PARENTS' AND SIBLINGS' SOCIAL BACKGROUND
   A. PARENTS

   1. Did your parents live together until you were 18? _____
      a. If not, how old were you when they were separated? _____
      b. If not, who were the adult males in the household after
         separation?

      c. If not, who were the adult females in the household after
         separation?

2. MOTHER (or key adult female in household during childhood)

    a. Name _____

    b. Relationship (if not mother) _____

    c. Date of birth _____

    d. Place of birth _____

    e. Ethnic background/nationality _____
       _____

    f. Number of years of school completed _____

    g. Major occupations of adulthood _____
       _____

    h. Religious affiliation as an adult, if any _____

3. FATHER (or key adult male in household during childhood)

    a. Name _____

    b. Relationship (if not father) _____

    c. Date of birth _____

    d. Place of birth _____

    e. Ethnic background/nationality _____
       _____

    f. Number of years of school completed _____

    g. Major occupations of adulthood _____
       _____

    h. Religious affiliation as an adult, if any _____

B. YOUR SIBLINGS

1. FIRST

    a. Name _____

    b. Date of birth _____

    c. Place of birth _____

    d. Sex _____

    e. Relationship to you: Full _____ Half _____ Step _____

    f. Present marital status _____

    g. Number of children, if any _____

h. Number of years of schooling _____

i. Current occupation _____

2. SECOND

a. Name _____

b. Date of birth _____

c. Place of birth _____

d. Sex _____

e. Relationship to you: Full _____ Half _____ Step _____

f. Present marital status _____

g. Number of children, if any _____

h. Number of years of schooling _____

i. Current occupation _____

3. THIRD

a. Name _____

b. Date of birth _____

c. Place of birth _____

d. Sex _____

e. Relationship to you: Full _____ Half _____ Step _____

f. Present marital status _____

g. Number of children, if any _____

h. Number of years of schooling _____

i. Current occupation _____

Appendix B

•———•

Career History Interview

A. <u>Legal training</u>

   1. Where did you go to law school?

   2. What voluntary organizational activities did you participate in while in law school?
     a. Within the law school (e.g., student government, law review, moot court competition, legal fraternity)?
     b. In the community (e.g., church, sports, political activity)?

   3. Did you hold any jobs during your years in law school? If so, what were they?

   4. Have you taken part in any formal legal training since law school (e.g., state bar seminars, law institutes)?

B. <u>Jobs between law school and your current judgeship</u>

1. The first three years out of law school

   a. What positions did you hold during the first three years after you graduated from law school?

   b. How did you happen to take those positions, rather than others (i.e. why those particular jobs)?

   c. Were there particular individuals who were important in influencing your career choices during this period (e.g., law

professors, firm members, judges, old friends, fellow
law students, spouses)?

2. From the first three years up to your present position.

   a. <u>After</u> those first three years out of law school, what positions did you hold?

   b. For what periods of time did you hold those positions?

   c. What sorts of legal concentrations or specializations were
   involved (e.g., criminal vs. civil; or if civil, was it
   personal injury, corporate, or commercial)?

C. <u>Other activities during the period between law school and judgeship</u>.

   1. Did you engage in any organized <u>professional</u> activity during
   that period (e.g., state bar association, legal associations)?
   If so, what did your activity consist of?

   2. Did you engage in organized <u>community</u> activity during this
   period (e.g., fraternal organizations like the Lions; church;
   charity)?

   3. During this period were you involved in organized political
   party activity (e.g., fund raising, campaigning, organizing,
   legal consulting)?

D. <u>Your position as a judge</u>

   1. How long have you been on the bench?

   2. Did you receive any formal judicial training any time soon
   after you became a judge (e.g., National College of Judges;
   seminars)?

   3. What judicial selection process was used for your appointment?

   4. In what professional activities, if any, have you participated
   since on the bench?

   5. In what nonprofessional activities, if any, have you participated since on the bench?

E. <u>The relation between your background and your "judicial behavior"</u>
   In this final section, I seek <u>your</u> views on some general issues
   that are relevant for this research project.

   1. In what ways, if any, have <u>you</u> seen your social or occupational
   background as affecting your functioning as a judge?

   2. What terms would <u>you</u> use to characterize your political orientation (e.g., liberal, conservative, Republican, apolitical)?
   Do you think your political orientation affects or is apparent
   in your courtroom behavior? If so, how?

   3. What connections, if any, do you see between your social or
   legal background and the way you use language in the courtroom?

Appendix C

•———•

Rule 17, *Arizona Rules of Criminal Procedure*: Pleas of Guilty and No Contest

Rule 17.1   Pleading by defendant

a. Personal Appearance; Appropriate Court. A plea of guilty or no contest may be accepted by a court having jurisdiction to try the offense. Such plea shall be accepted only when made by the defendant personally in open court, unless the defendant is a corporation, in which case the plea may be entered by counsel or a corporate officer.

b. Voluntary and Intelligent Plea. A plea of guilty or no contest may be accepted only if voluntarily and intelligently made. Except for pleas to minor traffic offenses, the procedures of Rules 17.2, 17.3, and 17.4 shall be utilized by all courts to assure the voluntariness and intelligence of the plea.

c. Pleas of No Contest. A plea of no contest may be accepted only after due consideration of the views of the parties and the interest of the public in the effective administration of justice.

d. Record. A verbatim record shall be made of all plea proceedings occurring in a court of record.

Rule 17.2   Duty of court to advise defendant of his rights and of the consequences of pleading guilty or no contest.

Before accepting plea of guilty or no contest, the court shall address the defendant personally in open court, informing him of and determining that he understands the following:

a. The nature of the charge to which the plea is offered.

b. The nature and range of possible sentence for the offense to which the plea is offered, including any special conditions regarding sentence, parole, or commutation imposed by stature.

c. The constitutional rights which he forgoes by pleading guilty or no contest, including his right to counsel if he is not represented by counsel.

d. His right to plead not guilty.

Rule 17.3   Duty of court to determine voluntariness and intelligence of the plea.

Before accepting a plea of guilty or no contest, the court shall address the defendant personally in open court and determine that he wishes to forego the constitutional rights of which he has been advised, that his plea is voluntary and not the result of force, threats or promises (other than a plea agreement) and that there is a factual basis for the plea.

Rule 17.4   Plea negotiations and agreements.

a. Plea Negotiations. The parties may negotiate concerning, and reach an agreement on, any aspect of the deposition of the case. The court shall not participate in any such negotiations.

b. Plea Agreement. The term of a plea agreement shall be reduced to writing and signed by the defendant, his counsel, if any, and the prosecutor. An agreement may be revoked by any party prior to its acceptance by the court.

c. Determining the Accuracy of the Agreement and the Voluntariness and Intelligence of the Plea. The parties shall file the agreement with the court, which shall address the defendant personally and determine that he understands and agrees to its terms, that the written document contains all the terms of the agreement, and that the plea is entered in conformance with Rules 17.2 and 17.3.

d. Acceptance of Plea. After making such determinations, the court shall either accept or reject the tendered negotiated plea. The court shall not be bound by any provision in the plea agreement regarding the sentence or the term and conditions of probation to be imposed, if, after accepting the agreement and reviewing a presentence report, it rejects the provision as inappropriate.

e. Rejection of Plea. If an agreement or any provision thereof is rejected by the court, it shall give the defendant an opportunity to withdraw his plea, advising him that if he permits his plea to stand, the disposition of the case may be less favorable to him than that contemplated by the agreement.

f. Disclosure and Confidentiality. When a plea agreement or any term thereof is accepted, the agreement or such term shall become part of the record. However, if no agreement is reached, or if the agreement is revoked, rejected by the court, or withdrawn or if the judgment is later vacated or reversed, neither the plea discussion nor any resulting agreement, plea or judgment, nor statement made at a hearing on the plea, shall be admissible against the defendant in any criminal or civil action or administrative proceeding.

g. Automatic Change of Judge. If a plea is withdrawn after submission of the presentence report, the judge, upon request of the defendant, shall disqualify himself, but no additional disqualification of the judges under this rule shall be permitted.

Rule 17.6   Admission of a prior conviction

Whenever a prior conviction is an element of the crime charged, an admission thereto by the defendant shall be accepted only under the procedures of this rule, unless admitted by the defendant while testifying on the stand.

Appendix D

•———•

Plea Agreement

IN THE SUPERIOR COURT OF THE STATE OF ARIZONA
IN AND FOR THE COUNTY OF PIMA

The <u>1st</u> day of <u>September</u>, 19<u>78</u>.

THE STATE OF ARIZONA,   )
)
          Plaintiff,   )
)   No. _____
   vs.   )
)
_____ ,   )
)   PLEA AGREEMENT
          Defendant.   )
_____   )

The State of Arizona and the defendant hereby agree to the following disposition of this case:

Plea: The defendant, _____, agrees
      to plead _____ <u>guilty</u> _____ to the charge of:

On or about the 9th day of June, 1978,   did unlawfully possess a narcotic drug, to wit: heroin, all in violation of A.R.S. §§ 36-1002 and 36-1002.10.

Terms: On the following understanding, terms and conditions:

1. The statutory range and special conditions regarding sentence, parole, and commutation imposed by statute are:

Two to ten years in Arizona State Prison and/or $50,000 fine.

2. That the following charges are dismissed, or if not yet filed, shall not be brought against the defendant.

Dismissal of allegation of prior conviction. (A-00000)

3. That this agreement, unless rejected or withdrawn, serves to amend the complaint, indictment, or information to charge the offense to which the defendant pleads, without the filing of any additional pleading. If, after accepting the plea, the Court concludes that any of the terms or provisions of this agreement are unacceptable, both parties shall be given the opportunity to withdraw from this agreement, or the Court can reject the agreement. If the plea is rejected or withdrawn, the original charges are automatically reinstated.

4. If the defendant is charged with a felony, that he hereby gives up his right to a preliminary hearing or other probable cause determination on the charges to which he pleads. In the event the Court rejects the plea, or the defendant withdraws the plea, the defendant hereby gives up his right to a preliminary hearing or other probable cause determination on the original charges.

5. That unless the plea is rejected or withdrawn, the defendant hereby gives up any and all motions, defenses, objections, appeals, or requests he has made or raised, or could assert hereafter, to or against the Court's entry of judgment and imposition of sentence upon him consistent with this agreement.

6. That the defendant understands the following rights and understands that he gives up such rights by pleading guilty :

a. his right to a jury trial;

b. his right to confront the witnesses against him and cross-examine them;

c. his right to present evidence and call witnesses in his defense, knowing that the State will compel witnesses to appear and testify;

d. his right to be represented by counsel (appointed free of charge, if he cannot afford to hire his own) at trial of the proceedings, and

e. his right to remain silent, to refuse to be a witness against himself, and to be presumed innocent until proven guilty beyond a reasonable doubt.

7. In the event that defendant appeals the judgment and/or sentence in this matter, the State is relieved of the obligations previously enumerated under subdivision 2 of this agreement dealing with the dismissal of pending charges and other charges not yet filed. Such pending charges dismissed as a result of this agreement shall be reinstated at the request of the State and the State shall be free to file any charges not yet filed as of the date of this agreement.

8. That this written plea agreement contains all the terms and conditions of this plea agreement; and the defendant understands that any promises made by anyone, including his lawyer, that are not contained within this written plea agreement, are without force and effect, and are null and void. Any prediction or promise as to what the possible sentence will be is understood to be voided by this Agreement.

9. That I, _____, am not on or under the influence of any drug, medication, liquor or other intoxicant, and that I, _____, am at this time fully capable of understanding the terms and conditions of this plea agreement.

I, _____, have read this agreement with the assistance of counsel, understand its terms, understand the rights I give up by pleading guilty in this matter, and agree to be bound according to the provisions herein. I fully understand that if, as part of this plea bargain, I am granted probation by the Court, the terms and conditions thereof are subject to modification at any time during the period of probation in the event that I violate any written condition of my probation.

_____   _____
Date   Defendant

I have discussed this case with my client in detail and advised him of his constitutional rights and all possible defenses. I believe my client understands this plea agreement including the range of sentence he faces and the constitutional rights he gives up by entering into this agreement. I believe that the plea and disposition set forth herein are appropriate under the facts of this case. I concur in the entry of the plea as indicated above and on the terms and conditions set forth herein.

_____   _____
        Date   Defendant's Counsel

I have reviewed this matter and concur that the plea and disposition set forth herein are appropriate and are in the interests of justice.

                                             STEPHEN D. NEELY
                                             PIMA COUNTY ATTORNEY

_____   _____
        Date   Deputy County Attorney

CA-53   5/78

Appendix E

•———•

Transcription Notations

Transcription notations were developed by students of spoken discourse to deal with the ways in which speech differs from written language. Over the last several decades, notational systems for dealing with speech have proliferated, and some are much more fine-grained than others in the way they capture properties of the voice. My notations are for the most part quite basic and indicate some of the most common features of speech represented in transcriptions. Most of these features are not in fact the focus of analysis in this book but will enable students of language to compare the discourse dealt with here with other kinds of discourse analyzed elsewhere. They will also enable others who do not study language to get a sense of how spoken language differs from written language. The highly routinized courtroom discourse I analyze in this book differs from conversation and from less routinized courtroom trials in several ways to which I direct attention in the following discussion of my notations.

Basic Notations

Fundamentals

Speaker overlaps   Where two speakers are speaking at the same time, that speech is set off by left-to-right slashes in the speech of both speakers: /   /. Where possible the two speakers' speech has been vertically aligned:

> Judge: *I'm sorry. Three/weeks/?*
>
> Defense Lawyer: */At least/*
>   *three weeks if not four*
>   *weeks.*

Inaudible or unclear speech   Parentheses are used to indicate speech that cannot be understood by the transcriber (   ). Where the transcriber is not entirely confident she has heard what is said, that speech is enclosed in such brackets (in this matter):

> Defendant: *I was gonna burn ('em and*
> *throw 'em away)* (   ).

Pauses and long silences   Where there are pauses in speech of two seconds or longer, they are indicated and enclosed in square brackets [4 secs]:

> Defense Lawyer: *I'm handing the court*
> *the original and two*
> *copies, one copy for*
> *each of the files in*
> *this case [45 secs].*
>
> Judge: *For the record, you*
> *are John T. Appleton?*

Change of plea discourse reveals many more long pauses than one usually sees in transcripts of other kinds of speech. These pauses often reflect the fact that the judge is constantly looking at the written record of the case and feeding or plugging in information in that written record into the spoken change of plea.

Explanations of activity in courtroom   Curly brackets {   } are used in a few places to describe nonverbal activity or speech that cannot be captured in the transcript by other notations:

> Defendant: *What's my past record got*
> *to do about this shit?*
> *{Can hear other voices in*
> *the background during this}*

However, I do not explain all the legal jargon that appears in the transcripts, and I explicate it in my prose discussion only when it is necessary for my analysis. After all, much that we hear in talk we do not understand because of lack of shared knowledge with other parties to our interactions.

Punctuation

Dashes   The dash - is used for several different purposes:

- To indicate where there is a very slight pause in the flow of a speaker's speech:

> Judge: *CR-00000. State of Arizona*
> *against Wilbur Southcutt, this*
> *is the time set for- change of*
> *plea hearing.*

These "hitches" are again more common in changes of plea than in many forms of discourse, because of the way the judges must constantly plug in written information into their speech and because they must constantly plan what to say next.

- To indicate where a speaker repairs his own speech—that is, starts to say one thing and then (maybe) says another, or repeats the same thing again, and to indicate where the trajectory of speech goes off in a new direction from what was begun.

> Judge: *And that you do agree to uh*
> *the cont- to what this*
> *agreement says you agree*
> *to.*

- To indicate where a speaker stops speaking but the intonation pattern is not utterance final. This happens most commonly when the speaker is interrupted by another's speech.

> Judge: *You were debating about*
> *whether to go ahead and-*
>
> Defendant: *Right.*

Dots   Dots are used in excerpts from transcripts in the body of the book to indicate where material has been excised. Three dots . . . indicate that the excision is midsentence. Four dots . . . . indicate that the excision is at the beginning or end of a sentence.

Nongrammatical "sentences"   When a speaker runs on intonationally past the end of what we typically think of as a sentence, or intonationally creates a complete unit that in writing would not be a sentence, such units are written as if they were sentences—that is, begun with capital letters and ended with periods or question marks.

> Judge: *And uh similar(ly)- that would*
> *be the- apparently uh relating*
> *to incidents uh occurring uh*
> *last- late last summer and fall,*
> *and then again uh as to the*
> *charge involving the*
> *prescription drug that uh uh you*
> *either obtained or attempted to*
> *obtain, in this case some Valium*
> *uh by means of some uh false*
> *representations or some scheme,*
> *in other words without a*
> *prescription.*
>
> Judge: *Has anyone uh used any force or*
> *made any threats against you?*
> *To get you to change your plea*
> *(in this matter).*
>
> Defendant: *They tried to call the medic,*
> *but the medical care, you know,*
> *at the annex (in) Pima County*
> *jail isn't up to par, so I*
> *waited from Friday night until*

*Sunday afternoon to get to see
the jailhouse doctor (at- at the
main jail) and when I saw him,
this Dr. Schatz, he's he's he
has my uh record of (all) the
time I've been in custody of-
of Pima County sheriff's
department.*

Commas   Commas in transcribed materials here cannot always be interpreted as indicating that the speaker has paused or intonationally indicated a grammatical unit of some kind. Commas are also used as they are in written speech—that is, by convention or to make it easier for the reader to understand how the words are supposed to be related to one another to make meaning. This does not mean, however, that all such written conventions are adhered to. In general, then, sentence boundary punctuation more reliably indicates intonational units than clause boundary punctuation.

Defendant: *He said, "Don't go to Project
Create for a week. Just stay in
your bunk (for awhile)."*

Defendant: *And uh I thought, well, rather
'n go see a doctor here, or go
out on (the) streets and buy
those drugs, you know, I'd just
go see if I could get it
refilled.*

Defense Lawyer: *None, Your Honor.*

Underlining   Underlining indicates that a word or words are louder than those around them—that is, for what we usually call emphasis.

Defendant: *I'm in twenty-four lockup
for eight weeks. I'm
entitled to <u>some</u> rights.*

Question marks   Question marks usually appear at the end of questions, but when the question does not end with a question intonation, a period is used instead.

Judge: *Has anyone used any force
or any threats to cause you
to enter /pleas/ of guilty
at this time.*

Defendant: */No./*

More commonly, statements produced with a question intonation are ended with a question mark:

Judge: *That's your true name, Mr.
Appleton?*

> Judge: *You have a ten dollar money*
> *order which you changed to a*
> *hundred dollars or something*
> *like that?*

Capitalization

Capital letters are used as in general written communication to begin sentences and turns at talk. Where there is overlap between speakers, the first speaker's turn sometimes continues after as well as during the second speaker's overlap, and where that continuation looks like a second turn for the first speaker, the first word of that turn is not capitalized to indicate it is a continuation:

> Judge: *You did sign this agreement /uh,*
> *opposite/*
> Defendant: */Yes, sir/*
> Judge: *today's date on the back.*

Names, places, and dates are also capitalized conventionally, but some words that are capitalized in legal writing are not capitalized in transcript material (e.g., Court, Third Degree, State).

Spelling

Words commonly conspicuously contracted or run together are given unconventional spelling, for example, "didja" instead of "did you," "gonna" instead of "going to," and "th'offense," which makes "the offense" two syllables instead of three.

Speaker Identities

By Legal Roles

Speakers are identified by their legal roles in the change of plea: Judge, County Attorney, Defense Lawyer, and Defendant. When it is not possible to distinguish between the County Attorney and the Defense Lawyer, Lawyer is used. When the speaker cannot be identified, Speaker is used. When the transcriber is not certain of the identity, a question mark (?) follows.

Strategies for Preservation of Anonymity of the Participants

- All personal names in the transcripts were changed. Whenever possible, name similarity, in number of syllables and ethnicity, was created.
- Case numbers and other individual-identifying numbers were replaced by zeros (e.g. Case number CR-00000).

Guides to Legal Structure of Procedure in Appendix F

Subheadings

Subheadings in the transcripts in Appendix F, such as "Conditions of Plea Agreement" and "Constitutional Rights," indicate what written legal requirements are being met in different discourse segments of the change of plea and are discussed in detail in the body of the book.

Italicizing

Sections in italics indicate where the legal procedure is being collaboratively legally repaired by the judge and others, usually the lawyers. They can be thought of as side sequences that both depart from and yet are necessary for the legal validity of the sequential structure of the plea.

Appendix F

·———·

Four Changes of Plea / Guilty Plea Transcripts

Judge 8:   Robbery

1	*Opening*	
2	Judge:	Fine. [2 secs] A-00000, State
3		versus Denise Gonzalez.
4	Speaker:	( ).
5	Defense Lawyer:	Your Honor, Ed Martin, on
6		behalf of Miss Gonzalez. We are
7		here on a plea agreement which
8		is ent- been entered into by
9		Miss Gonzalez, uh Mr. Benton,
10		and myself. And we have, she
11		has signed and uh read the plea
12		agreement and has signed it. I
13		present that to the court now.
14	*Social Background Questions*	
15	Judge:	Thank you, Mr. Martin. [10
16		secs] For the record, you are
17		Denise Marie Gonzalez?
18	Defendant:	Yes, sir.
19	Judge:	How old are you? They call you
20		Neese? How old are you?
21	Defendant:	Eighteen.
22	Judge:	Where do you live?
23	Defendant:	One oh seven ( ) (Hart).
24	Judge:	How long have you lived in
25		Tucson, Neese?

26	Defendant:	Eighteen years.
27	Judge:	What education have you had? [4
28		secs] 'S how much edu-schooling
29		have you had?
30	Defendant:	Uhm [2 secs] Seven. [2 secs]
31	Judge:	Uhm do you read and understand
32		English?
33	Defendant:	Yes, sir.

34 *Plea Agreement Comprehension Questions*

35	Judge:	Did you read this agreement that
36		Mr. Martin just handed me over
37		carefully?
38	Defendant:	Yes, sir.
39	Judge:	Uhm I assume that you did
40		because your signature appears
41		on the back page opposite
42		today's date. Did you in fact
43		sign this agreement?
44	Defendant:	Yes, sir.
45	Judge:	And you did read it over before
46		you signed it?
47	Defendant:	Yes, sir.
48	Judge:	Do you understand what this
49		agreement says?
50	Defendant:	Yes, sir.
51	Judge:	Is there anything in here that
52		you don't agree to?
53	Defendant:	No, sir.

54 *Nature of Charge*

55	Judge:	If I understand it right, uh
56		Neese, you propose to enter a
57		plea of guilty to the charge of
58		robbery, uh is that your
59		understanding?
60	Defendant:	Yes, sir.

61 *Conditions of Plea Agreement and Sentencing*
62 *Possibilities*

63	Judge:	And in exchange for that uh
64		plea, the state is going to uh
65		uh dismiss the charge that's
66		presently against you, which is
67		armed robbery.
68	Defendant:	Yes, /sir/.
69	Judge:	/You/ understand that? Do
70		you realize that if I accept
71		this plea that uh you face uh
72		possible uh imprisonment-

73	*Repair*	
74	Defense Lawyer:	*Your Honor, may I interrupt*
75		*here, this plea agreement is*
76		*also posited upon the fact that*
77		*Miss Gonzalez will receive*
78		*probation.*
79	Judge:	*Uhm* [4 secs] *Assuming that you*
80		*received a probated sentence,*
81		*and then violated the probation,*
82		*it's a maximum of five years.*
83	Defense Lawyer:	*No, it's a minimum of five, (I*
84		*think) it's /five years/.*
85	Judge:	/Minimum of/ five.
86	Defense Lawyer:	*It's not a hard five. This /is*
87		( )/-*
88	Judge:	/Five to/ life? I can't
89		remember the /sen/ tence.
90	Defense Lawyer:	/Yes/.

91	Judge:	All right. [2 secs] Uh- Neese-
92		the possible punishment, I
93		understand that you've agreed
94		to uh a plea that stipulates
95		that you'll receive probation,
96		is that your understanding?
97	Defendant:	Yes, sir.
98	Judge:	But I want you to understand
99		that- uh if I go- first of all,
100		that provision isn't binding on
101		me. If I decided after I were
102		to receive uh probation report
103		that uh I couldn't go along
104		with it, then I would permit you
105		to withdraw your plea. Uh you
106		understand that? Assume that I
107		decide I can go along with it,
108		uh noting right off the bat
109		your age, uh and did put you on
110		probation, there would be a
111		number of terms and conditions
112		attached to your probation, uh
113		first of all, obviously, that
114		you're violating the law. 'N
115		there might be others that I
116		don't know anything about cause
117		I don't know anything about you.
118		Uh if you were to violate that
119		probation, <u>then</u> your probation
120		could be revoked, and you could
121		then be sent to prison. You
122		understand that?

123	Defendant:	Yes, sir.
124	Judge:	And if you were sent to prison,
125		uh the term would be uh five
126		years uh at a minimum. And how
127		much of that five years you'd
128		have to serve, I- uh minimum, I
129		can't really tell you now. But
130		it could be a substantial
131		period of time, now are you
132		aware of that? [2 secs] Did
133		Mr. Martin discuss that with
134		you?
135	Defendant:	Yes, sir. [4 secs]
136	Judge:	So in effect, you- I take it
137		your understanding and entering
138		into this plea agreement is that
139		you will receive probation and
140		you expect to abide by the terms
141		and conditions of probation that
142		the court would impose. Is
143		that right?
144	Defendant:	Yes, sir.
145	*Constitutional Rights*	
146	Judge:	Do you understand, Neese, that
147		you don't have to do this? You
148		have a right to go to trial on
149		the charges that are presently
150		ag- against you? [2 secs]
151	Defendant:	Ye/s sir/.
152	Judge:	/Uh/ and that if the state
153		failed to prove its case against
154		you at trial, uh that uh the
155		jury would be required to return
156		a verdict of not guilty?
157	Defendant:	Yes, sir.
158	Judge:	You understand there won't be
159		any trial if I accept this
160		plea?
161	Defendant:	Yes, sir.
162	Judge:	Uhm it says on page two and I
163		need to be sure for the record
164		that you understand all of the
165		rights that you're giving up,
166		uh'n what I was just uh
167		referring to uh specifically is
168		that you have a right to a jury
169		trial in this matter. Do you
170		know that?
171	Defendant:	Yes, sir.

172	Judge:	Do you understand that if you
173		can't afford a lawyer that the
174		court will appoint a lawyer to
175		defend you and to represent you,
176		uh both before the trial and at
177		trial?
178	Defendant:	Yes, sir.
179	Judge:	And do you realize that you have
180		the right to face uh cross-
181		examine, and confront the
182		witnesses that the state would
183		have to call to prove your guilt
184		in this matter?
185	Defendant:	Yes, sir.
186	Judge:	Uhm you would have the right to
187		present witnesses and evidence
188		in your defense, and to compel
189		the attendance of witnesses uh
190		if they wouldn't agree to appear
191		voluntarily?
192	Defendant:	Yes, sir.
193	Judge:	You have the right to have the
194		court tell the jury- instruct
195		the jury that uh you are to be
196		presumed innocent and that the
197		presumption of innocence uh
198		stays with you at all stages of
199		the trial uh until uh a jury
200		was satisfied under the law that
201		the state had borne the burden
202		which it has of proving your
203		guilt beyond a reasonable doubt.
204		Do you understand that?
205	Defendant:	Yes, sir.
206	Judge:	I believe uh that you'd be
207		entitled to a twelve-person
208		jury, and that each member of
209		the jury individually would have
210		to be satisfied that the state
211		had borne the burden of proving
212		your guilt beyond a reasonable
213		doubt. Do you realize that?
214	Defendant:	Yes, sir.
215	Judge:	And you could either remain
216		silent and rely on the
217		presumption of innocence and not
218		take the risk of incriminating
219		yourself, or you could choose to
220		testify in your defense if you
221		wished. That's an option that

222		you won't have either if I
223		accept this plea. Do you
224		realize that?
225	Defendant:	Yes, sir.
226	Judge:	Do you fully understand that the
227		reason you're giving up all
228		those rights if I accept this
229		plea is that that will end the
230		question of your your guilt or
231		uh- non-guilt, and there won't
232		be any trial, and then the
233		question uh is uh is the
234		sentence. That's all that's
235		left. Do you understand that?
236	Defendant:	Yes, sir.
237	Judge:	Okay. After all that, is it still
238		your desire that I accept this
239		plea?
240	Defendant:	Yes, sir. [11 secs]

241	*Repair of Condition of Plea Agreement*	
242	Judge:	*What attached notice uh is*
243		*/referred to ( )/?*
244	Defense Lawyer:	*/Your Honor, if there's/ a*
245		*notice in the file, we've filed*
246		*this case ( ) before you was*
247		*involving the juvenile /( )*
248		*presided over/.*
249	Judge:	*/Oh, yes, yes, yes, yes/ yes, yes.*
250		*[17 secs] All right, I d- I*
251		*thought I had remembered this*
252		*case. All right, do you*
253		*understand that as a part of*
254		*this agreement uh you must*
255		*testify truthfully uh if there*
256		*is uh a trial or an*
257		*adjudication proceeding*
258		*involving Johnny (Luna)?*
259	Defendant:	*Yes, sir.*
260	Judge:	*And that if you fail to uh uhm*
261		*to do that, that uh this*
262		*agreement isn't gonna be*
263		*binding on the state. You*
264		*understand that?*
265	Defendent:	*Yes, sir.*
266	Defense Lawyer:	*Your Honor, I think the record*
267		*should indicate that she has*
268		*already done that.*
269	Judge:	*Oh, you have. /All right/.*

270	Judge:	*/Yes, Your*
271		*Honor/.*
272	Judge:	*Is there any question in the*
273		*state's mind that uh uh*
274		*/defendant has/-*
275	County Attorney:	*/No, your Hon/or. That ( )*
276		*piece has been taken care of.*
277		*[2 secs]*
278	Judge:	*Alright. As I understand it,*
279		*Neese, in effect you've been*
280		*promised probation, in exchange*
281		*for your plea in this matter.*
282		*But, I think now you understand*
283		*that even if you get probation,*
284		*uhm that if you violate it you*
285		*could still go to prison. Now*
286		*you understand that?*
287	Defendant:	*Yes, sir.*

288	*Coercion Questions*	
289	Judge:	Did anybody else- did anybody
290		make any other promises than
291		just that to you?
292	Defendant:	No, /sir/.
293	Judge:	/In/ exchange for your plea?
294		Did anybody use any force
295		against you, or make any threats
296		against you
297	Defendant:	/No, sir/.
298	Judge:	/to get/ you to change your
299		plea? I have to be satisfied
300		that this is something you're
301		doing voluntarily. Uh is it?
302	Defendant:	Yes, sir?
303	Judge:	Have you discussed it fully and
304		carefully with Mr. Martin?
305	Defendant:	Yes, sir.
306	Judge:	D' you think he's giving you
307		good advice?
308	Defendant:	Yes, sir.
309	Judge:	You satisfied with his
310		representation?
311	Defendant:	Yes, sir.

312	*Factual Basis*	
313	Judge:	OK. Tell me what happened on
314		June sixth, 1978, I seem to
315		remember a little bit from a

316		juvenile proceeding, but uh I
317		wanna hear it from you.
318	Defendant:	Well, we went to my friend's
319		house and uh he told me to uhm
320		go down to uh Mantigo's, so I
321		went and he told me to wait for
322		him (uh) a couple of blocks
323		down, so I waited for him. And
324		I drove him around for awhile,
325		and waited for him, then he
326		came.
327	Judge:	Y- you knew he was gonna rob the
328		place?
329	Defendant:	Yes, sir.
330	Judge:	And you were gonna help him get
331		away?
332	Defendant:	Yes, sir.
333	Judge:	(All right). [2 secs] I'm
334		satisfied both because of the
335		defendant's statements and what
336		I recall of the juvenile matter
337		that there is a factual basis.
338	*Invitation to Repair*	
339	Judge:	Do either of you have a problem
340		with the record?
341	Defense Lawyer:	No, Your Honor, I don't.
342	County Attorney:	No, Your Honor.
343	*Findings*	
344	Judge:	Based on the record, the court
345		finds that there has been an
346		intelligent, voluntary,
347		understanding uh entry of a
348		plea by the defendant of guilty
349		to the charge of robbery,
350		committed on or about June
351		sixth, 1978, in violation of ARS
352		13-641 and 13-643 A, as amended.
353		That there is a factual basis
354		for the plea, and the plea is
355		accepted and entered in the
356		record.
357	*Closing*	
358	Defense Lawyer:	Your Honor, may we waive time
359		for sentencing, because uh Miss
360		Gonzalez's presently working.
361		She has to take time off from

362		work. Uh- the stipulated
363		sentence has been agreed to.
364		Uh- the state is familiar with
365		who she is, there's no previous
366		background of criminal record,
367		uh- she's eighteen years old,
368		the mother of a child. She
369		needs to work /and/-
370	Judge:	/Mr./ Martin, I
371		have no question in my mind,
372		cause it's come back to me a
373		little bit that I'm gonna go
374		along with that provision, but I
375		think there is uh uh definite
376		benefit for the defendant in
377		going through the pre-sentence
378		process, as well as uh
379		furnishing the court with
380		information I don't know what
381		particular terms and conditions
382		uh uhm I might wish to impose
383		uh I have no reason to believe
384		that there'd be any ones in
385		particular, but of course the
386		probation office has uh a lot
387		of discretion about that.
388	Defense Lawyer:	Fine.
389	Judge:	And I think at this point I'm
390		gonna order that a pre-sentence
391		investigation and report be
392		made. What uh what hours do
393		you work, Neese?
394	Defendant:	Uhm from eight to two-thirty.
395	Judge:	All right, if I were to uh provide
396		this time for sentencing at four
397		o'clock in the afternoon, uh uh
398		is there any reason you can't-
399		that's going to inconvenience
400		you?
401	Defendant:	No, sir.
402	Judge:	All right. It's ordered that uh
403		a pre-sentence investigation and
404		report be made by the adult
405		probation office of the court.
406		That uh sentencing in this
407		matter [2 secs] uh be Friday,
408		September twenty-ninth at four
409		P.M. Have to- rearrange your
410		weekend plans, Mr. Martin.

411	Defense Lawyer:	Your Honor, I'm always there.
412	Judge:	In division 0000. That's four
413		o'clock in the afternoon,
414		Neese. I want you to cooperate
415		with the adult probation office
416		in the making of that report.
417	Defendant:	Okay.
418	Judge:	Uhm it's to both your advantage
419		and to mine that they get
420		accurate information. I must
421		advise you if you don't appear
422		on uh uh [2 secs] September
423		twenty-ninth at four o'clock,
424		that uh I might very well vacate
425		this plea agreement and issue a
426		bench warrant for your arrest.
427		Do you understand that?
428	Defendant:	Yes, sir.
429	Judge:	Okay. Conditions of release
430		remain in effect.
431	Defense Lawyer:	Thank you. I'll take over, Your
432		Honor. [3 secs]
433	County Attorney:	May we be excused, Your Honor?

Judge 8:   Prescription Falsification

1	*Opening*	
2	Judge:	A-00000, A-00000, and A-00000.
3		State versus John T. Appleton,
4		aka Jack Appleton.
5	County Attorney:	( ) appearing for the state.
6	Defense Lawyer:	Dan ( ) from the public
7		defender's office appearing for
8		Mr. Appleton. Your Honor, we
9		have reached a plea agreement in
10		the case. I'm handing the court
11		the original and two copies, one
12		copy for each of the files, in
13		this case [45 secs].
14	Judge:	For the record, you are John T.
15		Appleton? That's your true
16		name, Mr. Appleton? I need you
17		to answer audibly.
18	Defendant:	Yes, I am Mr. Appleton.
19	*Nature of the Charge*	
20	Judge:	Uh Mr. Ripkin's handed me uh an
21		original and two copies of the

22		plea agreement which I take it
23		uh is to affect all three
24		cases. And if I understand it
25		correctly you propose to plead
26		guilty to two separate charges-
27		one charge being a violation-
28		well, being that you uh obtained
29		property uh by means of a false
30		or fraudulent uh pretense. [4
31		secs] Uh and the second one
32		being that uh you ob- obtained
33		or attempted to obtain a
34		prescription drug, to wit,
35		Valium, by fraud, deceit, or
36		misrepresentation. Uh that
37		would also be a felony. Is that
38		your understanding of what you
39		propose to /plead guilty to/?
40	Defendant:	/Yes, sir/.

41 *Conditions of Plea Agreement*

42	Judge:	And do I understand that in
43		exchange for this plea that uh
44		all charges uh in each of these
45		files on which uh uh a
46		determination of guilt is not
47		made will be dismissed. Is that
48		right?
49	Defense Lawyer:	Correct.

50 *Plea Agreement Comprehension Questions*

51	Judge:	You did sign this agreement /uh,
52		opposite/
53	Defendant:	/Yes, sir/
54	Judge:	today's date on the back. Did
55		you read it over carefully
56		before you signed it, Mr.
57		Appleton?
58	Defendant:	Yes, sir.

59 *Social Background Questions*

60	Judge:	Uh how old are you?
61	Defendant:	Thirty-four.
62	Judge:	Where do you live? Where is
63		your home?
64	Defendant:	Uh my hometown is ( ).
65		That's where my wife and family
66		[2 secs] /are right now./
67	Judge:	/All right./ How long
68		have you been in Tucson?

69	Defendant:	Totally, about one year, but
70		just before last Christmas, we
71		moved back to ( ).
72	Judge:	Uh these incidents uh
73		apparently relate to- Well, one
74		of them relates to an incident
75		that occurred last August of
76		seventy-seven, and the second
77		one uh ( ) prescription drug
78		charge to uh an incident on
79		July eighteenth, 1977. Were you in
80		Tucson at that time?
81	Defendant:	Right. That's from uh December
82		of last year almost the whole
83		year I lived in Tucson. I
84		worked for (that company).
85	Judge:	What kind of work (do) you do?
86	Defendant:	Uh (that's the) supervisor,
87		clerk. (Ordinarily I was) a
88		clerk and became a supervisor.
89	Judge:	/Uh what/-
90	Defendant:	/Most of/ my jobs have been
91		administrative type things.
92	Judge:	Where, specifically, were you
93		working here in Tucson?
94	Defendant:	For U-Totem stores. [2 secs]
95	Judge:	Uh you do read and understand
96		the English language.
97	Defendant:	Yes, I do.
98	Judge:	How much education have you had,
99		Mr. Appleton?
100	Defendant:	Two years ( ).

101	*Repair of Plea Agreement Comprehension Questions*	
102	Judge:	*Even though uh you tell me that*
103		*you have read this agreement*
104		*over carefully and believe that*
105		*you understand it uh there are*
106		*some things that uh I must for*
107		*the record be certain that you*
108		*do understand. Uh but*
109		*preliminarily uh from what*
110		*you've said I am assuming that*
111		*this agreement does not contain*
112		*anything that you did not agree*
113		*to. Is that correct?*
114	Defendant:	*That's correct.*
115	Judge:	*And that you do agree to uh*
116		*the cont- to what this agreement*
117		*says you agree to.*
118	Defendant:	*Yes, I do.*

119	*Constitutional Rights*	
120	Judge:	All right. Specifically, you do
121		not have to enter into this
122		agreement at all uh and if you
123		<u>do</u> enter into it, you give up
124		certain valuable constitutional
125		rights. Uh as matters now
126		stand, you have uh entered pleas
127		of not guilty in each of these
128		three files, and you have an
129		absolute right to uh a jury
130		trial in each of the files and
131		(on) each of the charges in
132		those files. Do you understand
133		that?
134	Defendant:	Yes, I do.
135	Judge:	Uh at any such trial you'd have
136		the right to the assistance of a
137		court-appointed attorney if you
138		could not afford uh a lawyer to
139		represent you, and of course
140		that assistance would be
141		available to you uh at pretrial
142		proceedings as well as a trial.
143		(You) give that right up. (Do
144		you) understand that? You'd
145		also have the right to uh face
146		and confront and to cross-
147		examine the witnesses that the
148		state would have to call to
149		prove your guilt. That right
150		would be lost to you as well.
151		(Do) you understand that?
152	Defendant:	Yes, I do.
153	Judge:	Uh you'd have the right to
154		compel the attendance of
155		witnesses in your defense, if
156		uh they would not appear
157		voluntarily. (You) understand
158		that?
159	Defendant:	Yes, sir.
160	Judge:	You'd have the right to have the
161		court instruct the jury uh that
162		you are to be presumed innocent
163		until the state had borne the
164		burden which it has of proving
165		your guilt beyond a reasonable
166		doubt. Are you aware of that?
167	Defendant:	Yes, sir.
168	Judge:	Uh you also have the right, of
169		course, not to incriminate

170		yourself. You could either take
171		the stand and testify yourself
172		or uh remain silent and rely on
173		the presumption of innocence uh.
174		That's a decision that you would
175		make uh together with your
176		lawyer. And that right you
177		would also give up. You
178		understand that?
179	Defendant:	Yes, sir.
180	Judge:	In other words uh you give up
181		all those rights because there
182		isn't gonna be a trial if I
183		accept these pleas uh this plea
184		uh. That will dispose of the
185		issue of your uh your guilt uh
186		and the state's ability to
187		prove your guilt. And all that
188		would remain then would be uh
189		for me to decide what
190		disposition to make (of that).
191		You understand that?
192	Defendant:	Yes, sir. [3 secs]
193	*Coercion Questions*	
194	Judge:	Have you discussed this matter
195		carefully with Mr. Ripkin?
196	Defendant:	Yes, sir.
197	Judge:	Do you feel that he's given you
198		good advice?
199	Defendant:	Yes, sir.
200	Judge:	Are you satisfied with his
201		representation to this point?
202	Defendant:	Yes, sir.
203	Judge:	Has anyone uh used any force or
204		made any threats against you?
ˋ205		To get you to change your plea
206		(in this matter).
207	Defendant:	No, sir.
208	Judge:	Uh has anyone made any promises
209		uh of benefit or reward uh in
210		some fashion to get you to
211		change your plea?
212	Defendant:	No, sir.
213	Judge:	( ) That being the case,
214		then, I uh uh must assume that
215		your willingness to plead guilty
216		is uh something that you're
217		doing voluntarily and uh after
218		thinking about it, exercising

219		your free will. Is that
220		correct?
221	Defendant:	Yes, sir.

222 *Repair/Repeat of Nature of the Charges*

223	Judge:	*Are you aware of the nature of*
224		*the charges that you're pleading*
225		*guilty to, Mr. Appleton? With*
226		*respect to the first charge uh*
227		*uh the state would have to prove*
228		*that you uh uh attempted to*
229		*obtain from the U-Totem markets*
230		*uh things of value,*
231		*specifically money orders uh as*
232		*a result of some fraudulent*
233		*scheme or trick or artifice uh*
234		*uh representations or promises,*
235		*which of course is against the*
236		*law. (Now) uh do you understand*
237		*that to be the charge you're*
238		*pleading guilty to?*
239	Defendant:	*(Yes, Your Honor).*
240	Judge:	*And uh similar(ly)- that would*
241		*be the- apparently uh relating*
242		*to incidents uh occurring uh*
243		*last- late last summer and fall,*
244		*and then again uh as to the*
245		*charge involving the*
246		*prescription drug that uh uh you*
247		*either obtained or attempted to*
248		*obtain, in this case some*
249		*Valium uh by means of some uh*
250		*false representations or some*
251		*scheme, in other words without*
252		*a prescription. Do you*
253		*understand that that's what*
254		*you're pleading guilty to? Do*
255		*you realize that regardless of*
256		*what disposition uh the court*
257		*might make in this matter that*
258		*uh your record is going to show*
259		*two felony convictions uh in*
260		*this matter?*
261	Defendant:	*Yes, sir.*

262 *Sentencing Possibilities*

263	Judge:	Uh it is possible that you could
264		be placed on probation uh as a
265		result of uh (your) conviction
266		in this matter if I accept the

267		plea. Um but if that were to
268		be the case- I'm not saying that
269		that is, but if that were to be
270		the case, uh (you'd) have a
271		number of terms and conditions
272		of probation that you'd have to
273		observe and if uh you were to
274		violate those terms and it were
275		brought to my attention, and
276		shown to my satisfaction, <u>then</u>
277		your probation could be revoked
278		and you could be uh uh
279		imprisoned and subject to the
280		same sanctions uh you (are)
281		subject to if I accept these
282		pleas. Do you understand that?
283	Defendant:	Yes, sir.
284	Judge:	With respect to those sanctions,
285		uh the uh charge of obtaining
286		property by uh uh scheme or
287		artifice or fraudulent uh
288		preten- tenses is punishable by
289		imprisonment in the state prison
290		for uh not more than twenty
291		years uh or by a fine of uh up
292		to twenty thousand dollars or
293		both. Now do you understand
294		that?
295	Defendant:	Yes, sir.
296	Judge:	You're aware of that? And the
297		second charge, uh the uh
298		prescription drug charge is also
299		punishable by imprisonment in
300		the state prison for up to three
301		years or a fine of up to ten
302		thousand dollars or both. Did
303		you understand <u>that</u>?
304	Defendant:	Yes, sir.
305	Judge:	After we've gone through all
306		that, is it still your desire to
307		enter pleas of guilty to those
308		two charges?
309	Defendant:	Yes, sir.
310	*Repair of Sentencing Possibilities*	
311	Judge:	*Tell me what happened uh with*
312		*respect to- well, one other*
313		*thing- Are you presently on*
314		*probation or parole, either here*
315		*or anywhere else?*

316	Defendant:	*No, sir. [5 sec]*
317	Judge:	*And uh you do understand that*
318		*with respect to the matter of*
319		*punishment, that's strictly up*
320		*to the court and if I accept*
321		*these pleas, it'll be up to me*
322		*and uh uh since I don't know*
323		*anything about you- ab- or*
324		*these cases uh I don't know what*
325		*the disposition (would) be,*
326		*therefore no one else knows*
327		*what it would be, so no one*
328		<u>*could*</u> *represent to you what*
329		*you'd receive. Do you*
330		*understand that?*
331	Defendant:	*Yes, sir.*

332	*Repair of Coercion Questions*	
333	Judge:	<u>*Did*</u> *anyone make any*
334		*representations to you as to*
335		*what the sentence or disposition*
336		*would be?*
337	Defendant:	*Did (who) sir?*
338	Judge:	*Did* <u>*anyone*</u> *make any*
339		*representations to you to get*
340		*you to change your plea uh uh as*
341		*to what the uh punishment would*
342		*be?*
343	Defendant:	*No, sir.*

344	*Factual Basis*	
345	Judge:	Okay. Tell me about the uh- the
346		first charge. Apparently
347		incidents occurring uh on or
348		about August twenty-fourth of
349		1977 and November twentieth,
350		1977, I take it with respect to
351		some American Express trav- uh
352		money orders. Is that correct?
353	Defendant:	Right. Yes, it is.
354	Judge:	Tell me about it.
355	Defendant:	What would you like to know
356		about it?
357	Judge:	Well, I need to know if in fact
358		you uh did commit the offense
359		that you /are pleading guilty
360		to/.
361	Defense Lawyer:	/( )/
362	Defendant:	( ).
363	Defense Lawyer:	What happened?

364	Defendant:	Okay uh I worked for U-Totem.
365		(N') I was a supervisor. And,
366		uh uh I had a few oh personal
367		problems, but (uh you know) I
368		hate to- say that's the reason
369		(why) I did what I did, but ( ).
370		Uh basically, what it it
371		involved was just falsifying
372		the uh amount of money (on the)
373		money orders and then I kept
374		them. I kept them ( ) period
375		of three or four or five months,
376		debating whether I should cash
377		them or not. But I had some- I
378		was having marital problems,
379		(and uh) drug problems (and
380		things).
381	Judge:	When you made those
382		falsifications, I take it you
383		ultimately did cash the uh?
384	Defendant:	I did uh I uh I believe I
385		cashed the first uh one just
386		before Christmas and uh in a
387		matter of ten days I cashed
388		nineteen.
389	Judge:	So over some period of time uh
390		last fall then, you <u>did</u> cash a
391		total of nineteen. Is that
392		right?
393	Defendant:	Yes.
394	Judge:	You obtained the money by means
395		of your having falsified uh
396		either the applications or the
397		money orders themselves. Is
398		that right?
399	Defendant:	I falsified the amounts ( ).
400	Judge:	Uh, how did you do that? ( )
401		You have a ten-dollar money
402		order which you changed to a
403		hundred dollars or something
404		like that?
405	Defendant:	(Well) unfortunately, U-Totem is
406		pretty lax (you know in) that
407		aspect of uh selling money
408		orders. They just require one
409		(um) slip, you know, one record.
410		When you get the money order,
411		there's just the top part that
412		you fill in. (Then you have
413		employees) watch em punch it,

414		and then the bottom slip that
415		they tear off goes in to the
416		company. And uh [5 secs]
417		actually a customer put the idea
418		into my head, because uh you can
419		just fill out the bottom slips,
420		send it into the company and
421		then fill the money order out,
422		uh stamp the machine for (you
423		know) a hundred dollars more,
424		twenty-five dollars more than
425		what the actual figure the
426		company has in their records.
427	Judge:	Okay, so you knew when you did
428		that though that uh you were in
429		fact uh uh gonna- defrauding the
430		American Express Company and U-
431		Totem ( ). You were gonna
432		get more money than uh you were
433		paying for the money order?
434	Defendant:	( ) Yeh, I knew it, uh yeh.
435		I knew.
436	Judge:	Did it occur to you at that time
437		that that was uh a violation of
438		law?
439	Defendant:	Oh, I was well aware that it was
440		a violation of the law. But uh
441		you know, it's- I held those
442		(money cards) for that period
443		of time although I was, you
444		know, somewhat uh broke and
445		stuff and could have used the
446		money (and taken the cash in the
447		till).
448	Judge:	You were debating about whether
449		to go ahead and-
450	Defendant:	Right. I was gonna um-
451		/I didn't/
452	Judge:	/negotiate/
453	Defendant:	even tell my wife about what
454		happened. I was gonna burn
455		('em and throw 'em away) ( ).
456	Judge:	Tell me about the uh incident
457		this summer, July eighteenth uh
458		involving apparently some
459		Valium. What happened there?
460	Defendant:	Well, I was at the annex (at
461		Project Create). I was
462		hardship, you know, and I'd go
463		out to (Project Create) and

464		work, counsel, and stuff. And
465		uh I'd spend my nights and
466		weekends at the annex as a
467		condition of third-party
468		release. While lifting weights
469		one night at the annex- it was a
470		Friday night- I hurt my back a
471		bit ( ) (recurrent) back
472		problems for fifteen or sixteen
473		years. And uh all they gave me
474		was aspirin and Tylenol and I
475		was- it was pretty- pretty bad
476		and (the head PO just said) to
477		go lay in the bunk for awhile or
478		something. They tried to call
479		the medic, but the medical care,
480		you know, at the annex (in) Pima
481		County jail isn't up to par, so
482		I waited from Friday night until
483		Sunday afternoon to get to see
484		the jailhouse doctor (at- at the
485		main jail) and when I saw him,
486		this Dr. Schatz, he's he's he
487		has my uh record of (all) the
488		time I've been in custody of-
489		of Pima County sheriff's
490		department. But he wanted uh-
491		he was gonna put me in traction.
492		He didn't do that. He gave me
493		a double doses of Tylenol with
494		uh codeine in it (or) Valiums.
495		He said, "Don't go to Project
496		Create for a week. Just stay in
497		your bunk (for a while)." That
498		wasn't real effective. I was
499		used to uh taking stronger
500		medication and stuff like that.
501		It helped somewhat. I
502		remembered I had an old
503		prescription from (General)
504		Pharmacy in Tucson. It was a
505		prescription I'd brought to
506		Tucson, or my doctor from
507		Wisconsin had sent out here,
508		with-
509	Judge:	Was that for Valium?
510	Defendant:	It was for Valium, and it had
511		three refills on it. (But uh)
512		I only filled it one time for
513		one hundred and twenty ten

514		milligram Valium. And uh I
515		thought, well, rather 'n go see
516		a doctor here, or go out on
517		(the) streets and buy those
518		drugs, you know, I'd just go see
519		if I could get it refilled. But
520		in the meantime uh the effect
521		of the codeine (happened). (It
522		was uh a little like) banging on
523		the head. I'd never- in all
524		honesty, I've taken- [2–3 secs]
525	Defense Lawyer:	(Just tell him about the
526		prescription [7 secs] That's
527		what he wants to find out.)
528	Defendant:	Oh, wow. Um okay. I wanted to
529		see if I could refill that
530		prescription. And it's uh- [2
531		secs] It was no longer the
532		statu- uh the time (limit had)
533		run (out).
534	Judge:	More than a year old?
535	Defendant:	More than a- well no- yeh, it
536		was. I guess it was about
537		fourteen months or so- fifteen
538		months. (So) basically that's
539		it.
540	Judge:	Didja actually as a result of
541		that uh obtain any Valium, or-
542		or simply attempt to and
543		/apparently uh/
544	Defendant:	/Just an attempt./
545	Judge:	the druggist uh uh must have
546		re- reported that attempt to the
547		authorities?
548	Defendant:	The druggist called back to
549		Wisconsin to see if uh- that
550		was if it could be refilled and
551		stuff and uh wasn't all ( ).
552		In the meantime uh [2 secs] I
553		uh called (Gerald's) Pharmacy
554		and impersonated someone from
555		the doctor's office.
556	Judge:	I see.
557	Defendant:	And the DPS came and, as a
558		result. /( )/
559	Judge:	When /you uh/ took that move,
560		I take it you knew that was
561		against the law.
562	Defendant:	Uh well now we can get into the
563		(huhnh huhnh).

564	Judge:	Well, does it surprise you that
565		that is a violation?
566	Defendant:	No, it doesn't surprise me that
567		it was a violation.
568	Judge:	I think there's a sufficient
569		factual basis uh gentlemen. Do
570		either of you have any problems?
571		[3 secs]
572	Defense Lawyer:	None, Your Honor.
573	Judge:	Anything you want to ask uh Mr.
574		Ripkin uh privately perhaps,
575		before (I) accept uh these
576		pleas?
577	Defendant(?):	No.
578	*Findings*	
579	Judge:	Based on the record the court
580		finds that there has been uh an
581		intelligent, uh understanding,
582		(and) voluntary change of plea
583		and the pleas of guilty to the
584		charges of obtaining property
585		by uh fraudulent scheme or
586		artifice uh between August twenty-fourth,
587		1977 and November twentieth, 1977,
588		violation of ARS 13-320.01.
589		Uh that plea is accepted and the
590		plea of guilty to the charge of
591		of obtaining or attempting to
592		obtain prescription drug uh
593		(on) or about July (eighteenth), 1977,
594		in violation of ARS 32-1971
595		and 32–1996 A, uh is also
596		accepted. That there is a
597		factual basis for each of the
598		charges and the pleas are
599		therefore accepted and entered
600		of record.
601	*Closing*	
602	Judge:	Uh what is Mr. Appleton's status
603		with respect to release at the
604		present time?
605	Defense Lawyer:	Presently he is being held in
606		the Pima County jail (so there's
607		no release status). We are
608		going to be needing to get some
609		letters (and) recommendations
610		from the state of Wisconsin.
611		Uh (it) might be good to have at
612		least three weeks, if not four.

613	Judge:	I'm sorry. Three /weeks/?
614	Defense Lawyer:	/At least/
615		three weeks if not four weeks.
616		[2 secs] (Before the) ( ).
617	Judge:	All right. I'll set the time for
618		sentencing in this matter for
619		Friday, September twenty-second,
620		1978, in division 0000 at nine
621		A.M. [8 secs] Order that a pre-
622		sentence investigation report be
623		made by the adult probation
624		office of this court and
625		continue uh conditions of
626		release pending that. I must
627		advise you, Mr. Appleton, that
628		uh that is the time when I will
629		decide what disposition to make
630		in this matter. You must be
631		present um at that time which is
632		uh thirty days from today and if
633		you fail to be present uh you
634		could be sentenced even though
635		you aren't present and uh a
636		bench warrant (could) issue for
637		your arrest. It's to your
638		advantage to cooperate with the
639		adult probation office so that
640		uh I get the best information
641		possible to use in deciding what
642		to do. Obviously the better the
643		information the more
644		intelligently I can attempt to
645		assess what to do. I'm sure you
646		understand. Is there anything
647		else ( )? (All right). The
648		original and copies are to be
649		filed in each of your three
650		files.
651	Defendant:	Thank you, sir. [5 secs]
652	Judge:	Are the parties ready on Rivera
653		case?

Judge 4: Robbery

1	*Opening*	
2	Judge:	CR-00000. State of Arizona
3		against Wilbur Southcutt, this
4		is the time set for- change of
5		plea hearing.

6	*Repair*	
7	Judge:	*It's my understanding- is it to*
8		*be a- violation hearing in the-*
9		*A-numbered cases also?*
10	Defense Lawyer(?):	*That is being dismissed, Your*
11		*Honor.*
12	County Attorney:	*( ) for the /state/.*
13	Defense Lawyer:	* /( )/.*
14		*[2 secs] ( ) plea*
15		*agreements. [114 secs {Some*
16		*very soft whispering during part*
17		*of this period}]*
18	Judge:	*Should uh these offenses, and*
19		*I'm- I don't know, should these*
20		*offenses be designated as-*
21		*violent or non-violent under*
22		*the- /code?/*
23	Defense Lawyer:	*No, uh, /they/ they've they*
24		*dismissed the allegation of*
25		*dangerous nature of previous*
26		*hearing on a motion to strike.*
27	County Attorney:	*That's correct, Your Honor. At*
28		*a time when uh I think it was*
29		*raised, I agreed to dismiss the*
30		*allegation of dangerous nature*
31		*because the prior convictions*
32		*made a stiffer sentence.*
33	Judge:	*Should the uh should the uh [4*
34		*secs] crimes then uh- be*
35		*designated as nondangerous to*
36		*the contrary?*
37	County Attorney:	*No, Your Honor, they're just*
38		*straight class threes and, for*
39		*future use, uh it'd be class*
40		*threes of the nature that they*
41		*are being pled to today with-*
42		*without specific designation.*
43	Judge:	*Okay. Fine.*
44	*Nature of the Charges*	
45	Judge:	Uh Mr. Southcutt I've been
46		handed a written plea agreement
47		which [2 secs] indicates that
48		you wish to enter pleas of
49		guilty at this time to [2 secs]
50		the crime of burglary in the
51		first degree, a class three
52		felony with two prior felony
53		convictions, and to the crime
54		of attempted armed robbery, a

55		class three felony, with two
56		prior [2 secs] convictions.
57		[2 secs]

58 *Plea Agreement Comprehension Questions*

59	Judge:	Have you read this plea
60		agreement?
61	Defendant:	Yes, Your Honor.
62	Judge:	And have you discussed it uh
63		with uh Mr. Tabbitt?
64	Defendant:	Yes, sir.
65	Judge:	And do you understand the terms
66		and conditions of this plea
67		agreement?
68	Defendant:	I do.

69 *Constitutional Rights*

70	Judge:	Alright, sir. [2 secs] You do
71		understand, Mr. Southcutt, that
72		uh you're not required to enter
73		pleas of guilty at this time to
74		any charges, that you are
75		entitled to a trial by jury on
76		the charges that are filed
77		against you uh in this case, and
78		that by entering a plea of
79		guilty at this time you're
80		giving up, you're waiving your
81		jury trial rights.
82	Defendant:	Yes, Your Honor.
83	Judge:	You also understand that you
84		have the uh following specific
85		uh jury trial rights which you
86		are giving up, and that is the
87		right to confront the witnesses
88		who have made the charges
89		against you and to cross-examine
90		those witnesses, the right to
91		present evidence, to call
92		witnesses in your own defense,
93		to require the state to compel
94		those witnesses to appear and
95		testify. The right to re- be
96		represented by an attorney
97		appointed free of charge at the
98		trial of the proceedings, the-
99		right to remain silent, to
100		refuse to be a witness against
101		yourself and to be presumed
102		innocent until proven guilty

103		beyond a reasonable doubt. You
104		understand you're giving up
105		those specific jury trial
106		rights?
107	Defendant:	Yes. [3 secs]

108	*Coercion Questions*	
109	Judge:	Have any promises been made to
110		you uh to cause you to enter
111		pleas of guilty at this time
112		other than the promises
113		contained in the written plea
114		agreement?
115	Defendant:	No.
116	Judge:	Has anyone used any force or any
117		threats to cause you to enter /
118		pleas/ of guilty at this time.
119	Defendant:	/No./
120		[4 secs]

121	*Conditions of Plea Agreement*	
122	Judge:	The [2 secs] plea agreement, Mr.
123		Southcutt, uh provides that
124		probation is not available. [2
125		secs] The- plea agreement uh
126		further provides that [2 secs]
127		in the event this uh plea
128		agreement is accepted by the
129		court, uh you shall receive a
130		sentence of ten years in the
131		Arizona state prison, there
132		being a mitigating factor, and
133		there being no additional aggra-
134		aggravating factors. Is is
135		that your understanding of the
136		agreement?
137	Defendant:	Yes, sir.

138	*Sentencing Possibilities*	
139	Judge:	You further understand that the-
140		statute uh provides that uh [2
141		secs] for the crime of burglary
142		of first degree, a class three
143		uh felony, the crime carries a
144		presumptive sentence of uh
145		eleven and one quarter years and
146		a minimum sentence of ten years,
147		and a maximum sentence of uh
148		twenty years. Do you

149		understand that that is the
150		/statu/tory provision?
151		[6 secs]
152	Defendant:	/Uhmhm./
153	Judge:	You further understand that uh-
154		if you are sentenced uh to
155		prison, uh pursuant to this plea
156		agreement if accepted by the
157		court, that uh you must serve
158		two-thirds of the sentence,
159		which would be two-thirds of ten
160		years before you would be
161		eligible for release on parole
162		or on any other basis?
163	Defendent:	I understand that.
164	Judge:	And that two-thirds of ten years
165		is uh straight time, flat time,
166		calendar time, do you
167		understand that?
168	Defendant:	Yes, sir.
169	Judge:	All right. [4 secs] By- do you
170		further understand that the
171		statute provides that a fine of
172		up to one hundred fifty thousand
173		dollars can be imposed?
174	Defendant:	I understand that.
175	*Factual Basis*	
176	Judge:	By entering a- plea of guilty to
177		the crime of burglary, first
178		degree, a class three felony,
179		with uh two prior convictions,
180		are you admitting to the court
181		that- on the twenty-sixth day
182		of December, 1978, you entered
183		a- nonresidential structure-
184		located at 5070 East Sixth in
185		Pima County, Arizona, that the
186		time you entered that structure
187		you- intended to steal and that
188		at the time you entered that
189		structure you were armed uh with
190		a deadly weapon, to wit a gun.
191		You admitting that those facts
192		are true?
193	Defendant:	Yes, sir.
194	Judge:	Further admitting by pleading
195		guilty to crime of attempted
196		armed robbery, a class three

197		felony, with two prior
198		convictions that [2 secs] on the
199		twenty-sixth day,
200	*Repair*	
201	Judge:	*does the first uh degree*
202		*burglary offense still require*
203		*nighttime?*
204	Defense Lawyer:	*No.*
205	County Attorney:	*No, Your Honor.*
206	Judge:	*All right. Are you admitting by*
207		*pleading guilty to attempted*
208		*armed robbery uh* [2 secs]
209		Mr. Southcutt on December the
210		twenty-sixth, uh 1978, uh you
211		committed to- you attempted to
212		commit the crime of robbery,
213		that is, you attempted to take
214		property uh from uh the person
215		or under the control of Martha
216		O'Malley uh while you were armed
217		with a deadly weapon, to wit a
218		gun and that uh y- you attempted
219		to- rob uh Ms. O'Malley by
220		force or fear?
221	Defendant:	I attempted to it.
222	Judge:	You attempted to it. Uh you
223		admitting [6 secs] Mr.
224		Southcutt, that uh you [3 secs]
225		previously been convicted in uh
226		[2 secs] case number A-00 [2
227		secs] 000 [2 secs] of two counts
228		of first degree burglary-
229		felonies in the [2 secs]
230		Superior Court of Pima County?
231	Defendant:	Yes, sir.
232	Judge:	And at the time that you were
233		convicted uh for these crimes
234		you were represented by an
235		attorney?
236	Defendant:	Yes.
237	Judge:	Further admitting that uh [2
238		secs] in case number A-00000 uh
239		[2 secs] that you were convicted
240		of the crime of one count of
241		first degree burglary on
242		December the ninth, 1975, in
243		Pima County attorney, that you
244		were represented by an attorney

245		er at the time of that ( )?
246	Defendant:	(Yes, sir).
247	Judge:	And the date of the uh other
248		two convictions uh was also
249		December the ninth, 1975, you
250		admitting that's true? [5
251		secs]

252	*Repair*	
253	Defendant:	That's /three/
254	Judge:	/Marbury/
255	Defendant:	*s- that's three separate- or o-*
256		*two separate?*
257	Judge:	*Those're two ca/ses, three/*
258	Defendant:	*/Two cases, yes,/*
259	Judge:	*counts and uh they all were- you*
260		*were sentenced on the same date*
261		*/in both of those cases/.*
262	Defendant:	*/Yeah, two of them I/ believe*
263		*were first degree burglaries,*
264		*and the other one was a grand*
265		*theft. For the record. [3*
266		*secs]*
267	County Attorney:	*No, Your Honor, prior*
268		*convictions are all indicated*
269		*as first-degree burglaries. [2*
270		*secs] I have available to the*
271		*court the pleadings- (uh pardon*
272		*me, Your Honor,) the*
273		*indictments ( ) minute entry*
274		*( ) sentence (Your Honor).*
275		*[2 secs]*
276	Judge:	*Should be a copy of the-*
277		*sentencing in the file. [11*
278		*secs]*
279	Defendant(?):	*There it is, a third- first-*
280		*degree burglary, but it's in*
281		*another (county) at a different*
282		*time. [3 secs]*
283	Judge:	*I'll uh- show you, Mr.*
284		*Southcutt a uh with Mr.*
285		*Tabbitt's uh [4 secs] help here*
286		*a uh- phota- photocopy of the*
287		*conviction in those two cases*
288		*which um perhaps Mr. Tabbitt*
289		*has there (it was) uh before me*
290		*in both cases on December the*
291		*ninth, 1979, it does show uh two*
292		*counts burglary, first degree*

293		/in (00000) ( )/.
294	Defense Lawyer:	/That is correct. That's
295		correct./ (There are three
296		involved). [2 secs]
297	Judge:	So you are admitting that that
298		is /true/?
299	Defendant:	/Yes/ sir. [2 secs]
300	Judge:	You satisfied with the uh
301		factual basis, Mr. ( )?
302	County Attorney:	I am, Your Honor. Thank you.
303	Judge:	Mr. /Tab/-
304	Defense Lawyer:	/Yes/.
305	*Findings*	
306	Judge:	The court finds the defendant's
307		uh pleas of guilty are being
308		made knowingly /and/-
309	*Repair of Conditions of Plea Agreement*	
310	County Attorney:	/'Scuses/ me,
311		*Your Honor. There there were*
312		*two additional matters that I*
313		*don't recall the court having*
314		*covered. That is the petition*
315		*to uh revoke and a misdemeanor*
316		*complaint. (They are) part of*
317		*the plea agree/ment/.*
318	Judge:	*/Yes/, I'll I'll*
319		*revoke those er er dismiss those*
320		*conditionally, but- [2 secs] As*
321		*part of the agreement, Mr.*
322		*Southcutt, uh- it was your*
323		*agreement and the state's*
324		*agreement that the petition to*
325		*revoke probation in uh both of*
326		*these two A-number cases would*
327		*be uh dismissed, and upon*
328		*sentencing, your probation would*
329		*be terminated. And uh a*
330		*misdemeanor complaint would*
331		*also be dismissed, which*
332		*charges assault, uh is that*
333		*your understanding?*
334	Defendant:	*Yes, (Your Honor).*
335	County Attorney:	*May I- ask for additional*
336		*record as to the assault*
337		*charge, Your Honor. (It's) my*
338		*understanding the defendant has*
339		*limited his denial as to that*
340		*assault charge and continues to*

341		*deny his uh culpability in*
342		*connection with that assault*
343		*charge. [2 secs] And is not*
344		*admitting to that charge at all.*
345	Defense Lawyer:	*It's being dismissed!*
346	Defendant(?):	*( ).*
347	Judge:	*Being dismissed.*
348	County Attorney:	*(He's) maintaining a not guilty*
349		*to that charge (Your Honor).*
350		*That's my understanding from the*
351		*defendant.*
352	Defendant:	*Because I wasn't ( ).*
353	Defense Lawyer:	*Uh-*
354	County Attorney:	*All right. /That's- I ( )/*
355	Defense Lawyer:	* /I don't understand,*
356		*wh- what's the problem?/*
357	Judge:	*I don't think there's a*
358		*problem.*
359		Court finds the defendant's uh
360		pleas of guilty are being made
361		knowingly, and voluntarily, and
362		intelligently with an
363		understanding of the
364		consequences, and no promises
365		other than those contained in
366		the plea agreement, no threats,
367		no force were used to cause him
368		to enter his pleas of guilty.
369		That there- is a factual basis
370		for the- plea of guilty and the
371		uh allegation of uh two prior uh
372		felony convictions.
373	*Formal Plea*	
374	Judge:	You're accused uh Mr. Southcutt
375		by the state of Arizona of the
376		charge of burglary, first
377		degree, a cl- class three
378		felony with two prior
379		convictions committed on
380		December the twenty-sixth day-
381		1978 uh in violation of ARS
382		section 13- uh 701.
383	*Repair*	
384	Judge:	*Is that the substantive charge?*
385	Defense Lawyer:	*Yes, sir.*
386	County Attorney:	*Yes, sir.*
387	Judge:	*Uh and 702. [4 secs]*

388	County Attorney:	*N'Your Honor? Are you asking*
389		*is that the statute for the*
390		*substantive-*
391	Judge:	*Yeah.*
392	County Attorney:	*No. That's the sentencing*
393		*section.*
394	Judge:	*All right, which is the- which*
395		*is the burg/lary/-*
396	Defense Lawyer(?):	* /Uh/ it's uh 15 uh-*
397		*( ) [2 secs] It's 1508.*
398	County Attorney:	*That's correct, Your Honor.*
399	Judge:	*In violation of 13-1508.*
400	Defense Lawyer(?):	*All right.*

401	Judge:	And also charged uh with the
402		crime of attempted armed
403		robbery, a class three felony,
404		of two prior convictions,
405		committed on December twenty-
406		sixth, 1978, in violation of
407		ARS 13 dash-

408	*Repair*	
409	Defense Lawyer:	*It's 1904 and two.*
410	Judge:	*1904, 1902.*

411		How do you plead to uh both of
412		those uh-
413	Defendant:	Guilty.
414	Judge:	And you have admitted that the
415		allegations of the prior
416		convictions are true?
417	Defendant:	Yes, sir. [2 secs]
418	Judge:	The defendant's pleas of guilty
419		are accepted, the clerk is
420		directed to enter them of
421		record.

422	*Closing*	
423	Judge:	It is ordered setting this
424		matter for entry of judgment of
425		guilt and sentencing. [3 secs]
426	Defense Lawyer:	At the full thirty days.
427	Judge:	(Thirty) days. [2 secs] May
428		the uh twenty-fifth, at uh nine
429		A.M. in division 00000, it is
430		further dismissing the petition
431		to revoke probation. Case A-
432		00000 and A-00000. Further
433		ordered dismissing the
434		misdemeanor.

Judge 4:   Prescription Falsification

1   *Opening*
2   Judge: Uh CR-00000, state of Arizona
3   against Richard Farmer. This is
4   the time set for change of plea.
5   County Attorney: Tom Peters, for the state, Your
6   Honor.
7   Defense Lawyer: Emil Sawyer, appearing with
8   Richard Farmer, who's present in
9   the court. [10 secs]

10 *Repair*
11 County Attorney: (   ) [*16 secs*]
12 Defense Lawyer: *Your Honor, if I-*
13 Judge: *I think probably the u- the*
14   *should not the range of*
15   *sentencing be set forth*
16   */in written/-*
17 County Attorney: */Y- Your Honor/*
18   */I'm uh it's on/*
19 Defense Lawyer: */(It's on the) second page./*
20 County Attorney: *Uh I was gonna clarify that in a*
21   *moment, we didn't have room on*
22   *the first page /so/*
23 Judge: */Alright./*
24 County Attorney: *I probably should have*
25   */X'ed/*
26 Judge: */Alright./*
27 County Attorney: *that out. It it's on page two.*
28   [41 secs]

29 *Nature of Charge*
30 Judge: Mr. Farmer, I've been handed a
31   written plea agreement which
32   states that you intend to enter
33   a plea of guilty at this time to
34   the crime of obtaining or
35   attempting to obtain a
36   prescription-only drug or
37   dangerous drug by- fraud- in
38   violation of ARS sections 32–
39   1971 and 32–1996 A. [7 secs]
40   Committed on January the second,
41   1979.

42 *Conditions of Plea Agreement*
43 Judge: The- crime [2 secs] to be
44   treated as an open-ended-

45		offense [2 secs] that is, either
46		as a felony or as a- a class
47		five felony or as a class two
48		misdemeanor. Dependent upon
49		your performance during a an
50		agreed upon- uh two-year period
51		of probation. Is's that
52		correct, Mr. Sawyer? [7 secs]
53	Defense Lawyer:	Uhhm [4 secs] that is correct,
54		Judge.
55	Judge:	Mr. Peters?
56	County Attorney:	Yes, Your /Honor, that's my
57		understanding./
58	Judge:	/Is that the
59		agreement? All right/.

60	*Plea Agreement Comprehension Questions*	
61	Judge:	Have you read this plea
62		agreement, /uh/-
63	Defendant:	/Yes/ I have, Your
64		Honor.
65	Judge:	Mr. Farmer? And do you
66		understand the terms and
67		conditions of this plea
68		a/greement/?
69	Defendant:	/Yes, Your Honor./

70	*Constitutional Rights*	
71	Judge:	Do you understand that uh- you
72		are entitled to a trial by jury
73		on the charges that are filed
74		against you in this case?
75	Defendant:	Yes, Your Honor.
76	Judge:	And that by entering a plea of
77		guilty at this time, you're
78		giving up and waiving your right
79		to a trial by jury?
80	Defendant:	Yes, Your Honor.
81	Judge:	D'ya understand that you do have
82		the following specific jury-
83		trial rights which you are
84		giving up, and that is the right
85		to confront the witnesses who
86		have made the charges against
87		you, and to cross-examine those
88		witnesses, the right to present
89		evidence and to call witnesses
90		in your own defense, to require
91		the state to compel those
92		witnesses to appear and testify,

93		the right to be represented by
94		an attorney appointed free of
95		charge at the trial of
96		proceedings, the right to remain
97		silent, to refuse to be a
98		witness against yourself, and to
99		be presumed innocent until
100		proven guilty beyond a
101		reasonable doubt. Do you
102		understand that you're giving up
103		all of those- uh jury trial
104		rights by pleading guilty?
105	Defendant:	Yes, Your Honor.
106	*Coercion Questions*	
107	Judge:	Have any promises been made to
108		you in connection with your plea
109		of guilty, other than the
110		promises contained in this plea
111		agreement?
112	Defendant:	(Uh not that I know of).
113	Judge:	All right.
114	*Sentencing Possibilities and Conditions of Plea*	
115	*Agreement*	
116	Judge:	Uh- the plea agreement, Mr.
117		Farmer, as I read it, uh
118		provides that at the time of
119		sentencing, and that is if I
120		accept the plea agreement uh
121		after receiving a presentence
122		report from the probation
123		department, uh- that at the
124		time of sentencing, you <u>will</u> be
125		placed on probation for a period
126		of two years. Is that your
127		understanding?
128	Defendant:	(Uh right).
129	Judge:	If at any time during that two-
130		year period while you're on-
131		probation you violate the terms
132		and conditions of your probation
133		[2 secs] my understanding of
134		this plea agreement is that if
135		your probation is revoked during
136		the two-year period, based upon
137		violation, that the- crime can
138		be treated as a felony and as a
139		felony, you could be sentenced
140		to the Arizona state prison for

141		a presumptive term of two years
142		which could be increased up to
143		two and a half years, based upon
144		aggravating circumstances, or
145		decreased to a term of one year,
146		based upon mitigating
147		circumstances. U- is that your
148		understanding?
149	Defendant:	Yes, sir.
150	Judge:	All right. If [2 secs] your
151		probation is completed
152		satisfactorily- after a period
153		of two years, your probation
154		will- have been satisfied and
155		the- offense will be treated as
156		a- misdemeanor. Do you
157		understand that?
158	Defendant:	Yes, I do.
159	Judge:	I take it that the agreement can
160		also be read to provide that you
161		could [3 secs] not be revoked,
162		you could go through the two
163		year period of probation and
164		because of an unsatisfactory
165		performance while on probation,
166		for reasons that were not-
167		sufficient to justify
168		revocation, the court could
169		designate the offense as a
170		felony. Is that correct? Mr.
171		Peters?
172	County Attorney:	Yes, Your Honor, I believe so,
173		if- performance was /( )/
174		( ).
175	Defense Lawyer:	/Yes, I-/
176		[2 sec]
177	Judge:	And do you also understand that
178		uh if [2 secs] your probation
179		were to be revoked, it uh
180		th'offense could still be
181		treated as a misdemeanor, but
182		you could be sentenced to a term
183		in the Pima County jail of up to
184		four months, d'ya understand
185		that?
186	Defendant:	Yes, Your Honor.
187	Judge:	Also, understand that u- a fine
188		as a misdemeanor could be
189		imposed in the sum of seven
190		hundred fifty dollars.

191	Defendant:	Yes, Your Honor.
192	Judge:	A fine- as a felony could be
193		imposed up to one hundred and
194		fifty thousand dollars. Do you
195		understand uh all of those
196		provisions?
197	Defendant:	Yes, Your Honor. [2 secs]
198	Judge:	And, according to the plea
199		agreement, you are also to
200		furnish uh the Arizona
201		department of public safety
202		with a handwriting uh exemplar.
203		[2 secs] You-
204	Defendant:	Yeah, yes, sir.
205	Judge:	Good.
206	Defendant:	I haven't yet, but I s-
207	Judge:	Y- y- you're up to do that,
208		all right? [3 secs]

209	*Factual Basis*	
210	Judge:	What's the factual basis, Mr.
211		Sawyer, please?
212	Defense Lawyer:	Judge, I think we will just
213		agree with what the county
214		attorney will tell the court.
215	Judge:	All right. [5 secs]
216	County Attorney:	( ), Your Honor. [27 secs] The
217		uh factual basis in this
218		case, Your Honor, uh Mr. Farmer
219		obtained a prescription for
220		Tylenol number four uh which
221		falls under the prescription and
222		dangerous drug statute. And
223		uh the prescription was for the
224		amount of uh fifteen tablets,
225		the prescription was altered to
226		twenty-five tablets when
227		presented to the pharmacy. Uh-
228		Mr. Farmer has been charged
229		under the statute for altering
230		the prescription from fifteen to
231		twenty-five tablets of Tylenol
232		number four.
233	Judge:	Mr. Farmer, by entering a plea
234		of guilty, are you admitting
235		that on January second, 1979,
236		you did- alter a prescription
237		for Tylenol number four by
238		increasing the uh number of the
239		uh capsules, and presenting uh

240		that uh to a pharmacy in uh
241		Pima County, Arizona, with the
242		intent to obtain the altered
243		number of uh pills.
244	Defendant:	Yes, sir.
245	Judge:	You're admitting that that's
246		true?
247	Defendant:	Yes.

248 *Findings*

249	Judge:	Court finds the defendant's plea
250		of guilty is being made
251		knowingly and voluntarily and
252		intelligently with an
253		understanding of the possible
254		consequences that- no promises
255		other than those contained in the
256		plea agreement were made to
257		cause him to enter his plea of
258		guilty. That there is a- no
259		threats, no force were used to
260		cause him to enter his plea of
261		guilty. That there is a factual
262		basis for the same.

263 *Formal Plea*

264	Judge:	Charged uh Mr. Farmer with the
265		crime of obtaining or
266		attempting to obtain a
267		prescription-only drug or
268		dangerous drug by fraud. Open-
269		ended, either uh class five
270		felony or class two misdemeanor.
271		What is your plea?
272	Defendant:	Guilty.
273	Judge:	Court accepts the defendant's
274		plea of guilty. The clerk is
275		directed to enter it of record.
276		It is ordered setting this
277		matter for entry of judgment of
278		guilt and sentencing.

279 *Repair*

280	Defense Lawyer:	*'Scuse me.*
281	Judge:	*Yes.*
282	Defense Lawyer:	*Judge, uhm there's a- few*
283		*matters at the bottom there, I'm*
284		*not sure you've covered those.*
285	Judge:	*Uh the- written into the plea*
286		*agreement, Mr. Farmer was a uh*

287		*[3 secs] Part of the agreement*
288		*is that those charges arising*
289		*from the investigation*
290		*authorized in Arizona department*
291		*of public safety DR report*
292		*number 00–00000 were all charges*
293		*investigated by DPS up to and*
294		*until April seventeenth, 1979,*
295		*uh will be dismissed, or will*
296		*not be filed, if not now filed.*
297		*Is that /your/ understanding*
298	Defendant:	/( )/
299	Judge:	*part of the uh- terms of the*
300		*plea agreement? [3 secs]*
301		*/Sentence/ yes?*
302	*Closing*	
303	Defense Lawyer:	/L-/ l- logistically how do you
304		wanna do this, do you wanna
305		have- the sentence two years
306		from now, or the sentencing a
307		month from /now/?
308	Judge:	/No/ I would uh say
309		that uh that uh the proper
310		procedure would be in thirty
311		days. I will sentence him uh
312		uh to this crime uh uh [2 secs]
313		for this crime. As an open-
314		ended offense, which- and uh
315		with the-
316	Defense Lawyer:	Understanding that if it's
317		/punishable ( )/
318	Judge:	/Understanding that/ if
319		probation's violated or he
320		doesn't perform, then- uh it'll
321		be treated at the end of the uh
322		two years as a felony or a
323		misdemeanor. But I would think
324		that it would be appropriate to
325		him uh to uh have a pre-trial
326		investigation, (usual) pre-
327		sentence report.
328	Defense Lawyer:	All right, a- along those lines,
329		uh- Richard uh has a problem
330		with some of the people that he
331		knows in Tucson. His family
332		lives in Pennsylvania and he
333		has uh gotten a job now in
334		Phoenix. And uh uh we would
335		like to have some sort of

336		understanding that uh he would
337		be able to go back to
338		Pennsylvania or live in Phoenix
339		uh during this two-year period.
340		[5 secs] I don't think
341		/( ) be problem/ with it-
342	Judge:	/I- no I don't-/
343		No, I don't I don't
344		/( ) any problem with that ( )/
345	Defense Lawyer:	/But I just wanted ( )/
346	Judge:	a two-year period.
347	Defense Lawyer:	part of the record at this time.
348	Judge:	All right. Uh- sentencing on May
349		the uh [2 secs] seventeenth.
350		[2 secs] Nine A.M., Division
351		00000. But do report to the
352		probation department.
353	Defense Lawyer:	Thank you, Your Honor.
354	County Attorney:	Thank you, Your Honor. [2 secs]
355	Judge:	Stand at recess.

Appendix G

·———·

Refusal of Plea Agreement
in Aborted Sentencing Transcript

Judge 6: Aborted Sentencing

1	Judge:	Uh CR 00000 state of Arizona
2		versus Harry Dolan. This is the
3		time set for sentencing. Uh
4		present um-
5	Lawyer:	Todd True on behalf of ( ).
6	Lawyer:	Paul Coffman ( ).
7	Judge:	(Show) the defendant in custody.
8		Uh as I informed you gentlemen
9		in chambers, I have reviewed the
10		uh defendant's record and I
11		cannot go along with the plea
12		agreement with you. If I were
13		to sentence him I would sentence
14		him to the (uh) state prison and
15		certainly give him more than uh
16		time served. The plea agreement
17		provides that the defendant may
18		withdraw his plea uh.
19	Defendant:	I don't wanna withdraw my plea.
20	Judge:	All right (let) the record show
21		that the defendant has withdrawn
22		his plea and the court orders
23		that the matter be set for trial
24		um-
25	Defendant:	I don't wanna withdraw my plea!
26		{louder than last time;

27		basically a shout; he shouts the
28		rest of the time}.
29	Judge:	You don't wanna withd/raw your
30		plea?/
31	Defense Lawyer:	/Be quiet/ please. [2 secs]
32		Your Honor, I would request that
33		you withdraw his plea. If my
34		client doesn't want to, I don't
35		know what I can do about it.
36	Defendant:	Well I can't get probation, I
37		can't get ROR (if) I go to
38		trial. Uh I want to get this
39		taken care of right now. I'm in
40		twenty-four lockup for eight
41		weeks. I'm entitled to some
42		rights.
43	Defense Lawyer:	Your Honor I h- I had originally
44		filed a Rule 11 in this case and
45		had withdrawn it uh at the time
46		of the plea agreement. I would
47		reinstitute it at this time that
48		the [2 secs] that an examination
49		that examinations be had. [4
50		secs]
51	Judge:	You say- anything to say about
52		that Mr. True?
53	County Attorney:	Uh well I'm kind of in an
54		awkward position here Your
55		Honor. I don't know very much
56		about the case at all. Uh if
57		there is valid grounds for Rule
58		11 uh that Mr. Coffman has made
59		then certainly the state would
60		have no objections to
61		examinations /under/-
62	Defendant:	/I've/ had a Rule
63		11 already Your Honor.
64	Defense Lawyer:	No he hasn't.
65	Defendant:	I don't want a Rule 11. I want
66		to get this taken care of. I'm
67		in jail.
68	Lawyer:	Do you want to go to prison? [3
69		secs]
70	Judge:	Well, all right. (Let) the record
71		show that the court is with is
72		uh is vacating the entry of uh a
73		plea agreement by the um
74		defendant [3 secs] and orders
75		that the matter be set for trial
76		by the uh court administrator

77	Defendant:	/I don't want to go to trial./
78	Judge:	/not more than thirty days/ not
79		more than thirty days from um
80		from today.
81	Defendant:	Who is he to tell me how to
82		plead when I already pled
83		guilty?
84	Defense Lawyer:	Your Honor, can I just- with
85		regard to the trial date, we can
86		only do a trial date on the
87		seventeenth of May which was
88		within the thirty-day period of
89		( ). Can we stay within
90		that original trial date?
91	Judge:	Today is /( )/
92	Defendant:	/I don't/ want to go to
93		trial.
94	Judge:	Can can you be ready to go by
95		May the seventeenth?
96	Defense Lawyer:	Certainly ( ) if I can get
97		the mental examinations done,
98		Your Honor.
99	Defendant:	I'm not taking no mental
100		examination. I want this
101		/taken care of/ today. [3 secs]
102	Judge:	/Can we take-/
103	Defendant:	I know my rights. I pled
104		guilty. [4 secs] If he wants
105		to send me to prison for my past
106		record, let him. I'm tired of
107		waiting in that county jail (for
108		going to court). [3 secs]
109	Judge:	Who do you uh. Well, there's no
110		point to really even setting a
111		trial. Well I can go ahead and
112		set (the trial).
113	Lawyer:	All right?
114	Judge:	All right. /( )/
115	Defendant:	/( )I've been/ in
116		lockup for two months, twenty-
117		four-hour lockup.
118	Judge:	I will uh I will re/tain-/
119	Defendant:	/In/ a little
120		cell this big. Twenty-four-hour
121		lock-up.
122	Judge:	I will retain the May
123		seventeenth trial date and I
124		will uh order a Rule 11
125		examination.
126	Defendant:	I'm not taking no Rule 11.

127	Judge:	Who who do you want?
128	Defense Lawyer:	Your Honor, Dr. Madagan.
129	Defendant:	Fuck this shit.
130	Speaker:	(Settle down right now. Just
131		stop it.)
132	Judge:	Dr. /Madagan./
133	Defendant:	/Look at/ this shit. Look
134		at this.
135	Defense Lawyer(?):	Well just relax, will you
136		/please/?
137	Speaker:	/Sit down/.
138	Defendant:	I don't- I pled guilty. [2
139		secs]
140	Judge:	Um. [2 secs]
141	Speaker:	Just relax.
142	Speaker:	/( )/
143	Defendant:	/Why are they/ /sentencing me?
144		Why are they taking my past
145		record about this?/
146	Multiple Speakers:	/( )/
147	Judge:	You can move the uh-
148	Defendant:	What's my past record got to do
149		about this shit?
150		{Can hear other voices in the
151		background during this} [9 secs
152		{defendant is taken from
153		courtroom during this time}]
154	Judge:	( )
155	County Attorney:	May I be excused Your Honor? [2
156		sec]
157	Judge:	Certainly {laughs}. Um.
158	Defense Lawyer:	Excuse me Your Honor I I filed a
159		Rule 11 and and uh-
160	Judge:	Was it /( )/
161	Defense Lawyer:	/It was/ granted and I withdrew
162		it when we entered into the plea
163		agreement.
164	Judge:	Okay.
165	Defense Lawyer:	Uh we had Dr. Madagan set for
166		seeing the defendant on uh April
167		the twentieth which is uh two
168		days away.
169	Judge:	He didn't didn't-
170	Defense Lawyer:	I don't believe that
171		appointment was
172	Judge:	I-
173	Defense Lawyer:	was vacated, and also Dr.
174		Addison. They had already been
175		appointed by the court.
176	Judge:	/( )/

177	Defense Lawyer:	/We/ could make a new
178		appointment with Dr. Addison,
179		but I-
180	Judge:	Well, I'll have my secretary
181		check on that this morning and
182		see if we can still make those
183		appointments.
184	Defense Lawyer:	Okay ( ) the court's final
185		decision.
186	Judge:	Okay Okay [3 secs] Thank you,
187		Paul. Uh CR 00000 {he's
188		calling new case}.

Notes

1 Ideology in Discourse

1. For this reason, my earliest analysis focused on spatial relations and nonverbal communication in the courtroom (Philips 1986).

2. This work was part of a general public dialogue about how much leeway judges should have in their sentencing. It was followed by nationwide movements in states to constrain judges' sentencing practices through criminal code revisions. Such a revision was implemented in Arizona during the course of my study.

3. As tape recording in courts was not allowed by noncourt personnel, in part because more than the one court stenographer-produced record of the case could then be created, the associate presiding judge had to get an oral ruling (by phone) from the chief justice of the Arizona Supreme Court that my taping could come under the educational exception to the ban on recording. I also had to promise not to share my recordings with others, something I could not do anyway under personal and professional ethical guidelines that aim to preserve the anonymity and voluntariness of participation in social scientific research.

4. Anthropologists and legal scholars (e.g., Kondo 1990; Kelly 1991; Merry 1990; Fineman 1988) increasingly are using the term DISCOURSES to refer to multiple interpretive perspectives constituted by social actors within a common cultural framework, apparently following Foucault (1980). But these scholars tend to lift the ideational content meaning of these discourses out of their original contexts of production with little analytical attention to the contexts of production themselves. In this book I use the term IDEOLOGIES much as these scholars use the term "discourses" and reserve the term "discourses" for the actual productions of speech and texts, focusing on the nature of the microcontexts of ideological production.

5. See Thompson (1984) for a discussion of useful approaches to the role of language in the constitution of ideologies that is compatible with the treatment here of ideology in discourse.

6. For an understanding of the development of the concept of genre in anthropology, see Hymes 1967; Philips 1987b; Hanks 1987; Briggs & Bauman 1992.

7. Because the concept of genre is usually applied to forms of talk that are clearly structured in a variety of ways, there is some question of how appropriate it is to attempt to impose the term on all forms of talk. See Briggs and Bauman (1992) for a discussion of different approaches to conceptualizing genre. Conversation analysts, for example, see conversation as the basic form of talk from which all other forms of talk are derived (e.g., Goodwin & Heritage 1990).

8. Bakhtin's (1981) concept of voices is used to focus on interpretive frames associated with particular social identities being "voiced" in discourse. The concept of voices differs from and is more complex than concepts of interpretive shifts that see them as taking place one after another in the stream of discourse in part because of Bakhtin's idea that even a single utterance can embody many voices. This idea has influenced the concept of ideological polysemy developed in this book. The concept of voices does not in itself entail attention to the sequential organization of meaning in discourse, although Hill (1995) uses this Bakhtinian concept to show how voices can be sequentially organized.

9. This process is represented in different ways in different traditions focusing on meaning in discourse that are influential in anthropology today. Conversation analysts see each taking of a turn at talk as involving a reinterpretation of what went on before (Sacks [1967] 1993; Goodwin & Heritage 1990). Performance theorists see each performance of a text as uniquely linked to the context of the performance (Bauman 1986; Tedlock 1983). The concept of indexicality involves the idea that part of the meaning of a sign involves the way in which it can be understood to be linked to the actual context in which it is used and to the speaker–hearer's knowledge of past uses of that sign (Silverstein 1976; Ochs 1992).

10. Examples of work in this tradition that address the social ordering of speech genres and activities include Gossen 1974; Philips [1983] 1993; Sherzer 1983; Feld 1982; Schieffelin 1990; Ochs 1988; Briggs 1988; Duranti 1984; Irvine 1990; Watson-Gegeo & Gegeo 1990; Kuipers 1990; Urban 1988; Kulick 1992. There is interplay and tension in this work between using intertextual analysis to reveal cultural homogeneity, the dominant use in fact, and using it to reveal intrasocietal cultural diversity.

11. Paul Willis's *Learning to Labor* (1977) is an influential model for anthropologists' conceptualization of resistance in discourse. Examples of linguistic anthropological work involving the analysis of speech genres that illustrate the influence of Marxist attention to struggle and resistance include Hill 1995; Hendricks 1988; and Briggs 1992.

Recent linguistic anthropological work on language ideologies (e.g., Kroskrity, Schieffelin, & Woolard 1992) also draws on Marxist as well as non-Marxist traditions in the study of "ideology." In my own contributions on this emerging topic, I have argued, as I do here, for the need to keep relations of domination and subordination in view (Philips 1992, in press) and have demonstrated, as I do here, how ideologies are constituted in discourse (Philips 1991, 1995). Although the ideologies I discuss in this book all involve language centrally, I do not represent these ideologies here as "language ideologies" because they are centrally and primarily about something other than language. However, given that this book is about ideology in discourse, what I have to say about that topic applies in general to *language* ideologies as well as to other kinds of ideologies.

2   The Myth of the Trial Court Judge as Nonideological

1. In contrast to the texts from guilty pleas in later chapters, these quotes from career history interviews were edited to omit false starts, repetitions, and back-channel expressions from the interviewer. Parentheses (   ) indicate where the word is inaudible to the transcriber. . . . . indicates that the quote is not continuous and speech at this point was excised. Square

brackets [   ] indicate where I added explanatory material. All the names used by the judges in quotes from them were changed to preserve anonymity.

2. The nine judges are named Judge 1 through Judge 9 on the basis of the order in which they came on to the bench. Judge 1 has been on the bench for a number of years; Judge 9 for less than a year.

3. Although one of the judges in this study was a woman, all are referred to using masculine pronouns to preserve her anonymity and because the bench was predominantly male.

4. Since the origin of this system, the commissions were expanded in size to include 10 public and 5 attorney members (Commission on Judicial Performance Review 1994).

5. A number of social theorists (e.g., Lasch [1991] and Habermas [1989] see a broad trend away from popular democracy and toward rule by professional elites, which the organized bar would be considered a part of.

3   Intertextual Relations between Written and Spoken Genres of Law

1. This representation of repair does not encompass the full range of kinds of repair considered in the tradition of conversation analysis, the source of the term, but rather is fundamentally geared toward accounting for the nature of the sequential structure of the guilty plea. What "repair" refers to in conversation analysis is what the hearer understands as the speaker cycling back through discourse units of varying sizes, changing what already was said (Sacks, Schegloff, & Jefferson 1974). The kind of repair I direct attention to here, however, involves not only locally managed repairs but also the anticipation of the need to repair at the beginning of the procedure and the postponement of repair to the end of the procedure associated with REPAIR SLOTS. This suggests that the global schema of the sequential structure of topics of the guilty plea partially constrains the way repairs are done in the verbal version of the plea.

2. All the names were changed to preserve anonymity.

3. Only a few of the defendants were women, and because the defendants were so predominantly male, I sometimes use the generic he to refer to defendants in this book.

4. Because the case law helps explain what is *not* in the procedure rather than what *is*, it is less evident that the spoken procedure indexes the case law than that it indexes the procedural rule, yet arguably there is such an intertextual connection.

4   Two Ideological Stances in Taking Guilty Pleas

1. This excerpt and some others from Judge 9 are from one tape-recorded interview that focused specifically on why the judge did the procedure as he did.

2. There *are* aspects of the individual proceeding, some of which have to do with characteristics of defendants, that affect the length of the proceeding. For example, close scrutiny of the individual times of the procedures makes it clear that if the defendant does not understand English the procedure is lengthened—not only by the involvement of an interpreter but also because the judges elaborate on their English syntax when an interpreter is involved. When defendants were identified as mentally retarded, the judges did slow down their rate of speech and generally simplified and repeated what they were saying. However, the judges did not solely depend on social background questions to make the determination of the need for this greater care in any of these cases.

3. Elsewhere (Philips 1990) I discussed the links between the desire to get defendants to confess and Foucault's (1980) evidence that confessional discourses were elaborated on in Europe in the expansion of rationalized bureaucratic control over people in recent centuries.

4. What evidence I have suggests that the judges I worked with are *not* consistent across different kinds of judicial decision making in the expression of what could be taken as liberal versus conservative political positions. For example, procedure-oriented judges were not as a group known as more lenient sentencers (i.e., as more "liberal" in their sentencing practices) than record-oriented judges.

5. Hymes (1967), for example, in the development of the ethnography of communication, took the position that the context of an utterance will resolve for participants which of its possible functions it has at that moment. Some scholars (e.g., Tannen 1984; Schiffrin 1987) and lines of analysis, however, have consistently argued that utterances can have more than one meaning. Thus for example co-interactants from different cultural backgrounds may interpret the same utterances differently.

5 Judges' Ideologies of Courtroom Control

1. This situation can also be viewed as one in which the defendant lost control over himself. Greg Matoesian (personal communication) pointed out that judges may "strategically" lose control to display just how out-of-control a defendant is.

2. The trials of O.J. Simpson certainly offer a current illustration of the importance of courtroom control to a judge's reputation. During and after the murder trial of O.J. Simpson, the judge presiding over the case, Lance Ito, was frequently criticized in the media for his lack of control over the courtroom and even blamed for the jury's failure to convict Simpson. In the civil trial against Simpson, which began in the fall of 1996, the new judge was repeatedly lauded in the media for his "no nonsense" greater control of the court.

3. Of the three ideological frameworks discussed in this book—what I have termed LEGAL, POLITICAL, and EVERYDAY control ideologies—the courtroom control ideology seems most like those analyzed in the emerging anthropological literature on language ideologies (e.g. Kroskrity, Schieffelin, & Woolard 1992). The courtroom control ideology is openly and widely shared. It entails both practice and talk about practice (metapragmatics) and has both implicit and explicit dimensions. Still, language is subordinated to the ideas of both control and informality, which is why I have called this a CONTROL IDEOLOGY rather than a language ideology.

4. Comaroff (1985) describes indigenous South African Christian groups as resisting state domination. Kennedy and Davis (1993) describe the way butch lesbians have resisted exclusion from public spaces. In both studies the active creation of alternative cultures in segregated spheres provided the basis for resistance, in a manner consistent with Gramsci's vision of what must be done socially and culturally for alternative hegemonies to emerge within a society.

References

Abel, Richard, ed. 1979. *The Politics of Informal Justice.* Vol. I: *The American Experience.* New York: Academic Press.

Abu-Lughod, Lila. 1985. *Veiled Sentiments: Honor and Poetry in a Bedouin Society.* Berkeley: University of California Press.

Althusser, Louis. 1971. Ideology and Ideological State Apparatuses. In *Lenin and Philosophy and Other Essays,* pp. 127–186. New York: Monthly Review Press.

Amherst Seminar, ed. 1988. Law and Ideology, Special Issue. *Law and Society Review* 22(4).

Arizona Daily Star, November 6, 1978.

Arizona Revised Statutes tit. 1, §§ 36–38, 1976.

Atkinson, J. Maxwell, and Paul Drew. 1979. *Order in Court.* Atlantic Highlands, N.J.: Humanities Press.

Bakhtin, Mikhail. 1981. *The Dialogic Imagination.* Austin: University of Texas Press.

Barthes, Roland. 1972. *Mythologies.* New York: Farrar, Strauss and Giroux.

Bauman, Richard. 1986. *Story, Performance, and Event: Contextual Studies of Oral Narrative.* New York: Cambridge University Press.

Bennett, W. Lance, and Martha Feldman. 1981. *Reconstructing Reality in the Courtroom.* London: Tavistock Publications.

Bourdieu, Pierre. 1977. *Outline of a Theory of Practice.* New York: Cambridge University Press.

Briggs, Charles. 1988. *Competence in Performance: The Creativity of Tradition in Mexicano Verbal Art.* Philadelphia: University of Pennsylvania Press.

———. 1992. "Since I am a Woman, I will Chastise My Relatives": Gender, Reported Speech, and the (Re)production of Social Relations in Warao Ritual Wailing. *American Ethnologist* 19(2): 337–361.

Briggs, Charles, and Richard Bauman. 1992. Genre, Intertextuality, and Social Power. *Journal of Linguistic Anthropology* 2(2): 131–172.

Brown, Penelope, and Steven Levinson. 1987. *Universals of Politeness.* New York: Cambridge University Press.

Cameron, James. 1976. Merit Selection in Arizona—the First Two Years. *Arizona State Law Journal* 3: 425–435.

Carnoy, Martin. 1984. Structuralism and the State: Althusser and Poulantzas. In *The State and Political Theory.* pp. 89–127. Princeton, NJ: Princeton University Press.

Comaroff, Jean. 1985. *Body of Power, Spirit of Resistance: The Culture and History of a South African People.* Chicago: University of Chicago Press.

Commission on Judicial Performance Review. 1994. Phoenix: Arizona State Supreme Court.

Conley, John, and William O'Barr. 1990. *Rules versus Relationships.* Chicago: University of Chicago Press.

Danet, Brenda, Kenneth Hoffman, Nicole Kermish, H. Jeffrey Rafn, and Deborah Stayman. 1976. An Ethnography of Questioning in the Courtroom. In *Language Use and the Uses of Language, NWAVE 5.* Roger Shuy and Anna Shnukal, eds., pp. 222–234. Washington, DC: Georgetown University Press.

Dolbeare, Kenneth. 1967. *Trial Courts in Urban Politics.* New York: Wiley.

Dunn, Peter. 1967. Judicial Selection and Tenure—A Merit Selection Plan for Arizona? *Arizona Law Review* 9: 297–304.

Duranti, Alessandro. 1984. Lauga and Talanoaga: Two Speech Genres in a Samoan Political Event. In *Dangerous Words: Language and Politics in the Pacific.* Donald Brenneis & Fred Myers, eds., pp. 217–242. New York: New York University Press,

Eisenstein, James, and Herbert Jacob. 1977. *Felony Justice.* Boston: Little, Brown.

Feld, Steven. 1982. *Sound and Sentiment: Birds, Weeping, Poetics, and Song in Kaluli Expression.* Philadelphia: University of Pennsylvania Press.

Fineman, Martha. 1988. Dominant Discourse, Professional Language, and Legal Change in Child Custody Decisionmaking. *Harvard Law Review* 101(4): 727–774.

Foucault, Michel. 1972. *The Discourse on Language.* Appendix to *The Archaeology of Knowledge,* pp. 215–237. New York: Pantheon.

———. 1980. *The History of Sexuality.* Vol I: *An Introduction.* New York: Vintage Books.

Goffman, Erving. 1974. *Frame Analysis: An Essay on the Organization of Experience.* New York: Harper and Row.

Goodwin, Charles, and John Heritage. 1990. Conversation Analysis. In *Annual Review of Anthropology, Vol. 19.* Bernard Siegel, Alan Beals, & Stephen Tyler, eds., pp. 283–307. Palo Alto, CA: Annual Reviews.

Gossen, Gary. 1974. *Chamulas in the World of the Sun: Time and Space in a Maya Oral Tradition.* Cambridge, MA: Harvard University Press.

Gramsci, Antonio. 1971. *Selections from the Prison Notebooks.* New York: International Publishers.

Grossman, Joel. 1965. *Lawyers and Judges: The A.B.A. and the Politics of Judicial Selection.* New York: Wiley.

Gumperz, John. 1982. *Discourse Strategies.* New York: Cambridge University Press.

Gumperz, John, and Dell Hymes, eds. 1964. The Ethnography of Communication. [Special publication]. *American Anthropologist* 66(6): Part 2.

Habermas, Jurgen. 1989. Technology and Science as "Ideology." In *Jurgen Habermas on Society and Politics: A Reader.* Steven Seidman, ed., pp. 237–265. Boston: Beacon Press.

Hanks, William. 1987. Discourse Genres in a Theory of Practice. *American Ethnologist* 14(4): 668–692.

Hay, Douglas. 1975. Property, Authority and the Criminal Law. In *Albion's Fatal Tree.* Douglas Hay, Peter Linebaugh, John Rule, E. P. Thompson, and Cal Winslow, eds., pp. 17–64. New York: Pantheon Books.

Hendricks, Janet. 1988. Power and Knowledge: Discourse and Ideological Transformation among the Shuar. *American Ethnologist* 15(2): 216–238.

Hill, Jane. 1995. The Voices of Don Gabriel. In *The Dialogic Emergence of Culture.* Dennis Tedlock and Bruce Mannheim, eds., pp. 97–147. Urbana: University of Illinois Press.

Hirsch, Susan. 1994. Kadhi's Courts as Complex Sites of Resistance: The State, Islam, and Gender in Postcolonial Kenya. In *Contested States: Law, Hegemony and Resistance.* Mindie Lazarus-Black and Susan Hirsch, eds., pp. 207–230. New York: Routledge.

Hogarth, John. 1971. *Sentencing as a Human Process.* Toronto: University of Toronto Press.

Hymes, Dell. 1967. Models of the Interaction of Language and Social Setting. *Journal of Social Issues* 23(2): 8–28.

Irvine, Judith. 1990. Registering Affect: Heteroglossia in the Linguistic Expression of Emotion. In *Language and the Politics of Emotion.* Catherine A. Lutz and Lila Abu-Lughod, eds., pp. 126–161. New York: Cambridge University Press.

Jacob, Herbert. 1978. *Justice in America.* Boston: Little, Brown.

Joerges, Christian, and David Trubek, eds. 1989. *Critical Legal Thought: An American–German Debate.* Baden-Baden, Germany: Nomos Verlagsgesellschaft.

Just, Peter. 1992. History, Power, Ideology, and Culture: Current Directions in the Anthropology of Law. *Law and Society Review* 26(2): 373–412.

Kairys, David. 1982. *The Politics of Law.* New York: Pantheon Books.

Kelly, John. 1991. *A Politics of Virtue: Hinduism, Sexuality and Countercolonial Discourse in Fiji.* Chicago: University of Chicago Press.

Kennedy, Elizabeth, and Madeline Davis. 1993. *Boots of Leather, Slippers of Gold: The Story of a Lesbian Community.* New York: Routledge.

Kondo, Dorinne. 1990. *Crafting Selves: Power, Gender and Discourses of Identity in a Japanese Workplace.* Chicago: University of Chicago Press.

Kroskrity, Paul, Bambi Schieffelin, and Katherine Woolard, eds. 1992. Special Issue on Language Ideologies. *Pragmatics* 2(3).

Kuipers, Joel. 1990. *Power in Performance.* Philadelphia: University of Pennsylvania Press.

Kulick, Don. 1992. *Language Shift and Cultural Reproduction.* New York: Cambridge University Press.

Labov, William. 1964. Phonological Correlates of Social Stratification. *American Anthropologist* 66: 164–176.

Lasch, Christopher. 1991. The Politics of the Civilized Minority. In *The True and Only Heaven,* pp. 412–475. New York: W. W. Norton.

Lazarus-Black, Mindie, and Susan Hirsch. 1994. *Contested States: Law, Hegemony and Resistance.* New York: Routledge.

Lee, Stephen. 1973. Judicial Selection and Tenure in Arizona. *Law and the Social Order* 4(1): 51–80.

Levin, Martin. 1977. *Urban Politics and the Criminal Courts.* Chicago: University of Chicago Press.

Martin, Emily. 1987. *The Woman in the Body: A Cultural Analysis of Reproduction.* Boston: Beacon.

Matoesian, Gregory. 1993. *Reproducing Rape: Domination through Talk in the Courtroom.* Chicago: University of Chicago Press.

Maynard, Douglas. 1984. *Inside Plea Bargaining.* New York: Plenum Press.

Merry, Sally. 1990. *Getting Justice and Getting Even.* Chicago: University of Chicago Press.

Mertz, Elizabeth. 1992. Language, Law and Social Meanings: Linguistic/Anthropological Contributions to the Study of Law. *Law and Society Review* 26(2): 413–436.

Nader, Laura. 1972. Up the Anthropologist: Perspectives Gained from Studying Up. In *Reinventing Anthropology.* Dell Hymes, ed., pp. 285–311. New York: Pantheon Press.

Nagel, Stuart. 1961. Political Party Affiliation and Judges' Decisions. *American Political Science Review* 55(4): 843–850.

O'Barr, William. 1982. *Linguistic Evidence: Language, Power and Strategy in the Courtroom.* New York: Academic Press.

Ochs, Elinor. 1988. *Culture and Language Development.* New York: Cambridge University Press.

———. 1992. Indexing Gender. In *Rethinking Context.* Alessandro Duranti and Charles Goodwin, eds., pp. 335–358. New York: Cambridge University Press.

Packer, Herbert. 1974. Two Models of the Criminal Process. In *Rough Justice: Perspectives on Lower Criminal Courts.* John Robertson, ed., pp. 136–154. Boston: Little, Brown.

Philips, Susan. 1982. The Language Socialization of Lawyers: Acquiring the "Cant." In *Doing Ethnography in the Classroom.* George Spindler, ed., pp. 176–209. New York: Holt, Rinehart & Winston.

———. 1983. *The Invisible Culture: Communication in Classroom and Community on the Warm Springs Indian Reservation.* New York: Longman. (Reprint, Prospect Heights, IL: Waveland Press, 1993).

———. 1984a. Contextual Variation in Courtroom Language Use: The Structure of Noun Phases Referring to Crimes. *International Journal of the Sociology of Language* 49: 29–50.

———. 1984b. The Social Organization of Questions and Answers in Courtroom Discourse. [Special issue on Language in Law. Brenda Danet, ed.]. *Text* 4(1–3): 223–246.

———. 1986. The Role of Spatial Organization and Alignment in the Organization of Courtroom Discourse. In *Discourse and Institutional Authority: Medicine, Education, and Law.* Susan Fisher and Alexandra Todd, eds., pp. 223–233. Norwood, NJ: Ablex.

———. 1987a. On the Use of Wh Questions in American Courtroom Discourse. In *Power through Discourse.* Leah Kedar, ed., pp. 83–111. Norwood, NJ: Ablex.

———. 1987b. The Concept of Speech Genre in the Study of Language and Culture. *Working Papers and Proceedings of the Center for Psychosocial Studies* 11: 25–34. Chicago: Center for Psychosocial Studies.

———. 1990, June 1. *Criminal Defendants' Resistance to Confession in the Guilty Plea.* Paper presented at the Law and Society Association Meetings, Berkeley, CA.

———. 1991. Tongan Speech Levels: Practice and Talk about Practice in the Cultural Construction of Social Hierarchy. In *Currents in Pacific Linguistics: Papers on Austronesian Languages and Ethnolinguistics in Honour of George Grace.* Robert Blust, ed., pp. 369–382. Pacific Linguistics series C, no. 117. Canberra: School of Pacific Studies, Australian National University.

———. 1992. A Marx-Influenced Approach to Ideology and Language. Special Issue on Language Ideologies (Paul Kroskrity, Bambi Schieffelin, and Katherine Woolard, eds.). *Pragmatics* 2(3): 377–386.

———. 1993. Introduction. In *The Invisible Culture*, pp. xi–xix. Prospect Heights, Ill.: Waveland Press.

———. 1994. Local Legal Hegemony in the Tongan Magistrate's Court: How Sisters Fare Better than Wives. In *Contested States: Law, Hegemony and Resistance.* Mindy Lazarus-Black and Susan Hirsch, eds., pp. 59–88. New York: Routledge.

———. 1995. *From Practice to Structure in Tongan Language Ideology: How Crimes of Bad Language Harm the Sister–Brother Relationship.* Edited Collection on Language Ideologies, Paul Kroskrity, ed. Manuscript submitted for publication.

———. In press. Language Ideologies in Powerful Institutions. In *Language Ideologies.* Bambi B. Schieffelin, Kathryn A. Woolard, and Paul V. Kroskrity, eds. New York: Oxford University Press.

Roll, John. 1990. Merit Selection: The Arizona Experience. *Arizona State Law Journal* 22: 837–894.

Sacks, Harvey. 1992. Lecture 3, Spring Quarter, April 10, 1967; Lecture 4, Spring Quarter, April 12, 1967. *On Proving Hearership.* Unpublished mimeograph copy.

Sacks, Harvey, Emanuel Schegloff, and Gail Jefferson. 1974. A Simplest Systematics for the Organization of Turn-taking for Conversation. *Language* 50: 696–735.

Sarat, Austin, and Thomas Kearns, eds. 1991. *The Fate of Law.* Ann Arbor: University of Michigan Press.

Schieffelin, Bambi. 1990. *The Give and Take of Everyday Life: Language Socialization of Kaluli Children.* New York: Cambridge University Press.

Schiffrin, Deborah. 1987. *Discourse Markers.* New York: Cambridge University Press.

Schmidhauser, John. 1979. *Judges and Justices: The Federal Appellate Judiciary.* Boston: Little, Brown.

Scott, James. 1990. *Domination and the Arts of Resistance: Hidden Transcripts.* New Haven, CT: Yale University Press.

Sherzer, Joel. 1983. Kuna Ways of Speaking. Austin: University of Texas Press.

———. 1987. A Discourse-Centered Approach to Language and Culture. *American Anthropologist* 89: 295–309.

Silverstein, Michael. 1976. Shifters, Linguistic Categories and Cultural Description. In *Meaning in Anthropology.* Keith Basso and Henry Selby, eds., pp. 11–55. Albuquerque: University of New Mexico Press.

Slavin, Francis. 1976. Judicial Evaluation in Arizona. *Arizona Bar Journal* 12(2): 40–45.

Starr, June, and Jane Collier. 1989. *History and Power in the Study of Law.* Ithaca: Cornell University Press.

Sumner, Colin. 1979. *Reading Ideologies: An Investigation into the Marxist Theory of Ideology and Law.* New York: Academic Press.

Tannen, Deborah. 1984. *Conversational Style: Analyzing Talk among Friends.* Norwood, NJ: Ablex.

Tedlock, Dennis. 1983. *The Spoken Word and the Work of Interpretation.* Philadelphia: University of Pennsylvania Press.

Thompson, John. 1984. *Studies in the Theory of Ideology.* Cambridge, England: Polity Press.

Tigar, Michael, and Madeleine Levy. 1977. *Law and the Rise of Capitalism.* New York: Monthly Review Press.

Ulmer, S. Sidney. 1962. The Political Party Variable in the Michigan Supreme Court. *Journal of Public Law* 11(2): 352–362.

Urban, Greg. 1988. Ritual Wailing in Amerindian Brazil. *American Anthropologist* 90(2): 385–400.

———. 1991. *A Discourse Centered Approach to Culture.* Austin: University of Texas Press.

Watson, Richard, and Rondal Downing. 1969. *The Politics of the Bench and the Bar: Judicial Selection under the Missouri Nonpartisan Court Plan.* New York: Wiley.

Watson-Gegeo, Karen, and David Gegeo. 1990. Shaping the Mind and Straightening out Conflicts: The Discourse of Kwara'ae Family Counseling. In *Disentangling: Conflict Discourse in Pacific Societies.* Karen Watson-Gegeo & Geoffrey White, eds., pp 161–213. Stanford, CA: Stanford University Press.

Williams, Raymond. 1977. *Marxism and Literature.* New York: Oxford University Press.

Willis, Paul. 1977. *Learning to Labor.* New York: Columbia University Press.

Winters, Glen. 1973. Judicial Selection and Tenure. In *Judicial Selection and Tenure.* Glen Winters, ed., pp. 19–28. Chicago: American Judicature Society.

Index

Aborted sentencing, 89–92

Bar associations. *See* Organized bar

Constitutional rights, xii, 36–38, 63–68
Courtroom control, 75–76, 91, 109
  and loss of control, 88–89, 89–93,
    112
Courtroom control ideologies, xiii, xvi–
    xvii, 87, 108–111
  language use in, 108–110
  and legal ideologies, 106–107, 111–
    115
  as non–legal, 107–108
Culture, xiv, 10–11

Defendants, criminal
  education of, 60–61
  involvement in procedure, 48–86, 88,
    117 (*see also* Resistance to
    confession)
  responses during procedure, 74–75
Discourse structure
  genres, xiv, 11–12, 44–47, 50, 117–120,
    123, 194 n. 7
  global and local, 11
  and ideology, 8–13, 116

legal genres, 12, 30
  and organization of ideological diversity,
    11–12, 46–47, 116–124, 193 n. 4

Factual basis, 40–41, 66–74, 93–106
  nailing it down, 95–97, 98
  and typicality, 97–99
Frozen dialectic, 114

Gramsci, Antonio
  alternative hegemonies, 196 n. 4
  hegemony, 9, 91, 114
  law as hegemonic, 10, 12
  role of state, 9
Guilty pleas, 28, 30, 50–51, 54–59, 80–81
  trouble in, 62–63

Hegemony. *See* Gramsci, Antonio

Ideological diversity, 111–112, 116–123
  as hidden, 28, 47, 80–82, 119, 122
Ideological polysemy, 50, 85–87, 114–115,
    117, 120
Ideological stances. *See* Stances, ideological
Ideology. *See also* Marxism
  consciousness, 84–85
  dominant ideologies, 47, 112, 117

Ideology (*continued*)
  explicit vs. implicit, 9, 80–81, 110–111, 119
  and language, 8–13
  as shared, 82
Indexicality, 28–30, 47
Interactional strategies. *See* Strategies, interactional
Interpretation of law, xii, 10, 28, 47–48, 53, 119
Intertextual relations
  as hiding ideological diversity, 47, 80–82, 118–119
  and interpretive field, 119
  intertextual gaps, 28, 47
  intertextuality and, xv, 12–13, 27, 118–119
  in method, 12, 52, 80
  between written and spoken genres, 27–47, 118–119

Judges
  appellate vs. trial court, xiii, xv, 7, 24–25, 47, 123
  appointed vs. elected, xv, 18–25
  as non-ideological, 14, 22
  procedure oriented vs. record oriented, xii–xvii, 48–86
  social background of, 4–5, 6
Judicial behavior, xi–xii, 3–4, 193 n. 2
Judicial selection
  appointive vs. elective, 14–16
  and Merit Selection, 15, 17–18
  organized bar influence on, 23–24
  political party influence on, 16, 22–25

Language and ideology, 8–13
Language ideologies, 194 n. 11, 196 n. 3
Law
  case law, 45–46
  case law vs. procedural rule, xv, 44–46, 118
  due process, xii, xiv, 12–13, 44–47, 78, 111–113, 117 (*see also* Constitutional rights)
  as ideology, 9–10
  Rule 17, 27, 29
  spoken vs. written, xv, 27, 123
Legal ideologies, xii, 27–47, 48–86
  and courtroom control ideologies, 106–107, 111–115
  and political ideologies, 78–80
Linguistic anthropology, 10–13

Marxism. *See also* Gramsci, Antonio
  dominant ideology, 8–9, 47
  domination and subordination, 8, 114, 116, 121
  dualism, 13, 46–47, 114, 116, 120–121
  hiddenness of ideology, 8–9, 25, 88, 113–114
  ideology, concept of, xiv–xv, 8–10
  ideological critique, 80–82
  oppositional relations, 82–83, 114, 121–122
  reconsidered, 116–123
Method
  career history interviews, 6, 52–53
  ethnographic context, 88–89
  ethnography, 3–4
  guilty pleas, 50–51
  pilot project, 5
  posttaping interviews, 6, 51–52
  role in critique of ideology, 80
  social background questionnaire, 6
  tape recording, 5–6
  texts in, 7

Organized bar, xiv, 123. *See also* Judicial selection
  in evaluation of judges, 17, 23, 93
  in opposition to political parties, 23, 82–83, 122
  as political, 23–26
  State Bar of Arizona, 14, 93

Personal scripts for guilty pleas, 54–55
Political ideologies
  of appointed vs. elected judges, 19–22
  and judicial behavior, 4–5, 81
  and legal ideologies, 78–80
  liberal vs. conservative, 49–50
  and organized bar, 24–25
  on role of state, 49–50, 123
  Tucson judges' views on, xii–xiii
Political parties, xii–xiv, 7
  influence on judges' ideologies, 24
  in opposition to organized bar, 23, 82–83, 122
  organizations of, 14
  in selection of judges, 22–25
Polysemy, ideological. *See* Ideological polysemy

Procedure-oriented judges
    and courtroom control, 88–89, 112
    courtroom control ideologies, 88–89,
        107–111
    ideological stances of, 110
Professional elites, 194 n. 5

Question forms, 74–76, 97, 117

Repair
    in conversation analysis, 195 n. 1
    repair slots, 31, 32, 41
    of topics, 31, 34, 38–39
Resistance to confession, 88–89, 93–106, 114
    denial, 93, 94–99
    effects of, 122
    mitigation, 101–106
    referential obscurity, 100–101

Social background questions, 32–33, 59–63
Speech genre. See Discourse structure
Stances, ideological, xiii, xvi, 87, 118–120
    on courtroom control, 110
    defined, 52

dominant, 121
on law, 77–78, 117–119
in legal vs. political ideologies, 70,
    117
on political role of state, 78–80, 123
procedure-oriented and record-oriented,
    117, 121
as responses to resistance, 113
and strategies, 78, 119
Strategies, interactional. See also
    Constitutional rights; Factual basis;
    Social background questions
in courtroom control, 111
elaboration of topics in, 49, 59–74
procedure and record oriented, 48–49,
    53–54, 77–78
quantified, 74–77
variation in, 54–59

Tailoring procedures, 58–59, 60
Topics
    coherency of, 30–31
    defined, 30
    sequencing of, 29–30, 31–43, 117